Atlas of

World War II
Battle Plans

Before and After

ATLAS OF
WORLD WAR II
BATTLE PLANS

BEFORE AND AFTER

General Editor
Stephen Badsey

BARNES
&NOBLE
BOOKS
NEW YORK

Contents

Notes on the Contributors

General Editor

Dr Stephen Badsey MA (Cantab) FRHistS is a Senior Lecturer at RMA Sandhurst, and a Senior Research Fellow of De Montfort University, Bedford. He is a specialist on military theory and on media presentations of warfare. He has made numerous appearances as a historian on television and in the press, and has written or contributed to more than a dozen books on warfare.

Contributors

Dr Duncan Anderson MA BA is Head of the War Studies Department at RMA Sandhurst, and a Senior Research Fellow of De Montfort University, Bedford. He is an authority on the British Army of the mid-19th century and on World War II in the Far East, and co-author of *The Battle for Manila*.

Dr Niall Barr is a Senior Lecturer at RMA Sandhurst. He has led military battlefield tours of El Alamein, and is presently researching a book on Bernard L Montgomery and the Eighth Army.

Tim Bean is a Senior Lecturer at RMA Sandhurst, and a specialist on 18th-century warfare and naval history.

Matthew Bennett MA FSA FRHistS is a Senior Lecturer at RMA Sandhurst. He is an expert on medieval warfare, and author of many works on the subject including *The Cambridge Atlas of Warfare: The Middle Ages 787–1485*.

Lloyd Clark is a Senior Lecturer at RMA Sandhurst, and has published widely on 20th-century conflict. He is a specialist on World War I and airborne warfare and is currently researching on command and control in 'Operation Market-Garden'.

Dr Stephen Hart is a Senior Lecturer at RMA Sandhurst, and a specialist on the Battle of Normandy.

Professor Andrew Lambert PhD MA FRHistS is a member of the War Studies Department at King's College, University of London. He is a specialist on both naval warfare and the Crimean War, and author of numerous works including *The Crimean War* and *The Last Sailing Battlefleet*.

Sean McKnight is Deputy Head of the War Studies Department at RMA Sandhurst and a Senior Research Fellow of De Montfort University, Bedford. He is a specialist on warfare in the Middle East, from medieval times to the present day, and is currently researching on the Mesopotamia campaign in World War I.

Aryeh Nusbacher MA is a Senior Lecturer at RMA Sandhurst. He was educated at the University of Toronto, the Royal Military College of Canada, and Somerville College, Oxford University.

David Pickup MPhil BA FRGS is a Senior Lecturer at RMA Sandhurst, a former lieutenant commander in the Royal Navy, and a serving officer in the Public Affairs Branch of the Royal Naval Reserve.

Dr Ian Stewart is a Senior Lecturer at RMA Sandhurst, and the co-editor of *War, Culture and the Media*.

Dr Simon Trew MA is a Senior Lecturer at RMA Sandhurst, and the author of *Britain, Mihailovic and the Chetniks 1941–42*.

Stephen Walsh MA is a Senior Lecturer at RMA Sandhurst. He is currently researching World War II on the Eastern Front.

Dr Edmund Yorke MA BA is a Senior Lecturer at RMA Sandhurst. He has published widely in defence, Commonwealth and African affairs. His recent publications include contributions to *Diplomacy of the Highest Order* and *Aspects of Peacekeeping* and co-editorship of *The New South Africa*.

key to symbols used on Plan and Outcome maps

		Castelforte	town or village
• town or village	〜〜〜 coastline	**Stalingrad**	town battle named after
built-up area	── river or stream	**FRANCE**	country
═══ road or track	≈≈≈ river	PACO	state or area
▬·▬·▬ railroad	⊥⊥⊥⊥ canal	*Rhine*	river, canal
	↙ marsh	*Monte Cairo*	peak, mountains
▲ peak	◇ lake	*Prinz Eugen*	ship

arrows on the Plan maps are shown in outline to show the planned direction of attack

on the Outcome maps solid arrows show the direction of actual attacks and counter-attacks

Allied deployment

Axis or Japanese deployment

Introduction
The Strategy of World War II

"Now at this very moment I knew that the United States was in the war, up to the neck and in to the death. So we had won after all! ... How long the war would last or in what fashion it would end no man could tell, nor did I at this moment care ... We should not be wiped out. Our history would not come to an end ... Hitler's fate was sealed. Mussolini's fate was sealed. As for the Japanese, they would be ground to a powder. All the rest was merely the proper application of overwhelming force."

WINSTON CHURCHILL, ON HEARING THE NEWS OF PEARL HARBOR

ON 7 DECEMBER 1941 the Japanese attacked the United States Pacific Fleet at Pearl Harbor, bringing the United States into World War II on the side of Britain and its Empire. On 11 December Adolf Hitler declared war on the United States on behalf of Nazi Germany, accompanied by Fascist Italy under Benito Mussolini. Germany and Italy were already fighting against Britain in North Africa, and against the Soviet Union. Hitler's decision to declare war on the United States linked this war in Europe with the war in the Far East, so creating the world's first truly global war.

Pearl Harbor is only one of 21 major battles of World War II described in this book. The outcome of each of these battles played a major part in deciding which side would eventually win the war. This introduction describes the wider events and national strategies of World War II, placing all these battles into a context so that their origins and their consequences can be better understood.

What convinced the British prime minister Winston Churchill that Pearl Harbor was the turning point from which victory would eventually come? Unlike his arch-enemy Hitler, Churchill had a good understanding of military strategy, and of what produces victory in war. Britain and its two major Allies in the war, the United States and the Soviet Union, also learned how to cooperate together despite their differences, and to produce a winning strategy of war on a global scale.

To put it at its most simple, a strategy of war is just a plan to defeat the enemy. Once a war has begun, strategy is concerned first of all with how to fight, and then with where and when to fight. Strategy sets basic objectives for a country at war and its armed forces, which its leaders hope will result in victory. In order to achieve these objectives it is almost always necessary to fight battles, and so victory in battle brings the objectives of strategy closer. It sounds simple enough. But even leading a country successfully in peacetime is one of the most difficult and demanding of all human endeavours. Mobilizing and channelling the immensely complex and powerful resources of the 20th century's industrial global empires, including the skills and determination of their people, so that they could fight a war on the scale of World War II through to success, was an achievement without parallel in history.

For the people of Europe, World War II began on 1 September 1939, when the armed forces of Nazi Germany invaded Poland. Shortly before this, Germany had signed a non-aggression pact with Poland's enemy to the east, the communist Soviet Union under its effective dictator, Joseph Stalin. Britain and France had both offered security guarantees to Poland, and two days later both countries declared war on Germany. Poland faced strong German attacks from the north out of East Prussia, from the west, and from the south. On 17 September the Soviet Union joined in with an attack on eastern Poland. With nothing that the British and French could do to help them, the Poles fought hard until their defeat on 28 September. This left Poland partitioned between Germany and the Soviet Union. However, Britain and France did not declare war on the Soviet Union, realizing the artificial nature of its agreement with Germany and hoping to secure its help.

Within Europe, all other countries stayed neutral, but this was already a war of considerable size. The British Empire at that date included Canada, South Africa, Australia, and New Zealand, as well as British India (which stretched from modern Iran almost to Thailand), and many other countries round the globe. With the second largest navy in the world after the United States, Britain also controlled much of the world's shipping and natural resources. The French Empire was not quite as large, but included much of North Africa as well as colonies in the Far East. Nazi Germany had, by 1939, absorbed Austria and the Czech Republic as the 'Third Reich' (Empire), and had alliances or close ties with many of the smaller countries of Eastern Europe. Most important was the three-power Axis between Germany, Italy, and Japan.

The world before the start of World War II had been far from peaceful. The Spanish Civil War, begun in 1936, had only ended in March 1939 with victory for the Fascists, while Italy had expanded its own empire to include Ethiopia and Albania as well as Libya. The Japanese had occupied Chinese Manchuria in 1931, and in 1937 had invaded China itself, where a protracted, if technically undeclared, war was already raging. In 1939 the Soviet Union fought an undeclared war with the Japanese at Nomonhan, on the border between its own territory in Mongolia and Manchuria, leading to a peace settlement between the two countries in 1941.

The war aims of Germany, Italy, and Japan, and the strategies by which they hoped to achieve them, have been subject to argument for the obvious reason that they eventually failed to carry them out. No strategy or plan of war can ever be so precise that it is written down exactly before the war and then followed in every detail. The same is true of any plan for a battle, if only because the enemy also has his own plans. But the broad shape of these plans and their associated strategies is clear for each of the three countries.

As *Führer* ('Leader') of Nazi Germany, a title that he gave himself in 1934, Adolf Hitler was the chief architect of German strategy. In the widest sense, its objectives were to spread and establish Nazi ideology, and with it the domination of the 'Superior Races' – of which the Germans were believed by Hitler to be the highest form – over the 'Inferior Races' of the world. This included the policies that produced the extermination camps of World War II. It is probable that Hitler's Germany aimed at eventual domination of the entire world. But his first ambition was *Lebensraum* ('space to live'), the creation of a Reich stretching into eastern Europe as far as the Ural Mountains, which would become an area of settlement for German peoples. The 'Inferior' peoples of occupied countries would either be wiped out – particularly the Jewish population – or kept in a condition of semi-slavery.

Aims on this scale would keep Germany at war for many years. But historically Germany (and its chief predecessor state Prussia) had won its wars if these had been short, fought against one enemy at the time, and if Germany had been able to attack first. Long wars against many enemies on more than one front – most obviously World War I – had produced defeats for Germany. So before World War II, Hitler had sought to dominate Eastern Europe by threats, without Britain or France intervening. Their declaration of war over Poland came as a genuine surprise to the Nazis.

For World War II, Germany also added new technology to its traditional strategy of fighting short aggressive campaigns one at a time. This new technology was based chiefly on tanks and aircraft, and became known as the blitzkrieg ('lightning war'). There was always a problem at the heart of German strategy between the desire to fight these short blitzkriegs, and the desire for large territorial conquests. The concentration on the blitzkrieg also meant that Germany had a fairly weak navy, dependent chiefly upon submarines ('U-boats'), and an airforce better suited to supporting ground attacks than to long-range bombing.

Italy and Japan had altogether lesser ambitions than Germany. Italy was the weakest of the Axis powers, and Mussolini's aims were to create an Italian colonial empire from the countries that border the Mediterranean Sea. Japan had rather greater ambitions to create an empire on the Asian mainland, largely from the disintegration of China. Emperor Hirohito, who traditionally took no direct part in politics, was powerless to stop the ambitions and rivalries of the Japanese Imperial Army and Navy. Japan boasted some of the largest and most modern ships in the world, but Japanese strategy was beset by problems of attempting too much with forces that were too small.

Given the strength of their fleet, the British had planned for a long war, with their military strength peaking in about 1943. They started with a small army, most of which was sent to France in 1939. The British Royal Air Force (RAF) had based its strategy largely on bombing industrial targets in daylight. The first few experiences made it clear that existing bombers were too slow and lightly armed to survive over Germany in daylight. This led the British to turn to bombing at night, and a debate began over bombing strategies that would continue throughout the war.

Unlike Britain, France had a powerful army in 1939, together with quite a strong navy and air force. But strategy was based on the defence of France, chiefly by the formidable system of concrete bunkers and emplacements along the common border with Germany, known as the Maginot Line. Germany also had a similar, if weaker, defensive system along its western border, known as the Westwall. The French, like the British, planned for a long war in which they would be ready to attack in one or two years.

The defeat of Poland therefore produced the odd situation that, of all the countries at war, none was ready to attack. Germany had no interest in a long war with Britain and France, and continued to hope for a peace settlement. Only limited fighting took place at sea and in the air. American journalists called this period 'the phoney war'. Instead, all sides worked to strengthen their positions politically, with the British in particular hoping to convince the United States to enter the war. The Soviet Union used threats of force to occupy more territory in Eastern Europe, and in November attacked Finland in the 'Winter War', which lasted until March. On 9 April the Germans invaded Norway and also Denmark, and after brief resistance both countries surrendered.

Then the situation in Europe, and the war strategies that went with it, changed dramatically. On 10 May 1940 the Germans launched their long-awaited attack in the west, striking at the French and British armies through neutral Belgium and the Netherlands in order to avoid the Maginot Line. The result of this battle, the first of the great armoured blitzkriegs of the war, was as unexpected as it was dramatic. The French forces were defeated and collapsed in a matter of weeks. **The Fall of France** led to a complete French surrender on 22 June. Germany occupied the Netherlands, Belgium, and northern France. A puppet French state, known as 'Vichy France', was established in the south, and was responsible for controlling the French colonial empire. As with other countries overrun by the Germans, a number of Free French escaped to Britain to continue the fight. The British faced their greatest test in July as the **Battle of Britain**, a German attempt to establish air superiority over southern England, began as a preliminary to an amphibious invasion. The German failure in this battle represented their first important defeat in World War II, and left Britain as a critical threat in the west.

Nevertheless, Germany now controlled Europe from the Arctic to the Mediterranean. Italy had also declared war on 10 June, meaning that the Italian fleet in the Mediterranean and troops in the Italian colony of Libya both threatened Britain's control of the Suez Canal and communications with the Far East. Most of the countries of Eastern Europe now joined the Axis. Britain had no allies, and was facing a much greater threat at sea as German submarines could now sail from French and Norwegian ports. The long campaign called the Battle of the Atlantic had already begun, with Germany attempting to starve Britain into surrender. But the Royal Navy remained very powerful, and the German attempt to win the war in the Atlantic by including battleships led to the dramatic **Sink the *Bismarck*!** chase in March 1941.

In response to all these events the United States under President Franklin D Roosevelt, while remaining neutral, started to rearm and to tilt strongly towards the British side by offering economic and naval support. In August 1941 Britain and the United States issued the 'Atlantic Charter', a statement of mutual beliefs and future policy.

The British could attack Germany directly only by building up their bomber fleet, while the Royal Navy imposed a limited blockade on the Reich. Neither of these methods would be very effective for at least another year. Instead, the main theatre of war shifted to the Mediterranean. On 28 October 1940 Italian forces from Albania invaded Greece, only to be repulsed. In December a major attack by British forces from Egypt defeated the Italians in Libya. The German response was to send their own forces to North Africa to support the Italians. For the next two years a series of armoured battles would be fought in the Western Desert along the North African coast.

The British also hoped for allies in southern Europe and offered military support, a hope that ended in April 1941 when the Germans overran both

Yugoslavia and Greece. This campaign ended with the German capture of **Crete** using airborne forces in May. Having to be rescued by the Germans in this manner confirmed Italy's position as a subordinate partner in the Axis.

Hitler now decided that Britain was no threat, and would eventually either make peace or collapse from defeat by the U-boats. It was time for the campaign that had always been at the heart of Nazi war aims. On 22 June 1941 Germany launched its attack on the Soviet Union, **Operation Barbarossa**. This massive land and air campaign grew to include troops from virtually all the Axis countries in Europe. At first the Soviet forces reeled back under this hammer-blow. Within a few weeks the Germans had reached the outskirts of Leningrad (St Petersburg), the largest Soviet city in the north. But Leningrad held out, and as winter approached, what had been planned as another German blitzkrieg became a slow slogging match across the entire Eastern Front. In December the Germans were held just short of Moscow, their second major defeat in the war and their first on land.

Meanwhile on the far side of the world, the Japanese were having no success in their war with China. Their strategic response was to widen the war. In July, Japanese forces moved into French Indo-China. The British and Americans countered by imposing an oil embargo. South East Asia was rich in economic resources, and mostly controlled by European powers, which were in no position to defend them. The Japanese planned one swift operation that would take them as far south as New Guinea, as far west as Burma, and as far east as the Philippines (which were under American control). To make this happen, they needed to eliminate the only fighting unit powerful enough to intervene: the United States Pacific Fleet. This is why on 7 December 1941 the Japanese attacked **Pearl Harbor**, bringing the United States into the war.

The main reason that the Japanese attack on Pearl Harbor caught the Americans by surprise was that they were absolutely convinced that Japan could not defeat them in war. Much of the formidable United States Navy was now in the Atlantic, and its Army (including the Army Air Force) was only slowly building up from small beginnings. But so great was American industrial strength that within two years they would have overwhelming superiority over Japan. In fact the Japanese knew this too, but they were not prepared to give up the chance of an Asian empire by backing down to the Americans. Part of the Japanese strategic plan was based on exploiting the riches of South East Asia with what they called the 'Pan Asia Co-Prosperity Sphere'. They also hoped to provoke uprisings by Asian independence movements, particularly against the British in India.

Out in the Pacific Ocean the Japanese occupied a chain of islands, which they called the 'Line of the Rising Sun'. Their strategy was based on the fact that fighting through the jungles of South East Asia was formidably difficult. In order to reach the Japanese home islands with either bombers or ground troops the Americans would have to conduct an 'island hopping' campaign across the Pacific, taking the important islands in turn. If the Japanese could inflict heavy losses on the United States for each island, then the Americans might decide that the loss was too great and agree a negotiated peace.

Pearl Harbor and the capture of so much territory by the Japanese coincided with the Germans almost reaching Moscow, and represented a high point of the war for the Axis. Even so, Hitler's decision to declare war on the United States ranks with his decision to turn east before defeating Britain as among the greatest blunders in the whole of military history. Although the Soviet Union remained at peace with Japan, even China formally declared war on 9 December 1941, joining the United States and Britain.

Also in December 1941, at a major planning conference in Washington, the British and Americans decided on their basic strategy for the rest of the war. First, Germany was seen as the most powerful and most dangerous enemy, and priority would be given to defeating Germany before Japan. On the Eastern Front the Soviet Union was fighting desperately. The sheer size of the country and terrible nature of the war was absorbing two-thirds of the entire German war effort. It would clearly be a catastrophe for the Allies if the Soviet Union was defeated, and Stalin called repeatedly for a 'Second Front', an Allied attack into Western Europe. The British, who had already fought almost alone for over a year, were fighting in North Africa, the Far East, in the Atlantic, and in the Mediterranean, and were beginning to develop a bomber offensive over Germany. The United States was creating what Roosevelt called the 'Arsenal of Democracy' in terms of weapons and troops to use them. But first it needed to construct a global transport system in the form of ships, trucks, and aircraft to get them to the fighting areas. The most immediate help that it could give was in the Atlantic, and by creating a daylight bomber force to attack Germany from British bases in coordination with the RAF. All this would take about another year, during which the Allies would still be vulnerable to Axis attacks.

1942 was the last year in which the Axis could hope to win World War II by defeating the major Allies outright before increased Allied strength made this virtually impossible. On the Eastern Front the year opened with another German offensive, aimed not at Moscow but south towards the oil-producing regions of the Caucasus. The continuing war in the Western Desert also swung the Axis way with a brilliant blitzkrieg victory over British forces at **the Battle of Gazala** in May. The Japanese overran the Philippines, pressed deep into

Burma, and even raided Ceylon with aircraft carriers.

If only on the biggest maps and for a few weeks, the prospect of Axis world domination beckoned. The Germans and Italians might defeat the British and drive on through the Middle East towards Iran, meeting other German forces coming south out of the Caucasus. With the Japanese in Burma so close, India might rise in revolt and overthrow the British, letting Japanese forces through to link up with the Germans and Japanese. Then all that would be left would be the final confrontation with the United States.

It cannot be said with certainty that this could *never* have happened, but the Axis forces were already reaching the limit of their strength. They were over-stretched against enemies who were growing stronger and who were no longer at a disadvantage. In the Far East the Japanese were losing control of the Pacific in a series of defeats by the Americans, while fighting continued in Burma and New Guinea. The Battle of the Atlantic was effectively won by November 1942, the record month for Allied sinkings of German U-boats. In the Mediterranean the hard fought success of **Operation Pedestal** in August, and many other convoys, helped preserve the British base on Malta in its efforts to harass Axis supplies.

The limit of the Axis advance westward across the desert came just inside Egypt at the **Second Battle of El Alamein** in October, a slogging match that forced a headlong Axis retreat back through Libya into Tunisia. In November American and British amphibious forces landed along the North Africa coast in the Vichy French territories of Morocco, Algeria, and Tunisia. Many of the French garrisons declared for the Allies, and all but Tunisia were soon pacified. The Germans occupied Vichy France and rushed reinforcements to Tunisia, but their position in North Africa was clearly doomed. Finally, and most terribly of all for the Germans, their entire strategy on the Eastern Front suffered catastrophic defeat in the great city battle of **Stalingrad**, which began in September.

In January 1943 the British and Americans met in Casablanca for one of their frequent strategic planning conferences. The war in North Africa was not over, and the Axis forces in Tunisia did not surrender until 12 May. Germany and its allies controlled by force of arms virtually the whole of Europe except for a handful of neutral countries, and in eastern Europe the death camps had been established for the 'Final Solution', the wiping out of Jews and other 'Inferior' people. But for the first time the Allies could think in terms of planning the battles that would defeat Germany and Italy, rather than fighting to prevent further Axis victories and expansion.

At Casablanca the importance of a strategic bombing offensive against Germany's heartland was first agreed. But the practical problems of mounting mass bombing raids deep into Germany were considerable. The disastrous USAAF **Schweinfurt Raid** in October showed just how much had to be overcome before strategic bombing became truly effective.

Also at Casablanca, the British and Americans announced their policy for the defeat of Germany: there would be no negotiation, and Germany must surrender unconditionally. This was understandable in the light of everything that had gone before, but meant that there would be no quick or negotiated end to the war.

As the western Allies prepared to launch their attack on mainland Europe, the German and Axis forces on the Eastern Front were as strong as they would ever be. Soon the need to defend in the west meant that the Germans must split their forces further. In July the Germans launched their last great attack in the east, the **Battle of Kursk**. This was the biggest armoured battle in history, a desperate slogging match resulting in a decisive Soviet victory. From this time on, few in the German high command had any doubt that the war itself was lost.

In order to enter occupied Europe, the western Allies needed the kind of cooperation between countries that had never been seen in war before. They had to consider the damage they might do to occupied countries in liberating them, and the need to keep their own casualties low. They also needed cooperation between navies, armies, and airforces in order to mount large amphibious operations. All these problems were being slowly, and sometimes painfully, solved through experience against the Germans and the Japanese.

Where to launch their next campaign caused a serious debate between the British and the Americans. The United States favoured the direct route into Europe, using Britain as a base for an amphibious force to liberate northern France, and so move directly into Germany from the west. This had the advantage of probably being the fastest way to defeat Germany, and so end the war with fewest American casualties. Stalin, still calling for his 'Second Front', also favoured this route. The British were more concerned with what Europe would look like after the war. They also knew how many months it would take to build up the forces for the liberation of France, and the catastrophic consequences if the attempt failed. Churchill and his senior officers argued for a continued Mediterranean strategy. The idea was that the western Allies would first defeat Italy and then press on northwards into central Europe. The main advantage of this strategy was that it would meet the advancing Soviet forces much farther east, and prevent Stalin dominating Eastern Europe after the war.

The result of this debate was a compromise. The liberation of France would go ahead in 1944, but until then the Mediterranean strategy would continue.

On 10 July 1943 Allied forces landed in Sicily. Italy was even more convinced than Germany that the war was lost, and on 25 July Mussolini was forced out of power and imprisoned. On 3 September the Allies landed in southern Italy itself, the new Italian government surrendered, and on 13 October Italy declared war on Germany.

The German response was to turn their armed forces in Italy into an occupying force to prevent the Allies overrunning Italy and quickly reaching the southern Alps. Mussolini was rescued by a daring German raid in September and set up in northern Italy as a German puppet. The geography of Italy, narrow and with a mountain spine, lent itself to solid lines of defence across the country from coast to coast. After a retreat through the autumn, the main German stand came just south of Rome on the 'Gustav Line' at the end of the year.

The Allies were now prepared for what would be the decisive year of the war, both against Germany and against Japan. By air, sea, and land, in 1944 they would launch coordinated campaigns all around the world, each planned to help each other and to prevent their enemies from switching forces. This was an incredible achievement in global strategy, something that had never been done or even planned before.

At their conference in Cairo in November 1943 the British and Americans announced that their policy towards Japan also would be one of unconditional surrender. At a further conference in Tehran with the Soviet Union later that month, the basic strategy for 1944 against Germany was agreed. Although Britain continued as an important member of the Allies, the industrial strength of the United States and the Soviet Union, and the power of their forces, was now reaching its height. For the rest of the war, these two countries would increasingly dominate Allied strategy.

By early 1944 Italy had become a secondary theatre, less important than the forthcoming liberation of France, which was given priority in equipment and resources. But it was considered important for the Allies to keep attacking in Italy. With virtually complete control of both the air and the sea, they looked for new ways to break the Gustav Line. The amphibious contribution, the landing at **Anzio** on the west coast of Italy just south of Rome in January, was a failure ending in stalemate. And although air power contributed to the Fourth Battle of **Monte Cassino**, which also began in January and succeeded in liberating Rome on 5 June, the contribution was a controversial one. Fighting continued into northern Italy until the end of the year, with Italian forces fighting alongside the other Allies.

The main British and American campaign of the year began on 6 June, with the **D-Day** amphibious landings on the French coast. The Allies, with their almost complete control of the air and sea, could move troops and equipment across the English Channel and into Normandy faster than the Germans could move their reserves from other parts of occupied Europe. The reward for the success of D-Day came two months later with a complete Allied victory in the Battle of Normandy. A second Allied landing took place in the south of France on 15 August. Paris was liberated on 25 August, and most of France within a few weeks.

The Germans were in full retreat in the west, with the Allies in pursuit, entering Belgium and the Netherlands in early September. It looked possible that they could reach the industrial heartland of western Germany, so probably winning the war before the end of the year. But the risks involved in this strategy were considerable, not least because it meant a single thrust into Germany that could be counter-attacked, rather than an advance on a broad front. In September an attempt at a single thrust was made, using Allied airborne forces to open up a route through the Netherlands, in cooperation with a British advance. But **Operation Market-Garden** failed, and the decision to continue the broad front advance remained in force. By the end of the year the Allies had closed up to the German frontier from the North Sea to Switzerland, and to the Westwall defences.

Normandy was the largest amphibious battle in history, but it was small compared to any of the great battles on the Eastern Front, which continued to demand the bulk of the German war effort. In January 1944 Soviet forces finally drove the Germans back from Leningrad, so ending a siege that had lasted for over 900 days. This was followed by a succession of hammer blows at every point of the Axis line. The most important of these, **Operation Bagration**, was planned to start in June to coincide both with the D-Day landings and with the Allied breakthrough in Italy. In a spectacular demonstration of their own style of blitzkrieg, the Soviets liberated the city of Minsk and drove as far as eastern Poland before halting.

In September Finland asked the Soviet Union for an armistice. Romania, whose oilfields were almost the only natural source of oil for the Axis, was overrun by the Soviets in the same month, followed by much of Hungary. In October Soviet forces entered Yugoslavia and the Germans had to retreat hurriedly from Greece. Other than territorial conquest, one of Stalin's concerns was to build a barrier of eastern European states between his country and an attack from the west in some future war.

Germany's position was now hopeless. On 22 June a group of German Army officers tried unsuccessfully to assassinate Hitler, hoping that his death might lead to a negotiated peace with the Allies. The Axis had virtually disintegrated, and Germany had no effective supporters left. Bombing of

German cities and industrial targets by the British and Americans continued round the clock. From the east, south, and west Allied armies surrounded the Reich. The defeat of a last German attack in the west in December, known as the 'Battle of the Bulge', left Germany without any reserves. For most Germans, the chief reasons for fighting on were that they had no choice, and in the hope of surrendering to the western Allies rather than the hated Soviets.

All this time the war against Japan had been a secondary priority for the Allies, although the Japanese could have been forgiven for thinking otherwise. The powerful United States Navy had inflicted multiple defeats on the Japanese at sea, often in great battles between aircraft carriers in which the two fleets never saw each other. In June 1943 the Americans began their campaign to liberate New Guinea. In November their 'island hopping' advance reached as far as the Gilbert and Marshal islands, the first landings coming at 'bloody Tarawa' atoll. The Line of the Rising Sun was broken.

But Japan was still capable of two last major campaigns, one in China starting in April 1944 and another in Burma against the British in the hope of finally reaching India. The Americans also had forces both in Burma and China, with the strategic objective of building and training a Chinese Army large enough to defeat the Japanese, so allowing the USAAF to use the east coast of China for a bombing offensive against Japan.

The Japanese attack in Burma began in February, culminating in the decisive battles at Kohima and Imphal. With the Japanese supply line running across the jungle mountains of central Burma, the British strategy was to defend until the Japanese ran out of supplies, and then counter-attack. The largest airborne operation mounted in the Far East, **Operation Thursday**, was part of this larger British plan. A large airborne force was inserted into central Burma in March using gliders and succeeded in cutting the Japanese supply lines. By September the Japanese had been completely defeated, and by May 1945 Burma had been almost completely retaken by the Allies.

In January 1945 American forces landed back in the Philippines, retaking the capital **Manila** next month in a city battle of great destruction. Even more than the Germans, the Japanese troops fought to the last, and often committed suicide rather than face capture. Also in February American troops made a landing on **Iwo Jima** in the Volcano Islands, followed by a landing on Okinawa Island in April. This completed the American plans to bring Japan under long-range bombing, and also provided bases for possible amphibious landings.

Japan had lost control of the seas around its home islands. Between the starvation caused by the Allied blockade and the bombing which had devastated most of its cities, it was clear that the country could not last long.

The only remote Japanese hope was that the Soviet Union, still at peace with Japan, might negotiate a settlement with the other Allies.

In February 1945 Stalin, Roosevelt, and Churchill met for the last time at the Allied planning conference at Yalta, near Sevastopol. (Roosevelt died shortly afterwards, while Churchill lost the 1945 British election.) Soviet troops had already overrun Poland in January, and although the last battles against Germany had to be fought, the issue was never in doubt. Attacked from east and west in the spring, Germany collapsed. On 27 April Mussolini was captured and shot in northern Italy. On 30 April, as Soviet troops fought their way through the **Battle of Berlin,** the last great city battle, Hitler committed suicide. Germany surrendered completely on 8 May 1945.

The end of Japan was also a foregone conclusion. At Yalta the Soviets had promised to enter the war against Japan three months after the defeat of Germany. At the Allied conference held in Potsdam near Berlin in July, the American government learned that its new secret weapon, the atomic bomb, had been tested successfully. On 6 August the first of these bombs destroyed the Japanese city of Hiroshima. On 8 August the Soviet Union declared war on Japan and overran Japanese-held Manchuria down as far as the Korean peninsula. On 9 August a second atomic bomb destroyed the city of Nagasaki. On 15 August Japan finally surrendered, so ending World War II.

STEPHEN BADSEY

THE ARMOURED BLITZKRIEGS

"For better or worse, soldiers will have to come to terms with the tank… It will be the main battle-winning weapon, wherever it is put into action, and other weapons must accommodate themselves to its needs." HEINZ GUDERIAN, 1937

THE BATTLES OF World War II will be forever associated with the dominance of the tank on the battlefield, replacing the infantry, which for centuries had held the dominant position as the most important of the arms of war. Although the tank itself was first invented and used in World War I, the interwar years saw the development of the genuinely *fast* tank, a machine that was both armed and armoured well enough to fight its way across the battlefield and also to drive deep behind enemy lines once it reached open and undefended country. This combination of speed and strength suggested new ways of fighting battles based on the tank, and the period before World War II saw the development of ideas forever associated with the German word *Blitzkrieg* – 'lightning war'. All three of these battles show the same use of tanks in combination with other forces – particularly airforces – to defeat the enemy by strength and speed, bringing about not only a defeat but a collapse into chaos.

The Fall of France
Blitzkrieg in the West
10 MAY – 22 JUNE 1940

The German Armed Forces under Führer Adolf Hitler

VERSUS

The French Army and British Expeditionary Force under
General Maurice Gamelin

CHRONOLOGY

10 May 1940 –	The start of the German offensive
13 May 1940 –	German forces cross the River Meuse
14 May 1940 –	The Netherlands surrenders
20 May 1940 –	German forces reach the English Channel
28 May 1940 –	Belgium surrenders
4 June 1940 –	End of the Dunkirk evacuation
22 June 1940 –	France surrenders and signs an armistice

"No one has ever achieved what I have achieved… I have led the German people to a great height, even if the world does hate us now." ADOLF HITLER

THE CLASH OF two warring equals often produces lengthy wars, but occasionally such conflicts are resolved rapidly because one of the belligerents better appreciates the potential of the military technologies of the time. If a superior grasp of how to wage war is joined with the advantages of surprise, an imaginative plan opposed to a poor plan, and good fortune, then the defeat inflicted is likely to be catastrophic. Such a defeat was suffered by the Allies – the French and British – in 1940; they were overwhelmed by German forces in just six weeks. So comprehensive was the

German victory that the Netherlands, Belgium, and much of France were occupied, what was left of France was reduced to a rump satellite state of the greater German Reich, and the victors and many neutrals expected Britain to sue for a humiliating peace.

The Rival Armies

So unexpectedly decisive was the Allied defeat that many commentators blamed British and French defeatism – a consequence of memories of the slaughter of World War I and, in the case of France, interwar political turmoil. Britain and France were reluctant to go to war with Germany, and Britain refused to pull its weight in continental land warfare, committing only ten divisions. Memories of World War I weighed heavily on both the Allied governments and people. However, reluctance to fight another great European war was common to all belligerents, and the public mood on the outbreak of World War II in Germany was bleak. Much more detrimental to the Allies than the horror with which they regarded the necessity to wage war again, was the impact of 1914–18 on how they wished to conduct this new war.

Far from being defeatist in 1940, the Allied governments believed that the Germans had already missed their opportunity for a quick victory. The Allies believed they were militarily the equal of the Germans in 1940 and this optimism was based on some powerful military assets. The Allies matched the Germans in troops, and had 5,600 more guns – mainly the excellent French artillery. On the Franco-German frontier, the Maginot Line – a powerful belt of fortifications named after the French minister of war André Maginot – rendered any direct German attack on the Allies problematic. The Allies believed they could withstand any German offensive in 1940; and that in a long war the balance of military power would inexorably shift against Germany. Allied confidence in the 'long game' of attritional war partly resulted from their naval supremacy, which kept Germany blockaded from most of the outside world, ensuring that the Allied economies would out-produce Germany. This belief that the Allies would win a long attritional war – often labelled the 'Maginot Mentality' – was not as unrealistic as some historians suggest. But Allied leaders failed to appreciate that mechanized forces and air power gave Germany the potential to wage a swift and decisive campaign.

Contrary to popular belief, the Allies did not intend to fight a static war, and with more tanks and vehicles than the Germans they were certainly capable of waging mobile war. Unfortunately, over half of Allied mechanized forces were 'penny-packeted' (scattered in small groups along the front).

Despite this dilution of their armoured strength, both the British and French possessed powerful mechanized formations. In 1940 the French had formed three heavy armoured divisions and were forming a fourth, as well as three light mechanized divisions; the British had one armoured division which fought in the later part of the campaign, and their infantry divisions were lavishly equipped with motor vehicles. However, Allied armoured formations were – compared to the Germans – 'tank heavy', and failed to coordinate well with other arms. Allied tanks were designed either to resemble a mobile version of the 'pillboxes' intended for defence, or to deliver a modern version of the cavalry charge. For instance, the French B-1 tank was armed with a 75-mm gun in its hull and a 47-mm gun in its turret – no other tank in 1940 possessed such firepower. But it was slow, mechanically unreliable, had a limited range, and as 75% of all such tanks had no radios, they found it difficult to coordinate with other arms.

The Allies were behind the Germans in 1940, both in terms of the numbers of armoured divisions and the requirement that these should be all-arms formations. In 1940 German tanks were concentrated into ten armoured divisions – known as Panzer divisions from *Panzerkampfwagen* (PzKw or tank). Each Panzer division possessed significant numbers of motorized infantry, artillery, engineers, and signallers, as well as tanks. Technically German tanks were not dissimilar to Allied vehicles – indeed, the PzKw I and PzKw II, the most numerous of the German tanks, were inferior. However, the best German tanks, the PzKw III, PzKw IV, and the Czech-manufactured PzKw 35/38t, all possessed a gun that enabled them to engage most Allied tanks with some prospect of success; they also were protected by adequate armour, and robust engines gave them a good range and an acceptable speed. German tanks had all-round qualities, and were better suited for a role in an all-arms mechanized formation. But it was the way in which the German Army deployed and used its tanks that best explains their contribution to the Allied defeat.

In contrast to the parity on the ground, in the air the *Luftwaffe* (the German airforce) possessed a numerical and technological edge over the Allies. By 1940 the French were producing good modern planes, but the belated French rearmament programme ensured this was too little too late. The British – who had put considerable resources into the Royal Air Force (RAF) in the 1930s – held back a large percentage of their airforce for home defence, and many of the planes deployed in France were obsolete. Despite the technical excellence of the most modern British planes, the RAF focused on the independent role of airpower and was unpractised in close coordination with ground forces. In contrast, the Luftwaffe was closely tied to the German ground forces, and close air support was integral to the way in which Germany conducted ground operations.

The Rival Plans

With the exception of the airforces, the Germans enjoyed no significant numerical or technical advantage. It was how the Germans used their forces that explains their success. Whereas the Allies' strategy was attritional and was predicated on the belief that the war would be lengthy, German strategy was to attempt to decisively defeat the enemy in just one campaign. Between the wars, German military thinkers focused on how to win wars quickly – a blitzkrieg (lightning war).

Blitzkrieg was attractive to Hitler, because he lacked faith in the German people's stamina for a long war. Waging blitzkrieg, Germany could hope to defeat enemies with greater military potential and avoid the drastic reduction in living standards that a lengthy attritional and total war demand. Many conservative German generals were sceptical that a single campaign could defeat the Allies. But in 1940 commanders who believed that a combination of mechanization, airpower, and boldness could deliver rapid results were given the opportunity to vindicate their faith.

Allied operational planning was driven by Belgium's decision in 1936 to abandon its military alliance with France and declare its neutrality (the Netherlands was traditionally neutral). This denied the Allies the chance to meet a German attack on the powerfully fortified, and relatively short, Belgian–German frontier. By selfishly adopting neutrality, Belgium made it certain that it would initially face any German attack alone, and in 1940 both Belgian and Dutch forces were so badly mauled that they made a negligible contribution to the defence of their countries.

The Allies expected an attempt to outflank the Maginot Line to the north, and could have abandoned any plan to defend the Low Countries, meeting the German offensive on the Franco–Belgian frontier. But the Allied supreme commander, the French general Maurice Gamelin, argued instead for an advance into Belgium to block the anticipated German attack. In November 1939, Gamelin persuaded both Allied governments to adopt his 'Plan D', named after the River Dyle in Belgium. However, Gamelin was not content to halt on the Dyle, and the final variant of 'Plan D' called for an Allied advance as far north as the Dutch city of Breda. Gamelin expected Allied forces to move forward quickly and occupy defensive positions prior to contact with any German forces.

Unfortunately, 'Plan D' was fatally flawed. It thrust most of the better Allied formations, including the British Expeditionary Force (BEF), dangerously deep into the Low Countries, while the Namur–Sedan gap was left weakly held by a modest number of third-rate French divisions. This gap ran through the Ardennes forest, and constituted the hinge between the Allied northern wheel into the Low Countries and the Maginot Line. The rugged and tree-covered Ardennes were deemed easily defensible, and unsuitable terrain for mechanized warfare. Gamelin believed that if there were a German thrust through the Ardennes it would take time to prepare, and Belgian defences would slow its execution. Making matters worse for the Allies, the advance into the Low Countries would use up Allied reserve forces, leaving them with little strength to deal with the unexpected. Although some Allied commanders had doubts about 'Plan D', particularly the problems of extracting their forces if things went wrong, Gamelin does not seem to have considered the problems of retreating if worsted by German forces.

The Allied 'Plan D' was designed to move their forces to a position that would strengthen their ability to wage a long war. In contrast, the German *Fall Gelb* (Case Yellow) was designed to knock the Allies out of the war in one swift and decisive campaign. Following the surrender of the Polish Army on 28 September 1939, Adolf Hitler ordered preparations for an immediate offensive against France. Hitler's order was regarded by his generals as unrealistic, but on 19 October the German Armed Forces High Command – *Oberkommando der Wehrmacht* (OKW) – issued the plan *Fall Gelb*. *Fall Gelb* envisaged an attack through the Low Countries with the main weight of the offensive north of the Ardennes. This was the direction of attack which Gamelin anticipated, and it seems unlikely that it could have delivered the decisive result Hitler desired.

The weather, and his generals' opposition, frustrated Hitler's hopes for a winter offensive, but this worked to Germany's advantage as the delay gave the critics of *Fall Gelb* the opportunity to modify the plan. One major criticism was that its line of advance seemed only to repeat the German attack of 1914 at the start of World War I, the Schlieffen Plan, which had failed. In particular, General Erich von Manstein, who was chief of staff of Army Group A, in the centre of the German line including the Ardennes sector, was highly critical of *Fall Gelb* and advocated moving the main thrust southwards.

Hitler, who in practice if not in name already acted as supreme commander of the German Army as well as titular head of the armed forces, also had his doubts about the *Fall Gelb*. As early as October 1939 he suggested that a successful attack launched south of Liège could well enable German forces to advance to the English Channel coast and cut off the Allied armies in the northeast.

Modifications of *Fall Gelb* which shifted the weight of the German attack southwards were already underway, when on 10 January 1940 a German courier aircraft crash-landed near Mechelen in Belgium and a partial copy of the German plan fell into Belgian hands. This incident increased the impetus for major changes. Finally, on 17 February, Hitler met von Manstein – newly promoted to the command of an army corps in occupied Poland – and, finding his views echoed by a military professional, he decided to impose a new plan on his generals.

The revised plan for *Fall Gelb* was bold, so much so that throughout the offensive significant elements of the OKW feared that its boldness could backfire. Army Group C, the weakest of Germany's three army groups opposing the Allies, with only 17 divisions, was deployed along the German–French frontier. Its role was ostentatiously to prepare to assault the Maginot Line, and to leak false plans for an outflanking movement through Switzerland. Army Group B, with over 26 divisions and 2 Panzer divisions, was deployed opposite the Dutch and northern Belgian frontiers. Its role was to invade the Low Countries with massive aerial support, enticing the Allied armies to advance rapidly into Belgium and then preventing their rapid withdrawal in good order. Because it was important for Army Group B to advance quickly in the initial stages of the offensive, it was assigned most of Germany's scarce airborne forces, and given the support of most of the Luftwaffe for the first three days of the attack. Army Group A – constituting the main thrust of the German attack – with over 37 divisions and 7 Panzer divisions was deployed opposite the southern Belgian and Luxembourg frontiers. It was to advance swiftly but stealthily through the Ardennes, cross the River Meuse, and then, if all went well, drive northwest to the coast to cut off the Allied forces in the Low Countries. Provided that operations to the north went according to plan, Army Group A could expect the support of the bulk of the Luftwaffe once it commenced its attempts to cross the Meuse.

The Blitzkrieg

The German offensive commenced at 5.35 a.m. on 10 May. The Luftwaffe quickly won air superiority, attacking Allied communications, formations on the move, and airfields, and destroying Allied planes on the ground. In the north, Army Group B advanced swiftly into the Low Countries, aided by parachutists, gliders, and other special forces. Belgium at once asked for Allied assistance.

The powerful Belgian fort of Eben-Emael was taken by the gliders of the Koch Assault Detachment landing on its flat roof – an action which Hitler personally helped plan. Elsewhere in Belgium and the Netherlands, German airborne forces seized intact bridges over the rivers Waal, Lek, and Meuse, and the Albert Canal. Dutch hopes of holding out in 'Fortress Holland' – the Dutch provinces of Holland which could be completely surrounded by wide belts of water – were dashed by German success in taking and holding the bridge at Moerdijk over the Waal. On 13 May, advanced elements of 9th Panzer Division crossed the Waal bridge northwards into 'Fortress Holland'. In just four days the Dutch were crushed, the bombing of Rotterdam on 14 May merely hastening their surrender.

To the south, the German Sixth Army rapidly smashed through the Belgian frontier defences, joining with the airborne forces to their west holding the bridges over the Albert Canal at Vroenhoven and Veldwezelt. In two days the Belgians lost both of their main fortified lines and were left holding a third line of poor fortifications running from Antwerp to Namur.

The intensity of the German assault in the north made it easy to believe that 'Plan D' was the correct response to the enemy's intentions. On the evening of 10 May, French 1st Army Group (including First Army and the BEF) started moving to the Breda–Dyle line. Allied forces moving into the Low Countries advanced with commendable speed, but contrary to Gamelin's expectations they were forced to confront the Germans in an encounter battle in the open, rather than in fortified positions. Indeed, many of the Belgian positions the Allies expected to occupy were barely fortified.

The Allied formation with the furthest to move was French Seventh Army, but once in the southern Netherlands it found itself subject to heavy air attack, and, lacking armoured support, it retreated in the face of 9th Panzer Division. To the south French forces did better and temporarily halted German Army Group B's thrust into central Belgium. For two days the French I Cavalry Corps under General Robert Prioux, consisting mainly of two light mechanized divisions, delayed XVI Panzer Corps, while French First Army, the BEF, and Belgian forces prepared to defend the Antwerp–Namur line. In the fighting on 15 May, German Sixth Army failed to breach the Allied line in Belgium, and for a few hours the Allied armies believed that they had blocked the German offensive. The rude awakening came that evening: a disaster had befallen French forces to the south, and orders were to retreat.

The German Breakthrough

As German Army Group B invaded the Low Countries, Army Group A was moving through the Ardennes. Two Belgian divisions in the area moved away to the northeast, providing no serious opposition. This lack of Belgian

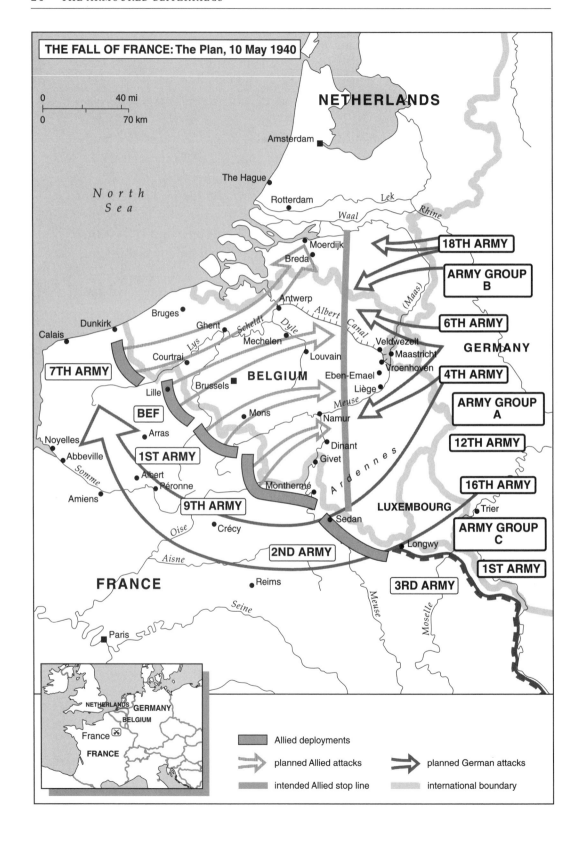

THE FALL OF FRANCE: The Plan, 10 May 1940

0   40 mi
0   70 km

NETHERLANDS

North Sea

Amsterdam

The Hague

Rotterdam

Lek

Waal

Rhine

Moerdijk

Breda

18TH ARMY

ARMY GROUP B

Antwerp

Albert Canal

(Maas)

Bruges

Ghent

Scheldt

Dyle

6TH ARMY

GERMANY

Calais

Dunkirk

Lys

Mechelen

Courtrai

Veldwezelt

Maastricht

Vroenhoven

7TH ARMY

Lille

BEF

Brussels

BELGIUM

Louvain

Eben-Emael

Liège

4TH ARMY

Mons

Meuse

Namur

ARMY GROUP A

Noyelles

Abbeville

Arras

1ST ARMY

Somme

Albert

Péronne

Amiens

9TH ARMY

Dinant

Givet

Ardennes

12TH ARMY

16TH ARMY

Monthermé

Oise

Crécy

2ND ARMY

Sedan

LUXEMBOURG

Trier

ARMY GROUP C

Longwy

1ST ARMY

Aisne

FRANCE

Reims

3RD ARMY

Seine

Meuse

Moselle

Paris

NETHERLANDS   GERMANY

BELGIUM

France

FRANCE

Allied deployments

planned Allied attacks   planned German attacks

intended Allied stop line   international boundary

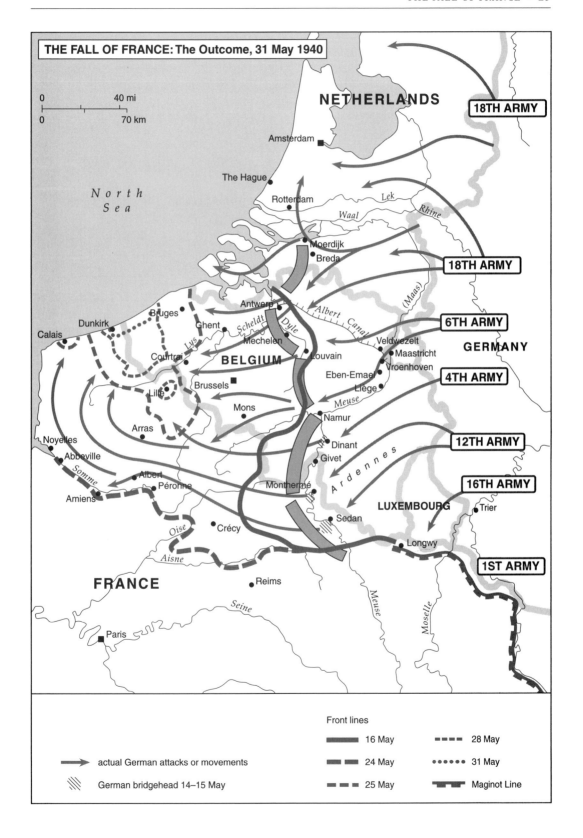

THE FALL OF FRANCE: The Outcome, 31 May 1940

0   40 mi
0   70 km

North
Sea

NETHERLANDS

18TH ARMY

Amsterdam

The Hague
Rotterdam

Lek
Waal
Rhine

Moerdijk
Breda

18TH ARMY

Bruges
Ghent
Dunkirk
Calais

Antwerp
Scheldt
Mechelen
Courtrai
Lys

Dyle
Albert Canal
(Maas)

6TH ARMY

Louvain
Veldwezelt
Maastricht
Vroenhoven

GERMANY

BELGIUM
Brussels

Eben-Emael
Liége

4TH ARMY

Lille
Mons

Meuse
Namur

Arras

Dinant
Givet

Ardennes

12TH ARMY

Noyelles
Abbeville
Somme
Albert
Péronne
Amiens

Monthermé

Sedan

LUXEMBOURG

16TH ARMY

Trier

1ST ARMY

Oise
Crécy

Longwy

Aisne

FRANCE

Reims

Meuse
Moselle

Seine

Paris

Front lines

━━━ 16 May   ▬ ▬ ▬ 28 May

▬ ▬ 24 May   ●●●●● 31 May

━ ━ 25 May   ▬▬▬ Maginot Line

⟶ actual German attacks or movements

⧅⧅ German bridgehead 14–15 May

resistance was bitterly criticized by French commanders, who were not warned of the move. A screen of French light cavalry divisions was rapidly swept aside by the Germans, and simple measures to block the roads – such as felling trees and destroying bridges – were not taken because Allied commanders wanted roads kept open for the forward movement of their own formations. Moving through the Ardennes, Army Group A suffered more delay from traffic jams than from any Allied military action, and it was only on 12 May that Allied bombers made a desultory attack on roads in the region.

By the evening of 12 May, German armour had reached the line of the River Meuse. The Allied High Command still thought that the main German attack was taking place further north, and expected about three days before the enemy was ready to attempt a river crossing. They were wrong: the next day the Germans assaulted the Meuse, the last formidable natural defensive line between them and the Channel coast.

For the 75 miles from Sedan to Namur the River Meuse was wide enough to constitute a formidable natural barrier, and, although in the north the river was overlooked by hills on the eastern bank, from Givet to Sedan the Meuse was dominated by wooded hills on the western (or Allied) bank. But the six overstretched French divisions that held this section of the river were mainly third-rate formations with obsolete equipment. In the north, where the river line was less defensible, French forces were disorganized and exhausted by their move forward to Belgian fortifications, which were found to be largely incomplete. In contrast, the Panzer divisions constituted the cutting edge of the Wehrmacht (German armed forces), and their all-arms mechanized structure – including artillery, engineers, and bridging equipment – meant that they could attempt an immediate crossing, with the Luftwaffe providing the additional firepower necessary to suppress French defences.

Typical of the successful German assaults over the Meuse on 13 May was the crossing of the river at Sedan, conducted by General Heinz Guderian's XIX the Panzer Corps – an operation that was especially important, as it constituted the southern flank of any subsequent advance. Defending the river line at Sedan was the French 55th Division, a 'Category B' division of third-rate reservists. The 55th Division's one potential advantage was its 140 artillery pieces – over double the normal divisional complement – which should have inflicted significant losses on any crossing. However, French artillery was neutralized by German airpower, as two Luftwaffe Flying Corps (roughly 1,100 aircraft) delivered a five-hour bombardment. Matters were exacerbated by French orders, issued in the expectation of a long, attritional slogging match, restricting the supply of shells.

German infantry crossed the river closely supported by Junkers Ju-87 'Stuka' dive bombers, and by nightfall they had neutralized the crucial heights of the Bois de la Marfée that dominated the western bank of this stretch of the Meuse. By midnight XIX Panzer Corps engineers had constructed their first bridge. Getting German heavy equipment and tanks over the river was essential for consolidation and rapid exploitation. French hopes of preventing disaster rested on launching a counterattack to destroy the German bridgehead before it was consolidated. But the two French attempts to destroy the German bridgehead were belatedly launched and ineptly conducted.

After the first small counter-attack had failed, the second planned French counter-attack involved their 3rd Armoured Division, which was available for action just after midday on 14 May. But the attack was postponed and the division dispersed into a defensive line; a fleeting window of opportunity disappeared, and, unable to reunite, the division fought in ineffective dribs and drabs. By 15 May, XIX Panzer Corps, with two other Panzer corps to the north, had consolidated its bridgehead and was ready to advance to the Channel coast.

The Allied Armies Collapse

Looking at the map showing the German advance to the coast, it is tempting to assume that the Allies ought to have been able to organize a counterattack to cut off the German armoured spearhead; indeed, this is what the more cautious among Hitler's generals feared. On both sides of the 'Panzer Corridor', the Allies had substantial forces, and only a few motorized formations defended the German lines of communication. However, the speed of the German surprise advance made it difficult for the Allies to make a coherent military response. The Germans were inside the Allied 'decision-making cycle', which meant Allied commanders were making decisions based on where the Germans had been, rather than where they were at that moment. Panzer divisions bypassed, or simply drove through, the courageous but ineffective attempts by Allied forces to halt their progress, reaching the English Channel coast near Abbeville on 20 May. Meanwhile, the Luftwaffe roamed the skies, launching attacks against Allied forces, hindering military movement, and compounding the chaos on the ground.

In the Low Countries, German Army Group B continued to press Allied forces, and the fall of Antwerp on 18 May undermined Allied efforts to conduct an organized fighting retreat. It is not surprising that Allied attempts to attack the 'Panzer Corridor' were spasmodic and poorly coordinated. There were small successes, such as the British attack against Major General Erwin

Rommel's 7th Panzer Division near Arras on 21 May, which caused the Germans great anxiety. But bolder councils held sway and their advance continued.

On the other side, military disaster exacerbated Allied military and political differences. Traumatized by the extent of the defeat, paralysis set in within the Allied higher commands. On 15 May Britain refused to transfer fighters from home defence to France, and King Leopold of Belgium ordered his forces to retreat north – a clear sign that he was contemplating surrender. Facing the possibility that French 1st Army Group would be completely cut off, the French planned to supply their forces by sea in the hope of attacking the 'Panzer Corridor'. But at the same time, the British planned to abandon the continent and evacuate through the Channel ports, eventually deciding on Dunkirk. On 23 May, the BEF abandoned Arras, and on 25 May French First Army ruled out any offensive action because its losses were too high. Threatened from all sides, French 1st Army Group held onto a strip of the Belgian coast and a narrow finger stretching roughly 80 miles down the French–Belgian frontier.

Allied defences were now disintegrating fast. On 24 May, German Sixth Army broke through the Belgian sector of the line on the River Lys, and the fall of Dunkirk seemed imminent. On 26 May the well-organized British began evacuating Allied forces from Dunkirk, joined rather haphazardly by the French. Matters were made worse on the evening of 27 May by the unilateral Belgian surrender, which briefly left a long gap in the Allied line. Increasingly, the Allied armies were starting to resemble an armed mob and the roads were clogged with defeated troops hoping to avoid capture. That the Allies were able continue evacuating until 4 June, long enough to rescue over 370,000 soldiers (60% of them British), was because Hitler halted the over-extended Panzers for two days, 24–26 May, and because French First Army's defence of the Lille area tied down seven German divisions, three of them Panzer divisions. However, the 'miracle' of Dunkirk must not be allowed to obscure the scale of the disaster: roughly 61 Allied divisions had been destroyed, including the best Allied armoured and motorized formations.

The End of the Battle

The destruction of the Allied armies in the northeast enabled the Germans to halt and replenish for a few days. But on 5 June the German offensive resumed, turning southwards. The newly appointed French supreme commander replacing Gamelin, the 73-year-old general Maxime Weygand, decided to defend the line of the rivers Somme and Aisne. However, this was more a gesture than a realistic strategy, as perhaps 60 demoralized French divisions faced over twice as many German troops, 9 times as many German tanks, and a rampant Luftwaffe dominating the skies.

Too late the French used an effective in-depth defence, showing that their previous debacle was by no means inevitable, but their troops were too thinly spread to prevent a German breakthrough and there were no armoured forces in reserve to launch counter-attacks. By 12 June, German forces had crossed the River Seine on either side of Paris and were moving south of Reims. Completing the defeat, Army Group C with Guderian's Panzers now in support, penetrated the barely defended Maginot Line in Lorraine. Political crisis and military defeat went hand in hand. The French government collapsed, and on 22 June a new government under the 84-year-old marshal Philippe Pétain signed an armistice with Germany, acknowledging total defeat.

SEAN MCKNIGHT

Further Reading

Bond, B *Britain, France and Belgium 1939–1940* (London, 1990)

Cohen, E A, and Gooch, J (eds) *Military Misfortunes* (New York, 1990)

Doughty, R *Breaking Point* (New York, 1990)

Horne, A *To Lose A Battle* (London, 1979)

The Battle of Gazala
Rommel's Masterpiece
26 MAY – 21 JUNE 1942

German and Italian *Panzerarmee Afrika* under
Field Marshal Erwin Rommel

VERSUS

British Eighth Army under Lieutenant General Neil Ritchie

CHRONOLOGY

26 May 1942 – Rommel begins his attack

29 May 1942 – Rommel withdraws into the Cauldron

5 June 1942 – Ritchie begins his counter-attack

12 June 1942 – Rommel renews his attack; Auchinleck assumes command

13 June 1942 – Eighth Army retreats or withdraws to Tobruk

21 June 1942 – Tobruk surrenders to Rommel

"It was only in the desert that the principles of armoured warfare as they were taught in theory before the war could be fully applied and thoroughly developed. It was only in the desert that real tank battles were fought by large-scale formations." ERWIN ROMMEL

THE WIDE OPEN spaces and lack of inhabited areas have always given desert warfare its own particular quality. In World War II, the campaigns fought in the coastal desert of Italian Libya had their own special importance for believers in the tank and in the blitzkrieg. They offered the chance of manoeuvre and the interplay of rapidly moving armoured forces almost in their purest form. It was in this arena that Erwin Rommel, perhaps the most famous of all the German generals of the war, earned his formidable reputation as a winner of armoured battles.

The battle that was fought south of Gazala in eastern Libya, between 26 May and 14 June 1942, is crucial in that it was Rommel's greatest victory over the British Eighth Army. His German *Afrika Korps*, combined with substantial Italian elements, took on and decisively defeated British, Imperial, and Allied forces which were dug-in behind minefields in a strongly defended position. Furthermore, the Eighth Army had a narrow superiority in numbers of men, tanks, and guns. This might seem unexceptional, were it not that orthodox tactics required a 3:1 advantage to the attacker, which was precisely what Montgomery demanded before he attacked Rommel at El Alamein 6 months later. Seen in this light, Rommel's victory was nothing less than miraculous. Yet it should also be remembered that it almost never came to pass, and that for 12 hours at the battle's crisis it was Rommel who contemplated surrender.

The British Plans

The British Eighth Army was no easy opponent for Rommel. Not only had it tasted victory over the Italians in late 1940 and early 1941, but it had also driven back an over-extended *Afrika Korps* to El Agheila in 'Operation Crusader' at the end of 1941. In May 1942 it was in position covering Tobruk (held by its 2nd South African Division), because it had been forced back there by Rommel's outflanking manoeuvre in January. Yet Rommel had been compelled to halt before the apparently well-planned defences of the Gazala Line. Almost 60 miles of minefields (known as the 'mine marsh') stretched south from the coast to the fortress at Bir Hacheim, designed to protect the desert flank of Eighth Army from encirclement.

About 100,000 strong, the bulk of Eighth Army formations were concentrated into 'boxes', independent strongpoints combining infantry and artillery. In the north, there was the 1st South African Division, then the British 50th (Northumbrian) Division, stretching as far as the Sidi Muftah box in the centre of the position. A brigade-sized force of Free French under Major General Joseph Pierre Koenig held Bir Hacheim, yet 20 miles of mine marsh between these two boxes was left uncovered by artillery.

In addition, the British commander Lieutenant General Neil Ritchie had forgotten the lessons of the early desert war. While one of his successful predecessors, Lieutenant General Sir Richard O'Connor, had recognized the need to keep a deep cushion of reconnaissance forces between him and the enemy, Ritchie had almost all his infantry in the front line. His tank formations, 1st Armoured Division, and the famous 7th Armoured Division (the 'Desert Rats'), were kept a little to the right rear of the main position, but they were not properly integrated into the defence and not capable of coordinating with the other arms to best effect. This was despite reforms instituted by the commander-in-chief in the Middle East, General Sir Claude Auchinleck (known as 'the Auk' to all). The 'Crusader' operation, although eventually successful, had proved the inflexibility of grouping armour and infantry in separate divisional formations, so Auchinleck broke them down into self-contained brigade groups with their own engineers and supporting artillery. By the start of the Gazala battle an armoured division was, theoretically at least, composed of an armoured brigade and two motorized infantry brigade groups, and the intention was to combine armour and anti-tank weapons in imitation of successful German tactics.

Yet the Eighth Army lacked the tactical doctrine to operate these novel formations effectively, and the infantry and armour were condemned to fight separate battles. Ritchie's unimaginative deployment was matched by the clumsy command structure. The area north of the Trigh Capuzzo highway he designated as under XIII Corps, commanded by Lieutenant General William ('Strafer') Gott. South of this line lay XXX Corps under Lieutenant General Baron Willoughby Norrie, who commanded troops in the boxes as well as the two armoured divisions, an unhappy arrangement further worsened by their scattered dispositions. Auchinleck advocated a concentration of armour centrally around the box code-named 'Knightsbridge', but Ritchie did not take this advice. Both British commanders were aware that a sweep around Eighth Army's left or desert flank was a likely option; but they were expecting an attack on the centre of their position along the Trigh Capuzzo.

The German Plans

The German attack was code-named 'Operation Theseus'. Field Marshal Rommel's plan, as expressed in his planning order of 1 May, was no less than the destruction of the enemy forces opposing him and the subsequent capture of Tobruk. This fortress had held out against an eight-month siege in 1941, and seizing it was crucial to the wider plan of Rommel's attack upon Egypt. Axis forces numbered about 90,000, including 561 tanks, although 228 of these were of Italian manufacture, known to the British as 'mobile coffins'. Rommel's 333 German tanks, or *Panzerkampfwagen* (PzKw), included 220 PzKw IIIs, most of the rest being PzKw IVs with short-barrelled guns more effective in the infantry support role. There were also upgraded versions of both types, known as 'Specials', whose long 75-mm guns gave them greater penetration, but Rommel had only 4 PzKw IV Specials and 14 PzKw Specials at the beginning of the battle. This was important because it meant that the Germans did not have the decisive qualitative superiority in armour with which they have so often been credited. The British possessed an enormous numerical superiority in armour – 849 tanks – although only 167 were the new US-built M3 Grants, which carried a 75-mm gun and were superior to the PzKw IIIs.

A crucial part of the Desert War was fought in the air. Field Marshal Albert Kesselring of the Luftwaffe, Rommel's immediate superior, was acutely conscious of the need to keep the *Panzerarmee* supplied with petrol, food, and other necessities. In order to do this he directed an intensive bombing campaign against Malta, the British island base which threatened the Axis supply route from Naples to Tripoli. The results led to Kesselring prematurely declaring on 11 April that: 'Malta as a naval base no longer demands consideration'. In the build-up to the Gazala battle, supplies reaching Rommel greatly increased. In January 1942, the *Afrika Korps* received 60,000 tons of fuel; in April this had risen to 150,00 tons. Also, on 26 May, Kesselring was able to assemble some 260 aircraft to support Rommel's attack. Against them, the British Desert Air Force could only muster 190 aircraft, and its US-built P-40 Kittyhawk and Hawker Hurricane fighters proved inferior to the new Messcherschmidt Bf 109F. As a result, the Germans were able to maintain a considerable air superiority throughout the battle.

The Opening Moves

Rommel launched his attack on the afternoon of 26 May. *Gruppe Cruewell* under Lieutenant General Ludwig Cruewell, himself a former *Afrika Korps* commander, consisting of four Italian infantry divisions under X Corps and XXI Corps, attacked the British and South African positions north of the Trigh Capuzzo. This was a feint to persuade the enemy that Cruewell's was the main point of attack.

In fact, Rommel was already leading 10,000 vehicles southeast. At about 9.00 p.m., on the pre-arranged codeword 'Venezia' (Venice), Rommel swung this force around Eighth Army's southern flank. On the inside of the wheel were the Italian Trieste Motorized Division, then their Ariete Armoured Division, then the German mobile forces: 21st Panzer Division, 15th Panzer Division, and, on the extreme right flank, 90th Light Division. The last named carried aircraft propellers to create more dust and convince the British that theirs was also a tank formation.

At 6.30 a.m. on 27 May the Ariete fell upon the surprised 3rd Indian Motorized Brigade and, although held up momentarily, dispersed it with the help of a few tanks from 21st Panzer Division. One hour later, 90th Light Division came into contact with the 7th Motorized Brigade (part of 7th

Armoured Division), which was also driven back, and by 10.00 a.m. it had reached the El Adem crossroads.

The heaviest fighting commenced at 8.30 a.m. in the centre of the armoured sweep. The two German armoured divisions were opposed by just one: 7th Armoured Division. The British were not properly concentrated, but still managed to inflict damage on the enemy formations. The Grants performed well, their 75-mm guns penetrated the panzers' armour, while the Germans were amazed that their own 50-mm anti-tank weapons' shells bounced off the new tanks. The confusion was exemplified by the capture and later escape of 7th Armoured Division's commander, Major General F W Messervy, when his headquarters was overrun, leaving the British cipher in enemy hands, and his division without a commander for two days.

The Cauldron Battle

By nightfall on 27 May, 90th Light Division had been forced off its position at El Adem by heavy bombing from the Desert Air Force. Also, 15th Panzer Division and 21st Panzer Division were still 15 miles short of their own target at Acroma. By now over a third of their tanks had been put out of action, and ammunition and fuel supplies were exhausted. Rommel had overreached himself, but Eighth Army was unable to react quickly or forcefully enough. There was an opportunity to counter-attack with a fresh unit, the 32nd Army Tank Brigade, together with elements of 1st Army Tank Brigade and both 1st Armoured Division and 7th Armoured Division; but it could not be properly exploited. Ariete Division fought off the combined attacks of 1st Army Tank Brigade and 2nd Armoured Brigade (part of 1st Armoured Division). The German panzer divisions had been severely disrupted, and dug in between Rigel Ridge and Bir el Harmat.

Rommel was now very worried and admitted to having underestimated the strength of the British armoured forces. The strike force of his *Panzerarmee* was now effectively surrounded and out of supplies, with no possibility of replenishment. Rommel was still trying to press on during 29 May, but 15th Panzer Division had been reduced to 40 tanks and was out of fuel, while 21st Panzer Division was only able to advance to the edge of the escarpment and shell troops below, and also attacked a position known as Commonwealth Keep. Here a small garrison put up a stubborn resistance before being overwhelmed.

On 29 May the British put in a substantial counter-attack with 2nd Armoured Brigade, later supported by 22nd Armoured Brigade, both part of 1st Armoured Division. Casualties were heavy on both sides, with one British armoured regiment, the 10th Hussars, being reduced to only four serviceable tanks. Rommel had to admit that he could make no further penetration. As a result, he was forced to withdraw into a position which became known as 'The Cauldron'. He was also unaware of the existence of 150th Infantry Brigade (part of 50th Division) in its 'box' in his rear. This meant that Rommel's entire panzer strike force was now effectively surrounded.

This could have been disastrous; although the efforts of *Gruppe Cruewell* in penetrating the minefield around the Trigh Capuzzo at least gave Rommel hope of being resupplied. He personally crossed the minefields to consult Kesselring as to how to regain the initiative. The British were jubilant at this point, yet failed to exploit the situation to their advantage. The German tactic of combining anti-tank guns – especially the formidable 88-mm – with their panzers meant that the British tanks were very vulnerable. In order to counter this the British needed to combine artillery support with the armoured thrusts, as the field guns' high explosive ammunition could have destroyed or suppressed the unprotected anti-tank guns. That this was not forthcoming was entirely due to the failings of British tactical doctrine and the absence of training for such a combined assault.

As a result, 2nd Armoured Brigade and 22nd Armoured Brigade were flung headlong at a strong position, and reduced to a third of their original strength. Meanwhile Rommel turned his attention to the destruction of 150th Infantry Brigade in his rear. It put up a stubborn a resistance, aided by the new 6-pounder anti-tank guns and a detachment of 4th Armoured Brigade from 7th Armoured Division. Each strongpoint within the box was only taken after hand-to-hand fighting, but with their ammunition exhausted the defenders finally surrendered on 1 June: 3,000 men, 100 tanks, and over 100 guns going 'into the bag'.

Rommel Attacks Again

In securing his line of supply, Rommel had made possible a renewed offensive. This took place in two directions on 2 June, against Acroma northwards (the original objective of 26 May) and towards Bir Hacheim at the extreme southern end of the Gazala Line. Crucial to this period of the battle was the inability of the British to react, as their commanders wavered over what to do. On 3 June, Ritchie wrote to Auchinleck that, 'I have decided that I must crush [the enemy] in "The Cauldron"', and planned 'Operation Aberdeen' to achieve this. But the moment had already passed. The British attack commenced on 5 June only to be handicapped by the lack of all-arms cooperation. For example, 9th Indian Infantry Brigade (from 2nd South

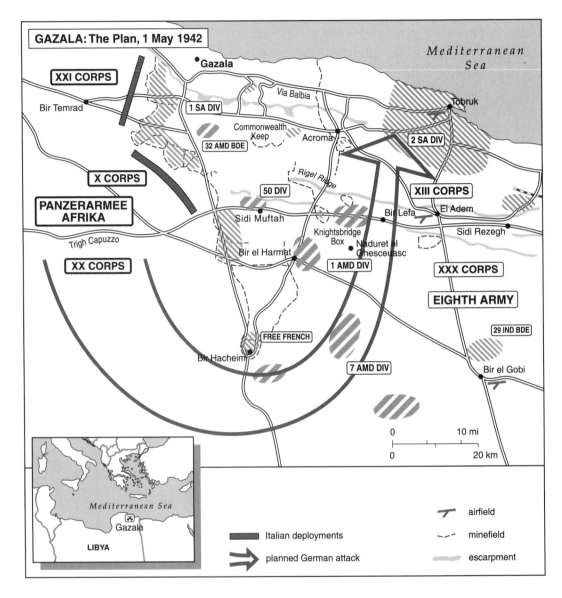

GAZALA: The Plan, 1 May 1942

Mediterranean Sea

XXI CORPS

Gazala

Bir Temrad

Via Balbia

1 SA DIV

Commonwealth Keep

Acroma

Tobruk

32 AMD BDE

2 SA DIV

X CORPS

Rigel Ridge

50 DIV

XIII CORPS

PANZERARMEE AFRIKA

Sidi Muftah

Bir Lefa

El Adem

Trigh Capuzzo

Knightsbridge Box

Naduret el Ghesceuasc

Sidi Rezegh

Bir el Harmat

XX CORPS

1 AMD DIV

XXX CORPS

EIGHTH ARMY

29 IND BDE

FREE FRENCH

Bir Hacheim

7 AMD DIV

Bir el Gobi

0   10 mi

0   20 km

Mediterranean Sea

Gazala

LIBYA

Italian deployments

planned German attack

airfield

minefield

escarpment

African Division) was supposed to coordinate with 22nd Armoured Brigade's 156 tanks, but this simply failed to happen because the infantry and armour had not trained together. In the north, an attack by 32nd Army Tank Brigade was struck in the flank by German panzers, and of the 70 Matilda and Valentine infantry tanks only 20 survived the attack.

On the afternoon of 5 June the Germans counter-attacked; a pincer movement with 21st Panzer Division and Ariete in the north and 15th Panzer from the south. That evening, Major General Messervy's headquarters was overrun again, and the Indian units' command and control broke down

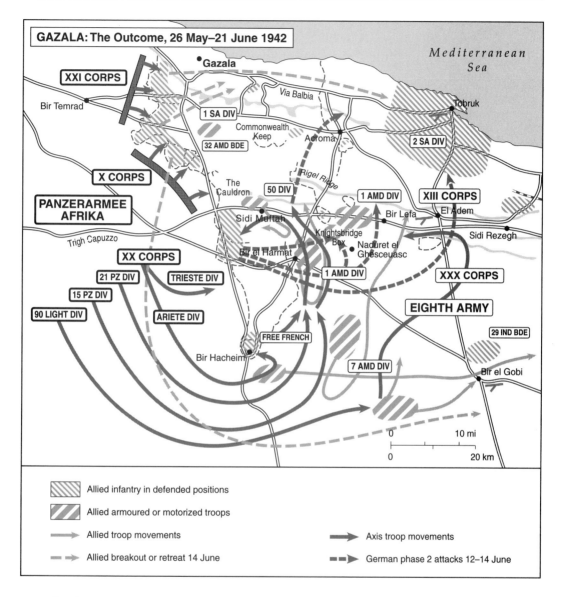

GAZALA: The Outcome, 26 May–21 June 1942

Legend:
- Allied infantry in defended positions
- Allied armoured or motorized troops
- Allied troop movements
- Allied breakout or retreat 14 June
- Axis troop movements
- German phase 2 attacks 12–14 June

completely; 22nd Armoured Brigade was unable to provide any support, having already been withdrawn into leaguer for the night. It too had been severely handled, losing 60 tanks. The following day 15th Panzer struck through Bir el Harmat to close the line of retreat: 3,100 prisoners, 96 guns, and 37 anti-tank guns fell into German hands. Eighth Army had lost over half its cruiser tanks (down from 300 to 132), and 50 out of 70 infantry support tanks. Rommel's assessment of the situation was that Ritchie had missed a great opportunity to form a *Schwerpunkt* ('critical point of an attack') in front of 21st Panzer Division.

One area in which the British did enjoy success was in raids upon the German supply line. On 8 June, Italian positions were overrun by four troops from 8th Royal Tank Regiment supported by South African armoured car and reconnaissance units. On the same day an infantry column of 2nd Rifle Brigade destroyed over 40 lorries, 4 tanks, and 7 artillery pieces. Important though such moves were, they were no more than flea bites in comparison to the kind of response that was needed to hold Rommel in check. With the hapless British assault crushingly repulsed, he was able to turn his attention to the destruction of the isolated Free French at Bir Hacheim.

Crisis at Bir Hacheim

From 2 June to 9 June there were 1,300 German air attacks on the Bir Hacheim position, 120 on the last day alone. Rommel appreciated the difficulty of the task, since he considered the carefully prepared strongpoints within Bir Hacheim as 'practically proof against air and artillery attacks'. Effective ground attacks began on 6 June, the day that Rommel broke out of 'The Cauldron', when two attacks by infantry with tank support were beaten off. On 8 June, 90th Light Division and the Trieste Division, combined with 15th Panzer Division and supported by heavy Junkers Ju-87 Stuka dive-bombing attacks, eventually began to the crack the position – 'the thorn in my side', as Rommel described it. Attacks the next day left 250 Axis dead in front one defending battalion's position alone. But by the end of 9 June it was apparent to Koenig that Bir Hacheim could no longer be held.

Still, Rommel was unwilling to try and overrun the position with tanks because of the heavy losses which he knew he would have to take. On 11 June, Koenig engineered a breakout which left only 500 men in German hands, although losses in equipment had been heavy. By holding on so determinedly the Free French had bought time for their Allies. Could this now be used to the best advantage? Although Rommel had turned Eighth Army's flank, all was not lost for the British. They held a strong defensive position stretching from the original Gazala Line in its northern portion and along the Trigh Capuzzo from the Knightsbridge box over 20 miles east to Sidi Regezh. This was defended in depth, and behind lay the garrison of Tobruk, although crucially, the town's fortifications had not been repaired since its recovery six months earlier. Also, the *Afrika Korps* had taken substantial damage. It was below half its original strength and some infantry units were down to a third; the Germans had 160 tanks and the Italians 70 tanks, although the Axis artillery was almost entirely intact, and was to be increased in strength by the large numbers of captured British guns which were distributed to its units.

The End of the Battle

For the next phase of the battle, Rommel was determined to repeat the medicine as before. Once more he intended the total destruction of the enemy. On the afternoon of 11 June, 90th Light Division moved south and leaguered for the night 7 miles south of El Adem, while 15th Panzer followed as far as Naduret el Bhesceuasc. The new British plan was to break through southeast to Bir el Gubi with 2nd Armoured Brigade and 4th Armoured Brigade, which would bring them upon the flank of 15th Panzer as it attacked El Adem. But the British armour was still forming up on 12 June when it was attacked from the north by 21st Panzer and Ariete and counter-attacked from the south by 15th Panzer. Although 22nd Armoured Brigade came to the assistance, it was severely mauled by German tanks. The other armoured brigades were then surrounded and destroyed. Although the figures are uncertain, it seems that on the morning of 12 June there were some 250 cruiser tanks and 80 infantry tanks available to the British; by the next day these had been reduced to 50 and 30 respectively, with 4th Armoured Brigade having only 15 tanks, and 2nd and 22nd Armoured Brigades only 50 tanks between them.

On 12 June, Auchinleck flew up from Cairo to assume direct command from Ritchie, but he was too late to save the situation. Almost the only factor in Eighth Army's favour was the extreme exhaustion of the German forces, whose attacks began to falter towards the end of 13 June. The Gazala Line had become untenable. Auchinleck drew up plans for a new defensive position, centred upon Acroma, to prevent the investment of Tobruk, and Eighth Army troops west of this line were effectively abandoned to the enemy. On the night of 14 June, the South Africans in the north of the original line fell back down the Via Balbia to Tobruk. Elements of 50th (Northumbrian) Division actually broke through the Italians opposing them and swung through the desert, escaping to Egypt. For the rest of the British forces, Tobruk provided an illusory refuge. They fell back in disorder to a position that had not been maintained to provide an effective defence. Unlike the previous year when the garrison had held out for eight months, the situation was to prove impossible, and by 21 June the town had fallen. Some 35,000 British and Commonwealth troops (including over 13,000 South Africans) were taken prisoner, together with huge amounts of guns, ammunition, and especially fuel essential to the *Afrika Korps'* continued mobility.

After the Battle

Rommel's plan had succeeded brilliantly. Although it had come near to failure on 29 May, and he himself had been prepared to surrender, Rommel was able to rescue the situation and inflict upon Eighth Army the most severe defeat it had ever suffered. His signal of 21 June epitomizes his style of command: 'For all troops of the *Panzerarmee*... Fortress of Tobruk has capitulated. All units will reassemble and prepare for further advance'. Five days later he was at El Alamein, the last-ditch defence line before Egypt – but that is another story. Summer 1942 was the zenith of Rommel's career in North Africa. He himself summed up why the British could not beat him by asking, 'What is the advantage of enjoying overall superiority if you allow your enemy to smash your formations one after another; your enemy who manages in single actions to concentrate superior forces at a decisive point?' That was the essence of the kind of war he practised: blitzkrieg.

MATTHEW BENNETT

Further Reading

Agar-Hamilton J A I , and Turner, L C F *Crisis in the Desert* (London, 1952)

Barnett, C *The Desert Generals* (London, 1960)

Macksey, K *Rommel, Battles and Campaigns* (London, 1979)

Operation Bagration
The Soviet Sledgehammer
22 JUNE – 8 JULY 1944

German Army Group Centre under Field Marshal Ernst Busch

VERSUS

Soviet 1st Belorussian Front under Colonel General
K K Rokossovsky
2nd Belorussian Front under Colonel General G F Zakharov
3rd Belorussian Front under Colonel General
I D Chernyakhovsky
1st Baltic Front under General I K Bagramayan

CHRONOLOGY

22 June 1944 – 'Operation Bagration' starts
26 June 1944 – Vitebsk and Bobruisk encircled
28 June 1944 – Field Marshal Busch dismissed
30 June 1944 – The Red Army crosses the Berezina
3 July 1944 – Soviet troops enter Minsk
8 July 1944 – German forces surrender east of Minsk

"The destruction of 30 divisions, in other words almost the whole of the Army Group: the whole of the Fourth Army, the bulk of Ninth Army and the Third Panzer Army..."
LIEUTENANT GENERAL RUDOLF BAMBLER, CAPTURED IN THE BATTLE

AMONG THE BLITZKRIEGS of World War II, German offensives have often held centre stage. But their enemies also could master the planning and execution of great armoured drives, sometimes to an even greater degree. By the closing years of the war, no-one was better at this than the great Red Army of the Soviet Union, if only because of the sheer scale on which it could conduct its operations. On 22 June 1944, three years to the day that Germany had invaded the Soviet Union, Joseph Stalin unleashed the Red Army on the German Army Group Centre. 'Operation Bagration', a name chosen by Stalin personally after a heroic Russian commander of the war against Napoleon, was to prove devastatingly successful.

The Origins of the Battle

The Germans had lost the initiative on the Eastern Front at Kursk during July 1943 and, in the ensuing months, found themselves engaged in a desperate fight for survival as the Red Army launched a series of offensives, predominantly in the Ukraine. In October 1943 the Soviets crossed the River Dnieper and in November 1943 liberated Kiev, the capital of the Ukraine. In the teeth of tenacious resistance, the Soviets sustained their assault throughout the winter and by the end of March 1944 completed the liberation of the Ukraine. During the pause enforced by the spring thaw in April 1944, both sides regrouped and considered their strategy for the summer campaign.

The German Plan

Despite the defeats inflicted upon the Wehrmacht since July 1943, Hitler believed that the Soviet Union would still collapse, as the old Russian Empire had in 1917. He refused to acknowledge that the Red Army's strength was increasing while that of the Wehrmacht was declining. In late April 1944, based upon intelligence reports, Hitler and the German High Command decided that the main Soviet offensive would attack Army Group North Ukraine rather than Army Group Centre in Belorussia. The relatively open terrain of the Ukraine was more suitable for manoeuvre war than the marshy and forested ground in Belorussia. Equally, although Belorussia offered a direct route to Poland, the road and rail network was poor in comparison with the Ukraine, and the Germans did not believe the Red Army possessed commanders of the ability and flair to offset the difficult terrain. Furthermore, although German intelligence acknowledged that the Soviets might launch attacks in Belorussia to support those in the Ukraine, they were confident that the awkward going would undermine the Soviet's numerical advantage. German confidence was reinforced by Army Group Centre's success in defeating previous Soviet attempts to destroy it. In this strategic intelligence assessment, assiduously created and nurtured by Red Army deception plans, lay the roots of the German disaster. It was fatally flawed:

the Soviet aim was to strike in Belorussia while fixing German reserves in the Ukraine.

This strategic miscalculation ensured Army Group Centre was unprepared for 'Operation Bagration'. Under the command of Field Marshal Busch since October 1943, Army Group Centre numbered 800,000 men, of which 400,000 were experienced combat troops. It was primarily an infantry force due to the redeployment of armour, through expectations of the main Soviet blow coming in the Ukraine, and the terrain, which lent itself to defence. Army Group Centre lacked air power for reconnaissance and close air support. It was short of reserves, particularly armoured formations, in line with German strategic assumptions. However, these deficiencies were partially remedied by Army Group Centre's extensive defensive positions on a sector of the front that had been dormant since December 1943. Nevertheless, the German positions lacked tactical density and operational depth, leaving them vulnerable to a rapid Soviet attack.

The Soviet Plan

By 1944, although he continued to play a key role in grand strategy, Stalin had learned the importance of allowing his military commanders to display their own strategic, operational, and tactical abilities. As a result, during 'Bagration' Soviet commanders were able to operate in a more flexible and independent manner than their German counterparts. In mid-April 1944 Stalin and the Soviet High Command (STAVKA) decided Belorussia would be the decisive strategic axis for the Summer. German resistance, although broken, had been formidable during Spring 1944 and the Red Army was keen to avoid a frontal clash with the powerful armoured formations of Army Group North Ukraine.

Belorussia was an attractive strategic option for several reasons. A successful advance would drive out Army Group Centre, leaving Army Group North and Army Group North Ukraine, to the north and south respectively, in a difficult position. It would liberate millions of Soviet citizens, and bring the Red Army to the Polish border, only 400 miles from Berlin. If the Germans could be surprised, something Soviet intelligence indicated was likely, the difficult terrain was considered to offer as many opportunities as pitfalls. If the shallow German defences were quickly penetrated then it would be virtually impossible for the Germans to coordinate an effective mobile defence. The fact that German intelligence anticipated the main blow in the Ukraine indicated that German positions in Belorussia, although extensive, would continue to lack depth, thus increasing the chances of a Soviet breakthrough.

By 1944 the Red Army was a powerful instrument of war. The four Soviet Fronts allocated to 'Bagration' by STAVKA had a combined strength of 1,250,000 troops, giving them a significant, if not overwhelming, numerical advantage. (A Soviet 'Front' was an operational level fighting formation, and not an exact replica of a German Army Group, being smaller in size and role; a Soviet 'Army' also was much smaller than its German equivalent.) The main operational objective of 'Bagration', the capture of Minsk so trapping Army Group Centre in the forests of Belorussia, was given to 1st Belorussian Front under Colonel General K K Rokossovsky and 3rd Belorussian Front under Colonel General I D Chernyakhovsky. General I K Bagramayan's 1st Baltic Front was to guard the northern flank from interference by German Army Group North. The smallest formation, 2nd Belorussian Front, commanded by Colonel General G F Zakharov, had the relatively minor role of fixing German formations in place and clearing up pockets of resistance.

The key strengths of the Red Army in 1944 were armour, artillery, and air power as well as the ability to deceive the Germans as to where, when, in what strength, and with what objectives it would attack. This was to play a key role in creating the conditions in which the Red Army would deal a hammer blow to German hopes on the Eastern Front.

The Opening Moves

The Soviets appreciated that a quick tactical breakthrough and operational encirclement of Army Group Centre was dependent upon the Germans failing to reinforce the depth of their defences in Belorussia. By 1944, the Soviets were masters of *maskirovka* ('masking'), a process of systematic deception, camouflage, and disinformation designed to create optimum conditions for a Soviet offensive. It was regarded as a mandatory – not optional – form of combat support for all commanders. STAVKA set in motion a major strategic deception campaign designed to induce German reserves into the Ukraine.

The Soviets understood that German intelligence was heavily dependent upon identifying the location of the elite Soviet 'tank armies', the key to Soviet deep operations, of which there were six in 1944. STAVKA played on this by ensuring that all six tank armies were deployed in the Ukrainian region in May 1944. In addition, 3rd Ukrainian Front was instructed to simulate a major deployment, involving 13 divisions, while overt Soviet air reconnaissance was stepped up. The Soviets appreciated the impossibility of disguising the presence of front-line tactical formations in Belorussia, but sought to hide the true significance of their strategic intentions by concealing the scale of their operational reserves.

Soviet *maskirovka* was remarkably successful. On the eve of 'Bagration', Army Group Centre had identified 140 out of 168 front-line Soviet divisions in Belorussia, but had only marked three tank corps when there were in fact eight. German intelligence had also completely missed the presence of 6th Guards Army with 1st Baltic Front, and the formidable 5th Guards Tank Army with 3rd Belorussian Front. Although German intelligence anticipated some attacks in Belorussia, these were seen as minor tactical diversions and a clumsy Soviet attempt to lure the Germans from the Ukraine. The success of the Soviet deception plan was confirmed by the transfer of LVI Panzer Corps from Army Group Centre to Army Group North Ukraine on 30 May 1944, and by the staggering fact that Field Marshal Busch, the commander of Army Group Centre, flew to Hitler's headquarters literally hours before the launch of 'Bagration'.

Operation Bagration

In the early hours of 22 June, following a series of partisan raids against German communication lines starting on 19 June, the Red Army launched 'Bagration' with a series of incursions along the front, designed to probe German defences and force the German infantry to occupy their positions underneath the Soviet preliminary bombardment. At dawn on 23 June a two-hour Soviet artillery offensive began, ranging over the entire depth of the German defences, universally described by German survivors as being of a shocking intensity and effectiveness. It was initially intended that it should be accompanied by air strikes of a similar magnitude, but, as much of the battlefield was shrouded in mist, only 160 sorties were flown by aircraft from 3rd Belorussian Front, with little effect.

The Encirclement of Vitebsk

The Soviet assault made its first significant gains in the north, as 1st Baltic Front and 3rd Belorussian Front made a joint assault on Vitebsk, the northern anchor of Army Group Centre's position in Belorussia, held by Colonel General Georg-Hans Reinhardt's Third Panzer Army. By the morning of 24 June, 6th Guards Army had broken through German IX Corps to the north of Vitebsk, in conjunction with 43rd Army which had penetrated German LIII Corps. To the south, 39th Army was threatening to encircle and trap the rest of LIII Corps in the city.

In response, Reinhardt ordered IX Corps to begin a fighting withdrawal to the River Dvina, and that evening asked for Hitler's permission to withdraw

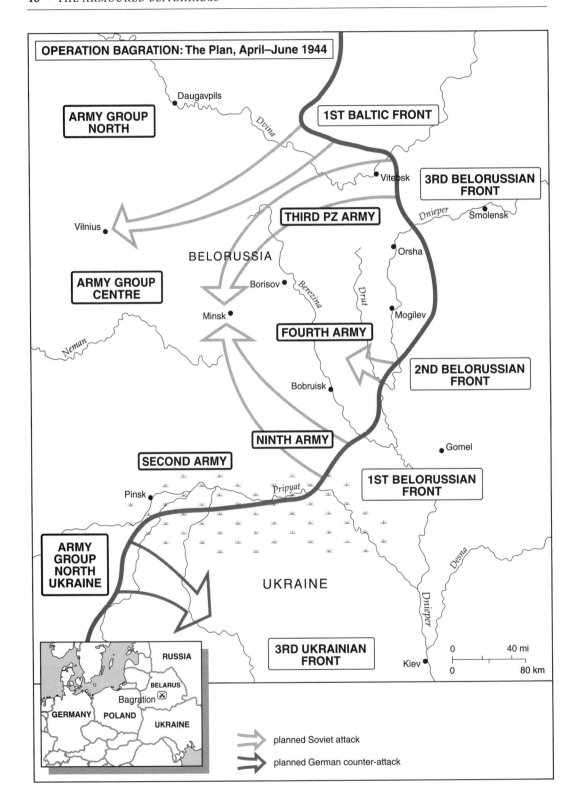

OPERATION BAGRATION: The Plan, April–June 1944

Daugavpils

ARMY GROUP NORTH

Dvina

1ST BALTIC FRONT

Vitebsk

3RD BELORUSSIAN FRONT

Dnieper   Smolensk

THIRD PZ ARMY

Vilnius

BELORUSSIA

Orsha

ARMY GROUP CENTRE

Borisov

Berezina

Drut

Minsk

Mogilev

Neman

FOURTH ARMY

2ND BELORUSSIAN FRONT

Bobruisk

NINTH ARMY

Gomel

SECOND ARMY

Pinsk

Pripyat

1ST BELORUSSIAN FRONT

ARMY GROUP NORTH UKRAINE

UKRAINE

Desna

Dnieper

3RD UKRAINIAN FRONT

Kiev

| 0 | | 40 mi |
| 0 | | 80 km |

RUSSIA

BELARUS

Bagration ⊠

GERMANY   POLAND

UKRAINE

planned Soviet attack

planned German counter-attack

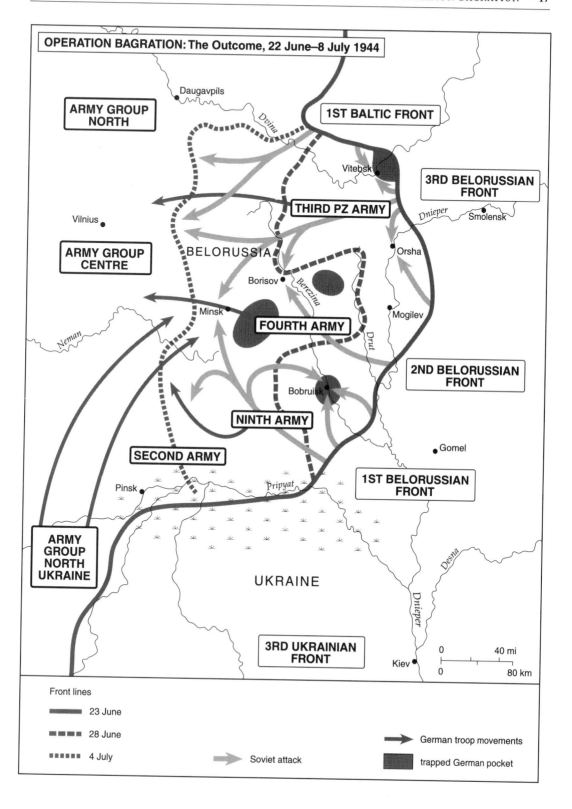

OPERATION BAGRATION: The Outcome, 22 June–8 July 1944

Daugavpils

Dvina

ARMY GROUP NORTH

1ST BALTIC FRONT

Vitebsk

3RD BELORUSSIAN FRONT

Dnieper   Smolensk

THIRD PZ ARMY

Vilnius

ARMY GROUP CENTRE

BELORUSSIA

Orsha

Borisov

Berezina

FOURTH ARMY

Mogilev

Minsk

Neman

Drut

2ND BELORUSSIAN FRONT

Bobruisk

NINTH ARMY

SECOND ARMY

Pripyat

1ST BELORUSSIAN FRONT

Pinsk

Gomel

ARMY GROUP NORTH UKRAINE

Desna

UKRAINE

Dnieper

3RD UKRAINIAN FRONT

Kiev

0   40 mi
0   80 km

Front lines

——— 23 June

▬ ▬ ▬ 28 June

▪▪▪▪▪ 4 July

➤ German troop movements

➤ Soviet attack

■ trapped German pocket

LIII Corps. This was initially refused, but at 8.25 p.m. Hitler relented, insisting only that a single division – 208th Infantry Division – was to remain in the city and fight it out to the last man if necessary. It was too late: the forces of 1st Baltic Front and 3rd Belorussian Front had already linked up, and IX Corps discovered to its dismay that 1st Baltic Front's troops had beaten it to the River Dvina.

The speed of the Soviet move stunned the German commanders. By the evening of 26 June, LIII Corps isolated in Vitebsk had ceased to exist as an effective fighting force. By the next day, Third Panzer Army's position in Belorussia had been irretrievably ruptured. The first nail had been hammered, with startling speed and intensity, into the coffin of Army Group Centre, as Soviet exploitation units raced west and southwest across Belorussia.

The Assault on Orsha

While this was happening, further Soviet gains were being made elsewhere. The town of Orsha on the River Dnieper was a critical tactical and operational position for both sides, a major rail as well as road junction. The region was defended by German Fourth Army under General Kurt Tippelskirch, who had 14th Infantry Division guarding the Moscow–Minsk road, supported by two of the strongest German divisions in Belorussia: 78th 'Sturm' Division ('assault' or 'storm' division, an honorary title granted in 1942) and 25th Panzergrenadier Division.

The southern wing of 3rd Belorussian Front had the task of securing the highway in the Orsha–Borisov sector. STAVKA intended that General K N Galitsky's heavily reinforced 11th Guards Army should break the formidable German tactical defences, opening a passage for 5th Guards Tank Army to transform the tactical victory into operational success by crossing the River Berezina near Borisov. STAVKA also ordered 2nd Belorussian Front to prevent German Fourth Army from diverting reserves north to Orsha by attacking on a broad front towards Mogilev. German units, as they were bypassed and outflanked, would then face a stark choice of retreating across the River Berezina or being crushed by the follow-up forces of 2nd Belorussian Front.

On 23rd June, 11th Guards Army began its assault on 78th 'Sturm' Division and 25th Panzergrenadier Division and, despite being reinforced with special assault formations, ran into fierce opposition. Next day, a reconnaissance patrol of 1st Guards Rifle Division managed to infiltrate a marshy and heavily wooded area between 78th 'Sturm' Division and its neighbour to the north, 256th Infantry Division. Galitsky immediately diverted his main reserve – II Guards Tank Corps – to develop this unexpected opportunity; 11th Guards Army fought a furious battle to defend and expand the opening, and by 25 June had broken the German line to the northwest of Orsha.

On the same evening, General Tippelskirch insisted that Fourth Army must withdraw to the west bank of the Dnieper. Field Marshal Busch reminded him of Hitler's uncompromising attitude to withdrawal, but Tippelskirch surreptitiously allowed the withdrawal. By 26 June the German position had crumbled and II Guards Tank Corps bypassed Orsha to the north, detaching a single brigade to envelop the town. Orsha fell to a combined assault by 11th Guards Army and 31st Army in the early hours of 27 June.

The Race for the Berezina

With the Dvina crossed, the Dnieper breached, and Orsha taken, the Red Army charged southwest towards the River Berezina and the town of Borisov, northeast of Minsk. A deadly race began between retreating German units and Soviet exploitation forces, led by 5th Guards Tank Army and II Guards Tank Corps.

It now became clear to the German high command that they had been duped as to the location of the main Soviet blow. German reserves were frantically despatched from Army Group North Ukraine back to Army Group Centre from whence they had come. The first of these, the powerful 5th Panzer Division, was deployed as a blocking force east of Borisov to hold the Berezina crossings long enough to permit the ragged remnants of Tippelskirch's Fourth Army, pounded mercilessly by the Red Air Force, to escape to the western bank of the river. On 28 June, 5th Panzer Division successfully fought a sharp encounter with Soviet III Guards Tank Corps on the main highway east of Borisov. But Soviet troops began to infiltrate the defences to the northwest of the town, and by the next day the rifle divisions of 11th Guards Army had caught up and cut the main Minsk–Smolensk road, preventing the escape of further German troops westward.

While Soviet troops were crossing the Berezina to the north of Borisov, to the south the commander of 35th Guards Tank Brigade forded the river by driving his tanks into it to act as a ramshackle but effective bridge. By 30 June the Soviets were across the river in strength, driving German 31st Infantry Division and 267th Infantry Division before them, and trapping the majority of the defunct Fourth Army to the east of the river.

The Annihilation of Ninth Army

As 3rd Belorussian Front's forces surged west across the Berezina, Colonel General K K Rokossovsky's 1st Belorussian Front was advancing towards Minsk from the south. On the first day of 1st Belorussian Front's attack, the northern assault group led by 48th Army struggled to make any progress in swampy conditions. The tactical success of German 134th Infantry Division in defending the northern position led General Hans Jordan, commanding Ninth Army, to commit his main reserve formation, 20th Panzer Division. As the tanks of 20th Panzer Division advanced, Rokossovsky seized his opportunity and ordered his southern assault group to attack.

In a matter of hours, 65th Army had demolished the German defences in the south, and Rokossovsky committed I Guards Tank Corps to exploit the breach. In response Jordan, recognizing that these developments threatened to trap the whole of Ninth Army, diverted 20th Panzer to deal with I Guards Tank Corps. As it struggled to overcome the difficult terrain, 20th Panzer's attack on the right flank of I Guards Tank Corps was unable to stem the rising tide, and its muddled diversion enabled 48th Army and 3rd Army to redeem their earlier failures in the north. The Soviet armoured forces, aided by engineers, infantry, and an unopposed Red Air Force, crashed northwards over marsh and stream and through forest towards Bobruisk. To the east near Rogachev, 3rd Army led by IX Tank Corps dashed for the Berezina, while 48th Army to its left pinned down desperate German formations.

On the morning of 27 June, IX Tank Corps seized bridgeheads over the Berezina northeast of Bobruisk. It was met by I Guards Tank Corps coming from southwest of Bobruisk, and the pincers closed trapping 40,000 troops of Ninth Army to the east of the Berezina, in a classic encirclement. Simultaneously, by moving northwards to the town of Berezino, 1st Belorussian Front forces, in conjunction with 3rd Belorussian Front, had pinned German Fourth Army on the eastern bank of the Berezina.

Army Group Centre was disintegrating, as brilliantly executed Soviet blows rained in from all directions. On 27 June, General Jordan was sacked and Busch was relieved the following day, as Reinhardt and Tippelskirch struggled to save their armies from complete annihilation. Rokossovsky ordered three of his rifle armies, 3rd Army, 48th Army, and 65th Army, to hold the Bobruisk pocket. The area east and southeast of Bobruisk became a killing ground, as German units were destroyed by the Red Air Force and Soviet artillery.

In response, Hitler ordered 12th Panzer Division to help Ninth Army, but it was intercepted on 28 June, about 12 miles west of Bobruisk, by the 'Cavalry-Mechanized Group' (a mixture of horsed cavalry and vehicles) that

Rokossovsky had deployed on 27 June to guard the western approaches of the Bobruisk pocket. As the Soviet infantry advanced into Bobruisk, on 28 June Lieutenant General Edmund Hoffmeister, commanding XLI Panzer Corps, led a breakout northwest from the city. Although initially successful, the breakout was repulsed by 3rd Army. In total 15,000 German troops eventually escaped the pocket, but such was their condition that they played no part in the defence of Minsk. The burning city of Bobruisk fell on 29 June amid desperate scenes. In a week 1st Belorussian Front had ripped apart Ninth Army, destroying the southern anchor of Army Group Centre's position and exposing the northern flank of Army Group North Ukraine.

The Liberation of Minsk

STAVKA urged on its commanders, ordering Rokossovsky to drive on Minsk where Chernyakhovsky's 3rd Belorussian Front would provide the northern arm of a huge pincer that would liberate the city, and destroy the remnants of Ninth Army and Fourth Army; while 1st Baltic Front harried Third Panzer Army. German troops streaming westward, demoralized and defeated, were still 60 miles from Minsk and were fighting between the rivers Drut and Berezina when the forward detachments of two Soviet fronts began their deadly race towards the city.

Once more, 5th Panzer Division sought to buy time for the retreating Germans by attacking east of Minsk. On 1 July the Soviets stormed Borisov, trapping Fourth Army's XII Corps and XXVII Corps on the eastern bank of the Berezina. Although 5th Panzer distinguished itself in defensive fighting on the Minsk–Borisov road over the next two days, it was to no avail as Rokossovky's forces pressed on in the south, with the rampaging I Guards Tank Corps only 15 miles from Minsk by 2 July.

Field Marshal Walter Model, who assumed command of Army Group Centre from Busch, realized there was no hope of rescuing the remaining Fourth Army units or of holding Minsk. Instead, he concentrated his remaining forces on holding open escape routes from the city to the west. However, in the early hours of 3 July, II Guards Tank Corps of 11th Guards Army finally broke 5th Panzer Division, and surged into the city from the northeast. They were joined by I Guards Tank Corps advancing from the south, while other units of 1st Belorussian Front severed rail escape routes to the southwest. The capture of Minsk on 4 July trapped 105,000 soldiers of Fourth Army behind Soviet lines in two vast encirclements. The mopping up of German troops, many of whom began to surrender from 8 July onwards, fell to 2nd Belorussian Front.

The Aftermath

The battle for Belorussia was over. In two weeks the Red Army, with a remarkable level of speed and skill, had carefully crafted a series of hammer blows which utterly annihilated Army Group Centre, inflicting 350,000 casualties and capturing over 150,000 German troops. Soviet losses for the operation totalled 178,501 men. 'Operation Bagration', the greatest Soviet victory of World War II, greater even than Stalingrad, inflicted twice as many casualties on the Germans in two weeks as the Anglo-American forces in six weeks' fighting in Normandy during the same period. A sledgehammer blow it was, but one delivered with poise, imagination, and daring ruthlessness. The Red Army had come of age.

STEPHEN WALSH

Further Reading

Erickson, J *The Road To Berlin* (London, 1985)

Glantz, D M, and House, J *When Titans Clashed* (Lawrence, Kansas, 1995)

Overy, R *Russia's War* (London, 1997)

THE AMPHIBIOUS LANDINGS

"In landing operations, retreat is impossible. To surrender is as ignoble as it is foolish… Above all remember that we as the attackers have the initiative. We know exactly what we are going to do, while the enemy is ignorant of our intentions and can only parry our blows. We must retain this tremendous advantage by always attacking: rapidly, ruthlessly, viciously and without rest."
LIEUTENANT GENERAL GEORGE S PATTON, JUNIOR, US ARMY, 1943

WORLD WAR II saw the perfection of amphibious landing techniques, especially by the Western Allies, whose particular strategic position meant that they were often obliged to land forces from the sea. Amphibious landings against prepared enemy defences were some of the most difficult military missions to accomplish. The invaders had to organize a complex interservice operation – often also a multinational one – just to deliver the troops onto the beaches, and to establish an initial beachhead against enemy resistance. Even when the landing forces achieved their beachhead on the first day, they often had to exploit inland against an enemy who could concentrate reserves faster by land than they could be brought by sea. A lot could go wrong both in the planning and the fighting. For all the help that they could be given, often success or failure hinged on the courage of the soldiers as they hit the beach.

Anzio

The Stranded Whale

22 JANUARY – 26 MAY 1944

United States VI Corps under Major General John P Lucas

VERSUS

German Fourteenth Army under General Eberhard
von Mackensen

CHRONOLOGY

3 November 1943 –	First Allied plans for the Anzio landings
2 January 1944 –	Alexander issues new orders for 'Operation Shingle'
20 January 1944 –	Fifth Army attacks the Gustav Line
22 January 1944 –	The Anzio landings take place
24 January 1944 –	German counter-attacks start
31 January 1944 –	Failed Allied breakout from Anzio
16 February 1944 –	Main German attack on the beachhead
26 May 1944 –	Final link up with advancing Allied forces

"I thought we were throwing a wildcat onto the beach to rip the bowels out of the Boche. Instead we have a stranded whale."

WINSTON CHURCHILL

AMPHIBIOUS LANDINGS IN World War II were always recognized as being among the most difficult of all operations of war. The nightmare for the attackers was that things could go completely wrong, and the landings could be destroyed on the beaches with massive loss of life. Against this, the surprise of an amphibious hook, opening up a new front against the enemy, could transform a campaign that was experiencing difficulty or had come to a halt. A lesser disaster was that a landing could get successfully ashore, but would be sealed off before it could develop its full potential. The balance in amphibious warfare between surprise and security, between risk and safety, was always a difficult one. In Italy in 1944, the Americans and British planned for a major amphibious success and produced only frustration, while their German opponents perhaps planned too well.

The Allied Plans

The Allied strategic concept for the Italian campaign in 1943–44 was to keep the Germans fighting in Italy, thus drawing German combat power away from the planned landings in northern France, 'Operation Overlord', and away from the Eastern Front where the Soviet Union was hard-pressed. In this context, any action in Italy which held German troops in place, or drew additional troops to Italy from other fronts, was a strategic success. This strategy was a precarious balance between the national aims of the three main Allies. The USA was very eager to concentrate Allied combat power for the invasion of northern France; the Soviet Union was eager to see a major second front opened in Europe as soon as possible; and Winston Churchill, as prime minister of the UK, had his own agenda.

The strategic aim in Italy was altered in December 1943, largely at Churchill's instigation. Not only must Allied forces in Italy occupy the Germans' attention, but they must maintain the initiative against German defences. Operations in Italy had to be seen as themselves successful in order to achieve this expanded strategic goal, particularly against the powerful German defences of the 'Gustav Line', which stretched across the Italian peninsula at its narrowest point, and in order to capture Rome.

The Allies had been unable to penetrate the Gustav Line in 1943, and their combat power in Italy was already being depleted in preparation for 'Operation Overlord' in France. In order to maintain the initiative, the British general Sir Harold Alexander, commanding 15th Army Group, had to consider alternatives. Because the Gustav Line's flanks were secured at either end by the sea, the only means of outflanking the line with significant forces was an amphibious landing on the Italian coast. Planning for an amphibious flanking attack was initially discussed by the staffs of 15th Army Group and US Fifth Army in mid-October 1943. By 3 November a plan was developed. The British Eighth Army under Lieutenant General Sir Oliver Leese would threaten German lines of communication around Pescara on the eastern side of the Gustav line. At the same time US Fifth Army under Lieutenant General

Mark W Clark would attack up the Liri and Sacco valleys to Frosinone, fighting through the Gustav Line and linking up with an amphibious force landing at the resort town of Anzio-Nettuno. This would link up with US VI Corps under Major General John P Lucas, which would conduct the amphibious operation with airborne support. The objective for the Anzio landing was the Alban Hills, dominating the roads between the Gustav Line and Rome.

At this point the Allied plans for Anzio became uncertain. The VI Corps operation was expected to begin by mid-December 1943. But as it became apparent that Fifth Army would not be likely to take Frosinone soon, the plan evolved into a larger force that could take the Alban Hills and hold a beachhead on its own. When the operation was shelved, shortly thereafter, Fifth Army's planning staff developed 'Operation Shingle', a diversionary attack with only one reinforced division, instead of a full corps, which would link up with the main body of the army at Frosinone. On 18 December, this plan too was shelved, but the 'Shingle' code name was retained.

Both these operations were set aside because most of the landing craft in the Mediterranean, their crews experienced from landings in North Africa, Sicily, and southern Italy, were scheduled to move to Britain by mid-January. Particularly important were the Landing Ship Tanks (LSTs), specially-built vessels which carried smaller landing craft close to their beaching sites, but which were also used to ferry heavy equipment all around the Mediterranean theatre. They were needed not only to execute the landing, but to maintain the flow of supplies, including ammunition, to the beachhead. The Allied strategic priority was the invasion of northern France, planned to commence in only a few months. Before they and their crews could take part in 'Operation Overlord', they would have to be sailed to Britain and refitted. Only the very highest levels of Allied military command, the Anglo-American Combined Chiefs of Staff, could change the allocation of landing craft away from 'Overlord' to devote them to an operational flanking movement in Italy. Their stay in the Mediterranean was extended one month to 15 January 1944, but then most of them would start their voyage northwards to Britain, en route to Normandy.

The Plans Change

At this point the plans for 'Operation Shingle' were dusted off at the instigation of Prime Minister Churchill and the operation rescheduled for around 20 January. In Tunis recovering from a bout of pneumonia, Churchill brought his unique brand of strategic vision to bear on the requirement for visible success in Italy. He convened a meeting of all members of the British War Cabinet then in Tunis – himself and Lord Beaverbrook, his trusted adviser – who approved the mission and arranged another month's availability for the landing craft.

The planning staff was drawn from Clark's Fifth Army, with an additional naval planning staff under Rear Admiral F J Lowry of the US Navy and an air planning staff under Major General J K Cannon of the US Army Air Force, commanding XII Air Support Command. The Joint Beach Intelligence Board of Allied Force Headquarters provided intelligence support. The old plans were converted into a new order from General Alexander, issued on 2 January 1944. As near as possible to 21 January, two reinforced divisions under VI Corps would land on the beaches of Anzio-Nettuno with the goal of taking the Alban Hills, thus cutting the German lines of communication and threatening the rear of German XIV Corps, defending the western sector of the Gustav Line. The operational concept sought to make the Germans fall back from the Gustav Line in order to defend Rome against the amphibious attack.

The new mission for 'Operation Shingle', as ordered by Lieutenant General Clark, was to seize and secure a beachhead at Anzio and to 'advance on' rather than 'advance to' the Alban Hills – a critical distinction. In Clark's estimate, the landing force of two divisions would be too small to take the Alban Hills, nor would it be expected to advance to Rome against the four German divisions reported to be in the area. Immediately before the landing, Clark's Fifth Army would make a strong attack towards Cassino and Frosinone in order to draw German reserves away from the Anzio beachhead, and if possible to break through the weakened Gustav Line to link up with the amphibious force. At the time the Allies did not know that Fifth Army's attack across the Rapido River on 20–21 January would fail, making it impossible for the rest of Fifth Army to link up with 'Shingle'. The Anzio force would be on its own for up to 28 days, when its supplies would run out.

Commitments in the Mediterranean theatre made it impossible to create a landing force that was either all American or all British. Under Major General Lucas's command in VI Corps would be US 3rd Infantry Division and 504th Parachute Regiment (from the 82nd 'All American' Airborne Division) and British 1st Infantry Division. The limited number of LSTs available meant that the two infantry divisions would land with significantly fewer vehicles than the recognized requirement for an assault. The air plan for Anzio was broken into three phases: the Allied Mediterranean Air Forces would conduct a preliminary bombardment of central Italy 1–14 January; isolate Anzio with attacks on roads and railways north of Rome as well as on roads to Anzio from the south; and finally, beginning on day of the attack, isolate Anzio by interdicting German reinforcements. A deception plan, using Brigadier Dudley Clarke's 'A Force', would create false radio traffic to convince the Germans that the likely point of landing would be at Civitavecchia rather than Anzio.

The German Plans

Bombardment by British naval forces was meant to lend credence to the deception, but the German theatre commander was not taken in. He had it on the best authority that there would be no amphibious attack within the next weeks. No less a personage than Admiral Wilhelm Canaris, head of the Abwehr (German military intelligence) gave assurance that there would be no amphibious flanking attack on the Gustav Line. Nonetheless, Field Marshal 'Smiling Albert' Kesselring, German Commander-in-Chief South, did prepare himself for the possibility. In December 1943 his headquarters selected five likely amphibious landing sites, and directed troops to be on 12-hour standby to contain and counter-attack. The plan which applied to Anzio, 'Case Richard', was intended to respond to an amphibious landing near Rome. Under 'Case Richard', 29th Panzergrenadier Division and 90th Panzergrenadier Division of motorized infantry stationed near Rome would be a rapid response force. Kesselring also had a deeper theatre reserve. German Fourteenth Army in northern Italy consisted largely of battle-hardened troops, who had rested and were training to go back into the Gustav Line as part of the Tenth Army. A directive from OKW (*Oberkommando der Wehrmacht*, the German forces' high command) also authorized reinforcements for 'Case Richard' to come from France, the Netherlands, and the Balkans. The plans for 'Case Richard' were comprehensive, taking into account the likely routes through the Alps, and crews were pre-positioned to de-ice the roads and to refuel reinforcing vehicles. Pontoon bridges were ready to replace crossings damaged by Allied interdiction bombing. Even the harbour facilities of a little resort town like Anzio would be destroyed – work by German engineers would begin soon after 19 January 1944.

In addition to the contingency plans, Kesselring had another tool. German soldiers had been trained, at least since the days of the pre-war Reichswehr, to execute missions independently without explicit instructions. German commanders would not need specific plans in order to respond to a landing on the Italian coast – their training and experience would enable them to do what was needed without orders. Likewise, German commanders were trained to cobble together formations on the spot rather than relying on existing organizational charts. This meant that even though reinforcement

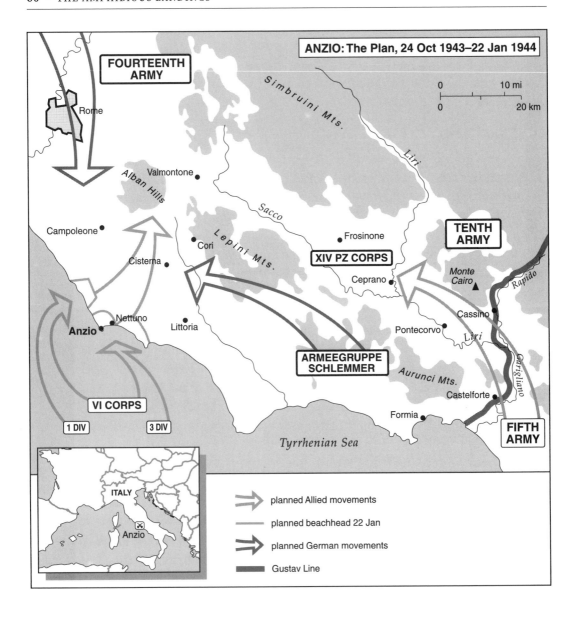

ANZIO: The Plan, 24 Oct 1943–22 Jan 1944

FOURTEENTH ARMY

Rome

Simbruini Mts.

Liri

0   10 mi
0   20 km

Valmontone

Alban Hills

Sacco

Campoleone

Frosinone

TENTH ARMY

Cori

Lepini Mts.

XIV PZ CORPS

Cisterna

Ceprano

Monte Cairo ▲

Rapido

Nettuno

Anzio

Littoria

Cassino

Pontecorvo

Liri

ARMEEGRUPPE SCHLEMMER

Aurunci Mts.

Gariglianо

VI CORPS

Castelforte

1 DIV   3 DIV

Formia

FIFTH ARMY

Tyrrhenian Sea

ITALY

Anzio

⇒ planned Allied movements

— planned beachhead 22 Jan

⇒ planned German movements

▬ Gustav Line

units and higher formation headquarters were not necessarily detailed to possible landing sites, they could be mated up effectively when it became necessary.

Kesselring's plan for 'Case Richard' was disrupted even before 'Operation Shingle' began. The attack on 20 January by Fifth Army's British X Corps and US II Corps on the Garigliano and Rapido rivers forced the German commander to commit his theatre reserve, the two panzergrenadier divisions,

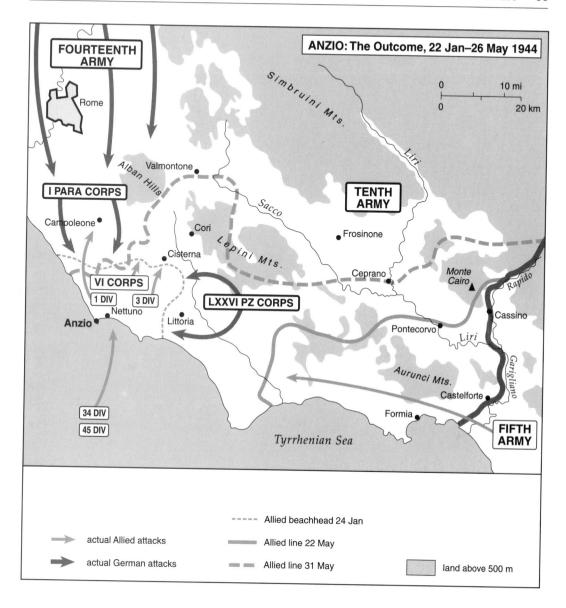

ANZIO: The Outcome, 22 Jan–26 May 1944

FOURTEENTH ARMY

Rome

I PARA CORPS

Campoleone

Valmontone

Alban Hills

Simbruini Mts.

Sacco

TENTH ARMY

Frosinone

Cori

Cisterna

Lepini Mts.

Ceprano

Monte Cairo ▲

Rapido

VI CORPS

1 DIV   3 DIV

Nettuno

Anzio

Littoria

LXXVI PZ CORPS

Pontecorvo

Liri

Cassino

Gargliano

34 DIV

45 DIV

Aurunci Mts.

Castelforte

Formia

FIFTH ARMY

Tyrrhenian Sea

→ actual Allied attacks

⇒ actual German attacks

----- Allied beachhead 24 Jan

Allied line 22 May

- - - Allied line 31 May

land above 500 m

0   10 mi
0   20 km

to the Gustav Line. 'Case Richard' did, however, permit Kesselring to use forces from the Gustav Line itself to counter-attack against an Allied landing on the coast, secure in the knowledge that as soon as the codeword 'Richard' was transmitted, OKW would rush reinforcements from all over Europe. As long as the Allies did not immediately break out of their beachhead, Kesselring could make do with Gustav Line troops until the reinforcements arrived.

The Allied Landings

On 22 January 1944, Lucas's VI Corps landed on the beaches of Anzio against little opposition. The only German troops in the area were three companies of engineers and one battalion of panzergrenadiers. So smooth was the landing that drunken German officers are reported to have driven on board a landing craft, mistaking it for their own garage. This allowed Lucas to follow his own plan without interference from enemy action. It was also in accord with Kesselring's plans – even had his theatre reserve not been committed to the Gustav Line, it would not have counter-attacked the 'Case Richard' beachhead for 12 hours. Fifth Army's fierce attack on the Gustav Line had bought Lucas more time, and Clark's orders to Lucas, both written and verbal, had made it clear to Lucas that the time was to be used to dig in and prepare to defend against the inevitable German counter-attack.

The German codeword 'Richard' went out immediately. The movements within Kesselring's own command had begun by nightfall on 22 January. The German Commanders-in-Chief West (France and the Low Countries), Southeast (the Balkans), and of the Replacement Army in Germany at once began moving the designated units towards the Rome area. In accordance with planning, all the staff work for the transfers had already been done, and the movements went like clockwork. The time spent by Lucas entrenching his position also gave the German theatre commander time to rapidly restructure his command. Kesselring directed the Tenth Army on the Gustav Line to continue to defend its positions. A task group under General Gustav von Zangen was assigned to look after Fourteenth Army's area of responsibility in northern Italy, while Kesselring ordered Fourteenth Army itself under General Eberhad von Mackensen to counter-attack the invasion force and 'throw the enemy forces landed south of Rome back into the sea'.

Now instead of only German Tenth Army facing the two Allied armies across the Gustav Line, two German armies faced two Allied armies. Hitler's order made their mission clear: 'The Gustav Line must be held at all costs for the sake of the political consequences which would follow a completely successful defence. The Führer expects the bitterest struggle for every yard'. Hitler viewed the Allied action in Italy as part of the overall plan for invading Europe in 1944, and joined Churchill in viewing success in Italy as necessary for success in the European war. This was exactly what Churchill had wanted Hitler to think.

The Battle

Throughout World War II, German commanders attempted to trap their Allied enemies into encirclements which could be destroyed in the *Kesselschlacht* (literally 'cauldron battle'), like a giant cooking pot – the English-language parallel would be to say that the Germans sought to shoot their enemies like fish in a barrel. On the beaches of Anzio-Nettuno, General Lucas methodically built a barrel and filled it with fish. Then he waited for the Germans to start shooting.

General von Mackensen arrived on 24 January with two instructions: first, to halt the Allies, and second, to drive them off the Anzio docks into the Tyrrhenian Sea. Mackensen's plan was to cut the beachhead in two, separating British 1st Division from US 3rd Division. Then the combat power of Fourteenth Army would be devoted to destroying each division individually.

General Clark watched decrypted German signals paint a picture of Mackensen's 90,000 troops massing to form the rim of the cauldron. Arriving from elsewhere in Italy were the 'Hermann Goering' Parachute Panzer Division, 16th SS 'Reichsfuhrer' Panzergrenadier Division, 35th Division, 26th Division, and 29th Panzergrenadier Division. By 24 January the desultory German bombing and scattered resistance began to escalate. Next day a group of Grenadier Guards from British 1st Division, patrolling towards the Alban Hills, were greeted with fire from German self-propelled artillery. The cauldron battle had begun.

The Anzio beachhead was brought under fire by German artillery, which became stronger as the battle escalated, until shells were striking the beach around the clock. Two German K5(E) 240-mm railway guns, built in the 1930s to blast through the Maginot Line, were brought from France to assist in the shelling. Called 'Leopold' and 'Robert' by their gunners, these guns hid in railway tunnels by day and fired their 250-kg high explosive rounds into Allied positions. Another battery of railway guns, 210-mm pieces, fired from railway tunnels nearby. Most important, however, were the many 170-mm guns positioned in the hills around Anzio-Nettuno. With a range of 30,000 yards, the German guns outranged the heaviest Allied artillery ashore – which had a range of 25,700 yards – enough to make a difference.

Preparing for a breakout battle, Lucas's 3rd Division attempted to attack outwards towards Cisterna, while 1st Division attacked towards Campoleone. Both attacks failed to gain positions for fighting onward, away from the beachhead. An attack by the combined VI Corps towards the Alban Hills was attempted on 31 January. By then, however, the two Allied divisions, augmented by US airborne troops, were facing 5 (smaller) German divisions with 48 batteries of artillery, well dug-in all around them; so VI Corps began to dig in again, preparing for Mackensen's counter-attack. On the night of 3 February 1944, Mackensen began an attack to split the beachhead, but was beaten back by the Allied defenders. The perimeter of the Anzio beachhead was now sealed.

The main German attack came on 16 February, by four divisions. The weary British 1st Division was in the process of being relieved by new formations, and the attack was only beaten back with the aid of massive air support and naval gunfire. The main German attempt to dislodge the beachhead had failed, and the Germans returned to their relentless bombardment, while the ruthless Canadian and US raiders of 1 Special Service Force cut German throats by night. Allied troops in the beachhead learned to walk in a special 'Anzio crouch' to avoid the gaze of German artillery spotters. Additional formations were funnelled into the beachhead during the following months, along with large supplies of ammunition to keep up the Allies' consumption of 2,700 tons per day. Naval forces increased their tempo of operations to allow the VI Corps to build up reserves of ammunition on the beach, and US 34th Infantry Division to join the beachhead.

One month after VI Corps landed on the beach, Major General Lucas was replaced, made the scapegoat for the Allied failure. After more German attacks in late February, the VI Corps beachhead at Anzio settled down to suffer until the Germans pulled back in May, in response to Allied victories elsewhere and the breaking of the Gustav Line.

The Consequences of the Battle

The Allied goal in Italy had been to keep the Germans fighting, robbing the defences of northern France of troops and equipment. Allied soldiers and equipment were being replaced and redoubled from the vast US and British empires, while Germany was incapable of making up its losses. Hitler's strategic plan, laid down inflexibly, was to maintain every bit of German-controlled ground no matter what the cost. The result of the operations on the Anzio beaches was that the Allied strategic aims were advanced, while the Germans preserved the illusion of success by holding onto the Gustav Line for a few more months. There might have been a lost Allied opportunity to deal a stinging reverse to the Germans by seizing the initiative in Italy, had a bold commander been in charge. Nonetheless, the bloody sacrifice of Anzio served the Allied strategic aims by moving German combat power to be wasted in Italy.

ARYEH NUSBACHER

Further Reading

Breuer, W *Agony at Anzio* (London, 1985)

D'Este, C *Fatal Decision: Anzio and the Battle of Rome* (London, 1991)

Kesselring, A *The Memoirs of Field Marshal Kesselring* (Novato, CA, 1988)

Vaughan-Thomas, W *Anzio* (London, 1961)

D-Day
The Longest Day
6 JUNE 1944

German Army Group B under Field Marshal Erwin Rommel
VERSUS
Allied 21st Army Group under General Bernard L Montgomery

CHRONOLOGY
4 June 1944 – First Allied invasion ships sail
5 June 1944 – Original date for D-Day, first Allied
aircraft carrying airborne forces take off
for Normandy
6 June 1944 – D-Day, main Allied landings take place
in Normandy
8 June 1944 – Montgomery comes ashore

"I am very uneasy about the whole operation. At the best, it will fall so very short of the expectation of the bulk of the people, namely all those who know nothing about its difficulties. At the worst it may well be the most ghastly disaster of the whole war." FIELD MARSHAL SIR ALAN BROOKE, CHIEF OF THE IMPERIAL GENERAL STAFF, 5 JUNE 1944

IN THE MILITARY terminology of World War II, the expression 'D-Day' was used simply to designate the planned starting day for any military operation. It was an entirely professional designation, used perhaps thousands of times in the course of the war. But for history, 'D-Day' also has a very particular resonance. It was made famous as the date of the start of 'Operation Overlord', 6 June 1944, the most important single day for the Western Allies during World War II in Europe, and the most critical amphibious operation of all.

The Origins of the Battle

In June 1940 the remnants of the defeated British Expeditionary Force escaped the clutches of the German Wehrmacht through the 'Miracle of Dunkirk'. Though the most forward-looking British senior commanders entertained thoughts of launching an invasion of Nazi-occupied northwestern Europe in the future, it would be years before Britain could seriously entertain such a strategy. In the meantime it had to survive against the onslaught of the German armed forces. During 1942–43, although the USA advocated ardently an invasion of Nazi-occupied Europe, the strategy selected was the British option that sought first to nibble away at the peripheries of the German empire, such as Vichy North Africa, to weaken the enemy. In March 1943 the Allies commenced planning for an invasion of Nazi-occupied France, code-named 'Overlord', due to commence in Spring 1944.

The Allied Plans

The D-Day invasion plan required the completion of various essential preliminaries, such as the assembly of the required forces. One such prerequisite was the Allied interdiction campaign in which bombers smashed the French railway network during the first half of 1944, to degrade significantly the enemy's ability either to redeploy forces to the invasion coast or to resupply those already there. In another preliminary, the Allied 'Fortitude South' deception scheme fooled the Germans into believing that the main Allied attack would come in the Pas de Calais, not in Normandy, which had been chosen for the landings.

The Allied invasion plan involved a vast naval armada of warships and landing craft crossing the English Channel through mine-free lanes to points offshore from the five designated invasion beaches. Prior to the assault, concentrated aerial and naval bombardments would neutralize the German defences. Around dawn, US First Army under Lieutenant General Omar N Bradley would start to land in the western sector on two beaches, 'Omaha' and 'Utah'. An hour later, British and Canadian forces of British Second Army under Lieutenant General Sir Miles Dempsey would start to land in the eastern sector on three beaches, designated (from west to east) by the code names 'Gold', 'Juno', and 'Sword'. All ground forces were under the command of the British general Sir Bernard Montgomery's 21st Army Group.

The Allies had planned the landings for 5 June, when the required combination of good moonlight and low tides was present. Any postponement of the invasion due to poor weather would mean a further two-week wait until satisfactory conditions reoccurred, a dangerous delay given the rapidly strengthening German defences in Normandy. Unfortunately, by 4 June a gale developed which forced Montgomery to cancel the attack. Later that day the Allied Supreme Commander in Europe, the US general Dwight D Eisenhower, accepted Montgomery's recommendation to commence the landings on 6 June.

Six hours before the amphibious landings commenced, 17,000 Allied airborne troops were to land in Normandy to secure the eastern and western flanks of the beachheads, US 82nd Airborne Division and 101st Airborne Division to the west close to 'Utah', and British 6th Airborne Division to the east of 'Sword'. This operation also served to both widen the frontage of the Allied invasion to 55 miles, and maximize the force strength committed against the enemy in those critical first hours.

Once the initial amphibious and airborne assault forces had established their beachheads, Allied follow-up forces would pass through to advance deeper into enemy territory. Their objectives were to widen and deepen their respective beachheads and begin the process of linking all five into one consolidated Allied-held sector. By midnight on 6 June the Allied forces were to have linked up the four eastern beachheads and the British airborne zone into a consolidated salient 39 miles wide and up to 10 miles deep, including the towns of Caen and Bayeux, and the Americans were to link up 'Utah' and 'Omaha' the next day. In addition, Montgomery ordered three armoured brigade groups to dash forward and seize three key communications nodes 15 miles inland, to prevent German armour from mounting a counter-attack.

The German Plans

Between Autumn 1943 and Spring 1944 the previously neglected German *Westheer* ('Western Army') feverishly strengthened its Atlantic Wall fortifications along the French and Belgian coasts. By mid-1944 the *Westheer* deployed 9 panzer divisions and one panzergrenadier division (with 1,510 tanks and armoured vehicles), plus 44 other divisions, mostly infantry. The Westheer was now commanded by Field Marshal Gerd von Rundstedt, whose *OB West* (*Oberfelshaber West* or 'Western Theatre Command') controlled two subordinate army group formations. In northeastern France, Field Marshal Erwin Rommel commanded Army Group B: Fifteenth Army in the Pas de Calais and Belgium, and Colonel General Friedrich Dollman's Seventh Army in Normandy and Brittany. In addition, von Rundstedt possessed a strategic armoured reserve, General Leo Freiherr Geyr von Schweppenburg's Panzer Group West of six panzer divisions.

Both uncertainty as to where Allied forces would land and command squabbles prevented the Westheer from developing a coherent plan to repel the Allied invasion. Rommel wished to hold German armour close to the coast for a swift counterstrike against the vulnerable Allies that would drive them back into the sea during the first 48 hours of the invasion. D-Day, he declared, would be 'the longest day' for both sides. But both von Rundstedt and von Schweppenburg wished to hold back the German panzer divisions to launch a decisive counterattack as the Allies advanced from their initial beachhead. As a solution to these disagreements, Hitler adopted an unsatisfactory compromise strategy which deployed just two panzer divisions forward.

The Allied Landings

During the night of 5–6 June, 7,000 aircraft and gliders transported the British and US airborne divisions to their drop zones in Normandy, with the landings starting just after midnight. British glider troops secured 'Pegasus Bridge' over the Caen Canal, the first piece of France to be liberated, while further east parachutists captured the Orne bridge and the village of Ranville. In addition, a parachute battalion landed to neutralize the Merville battery, 2 miles east of 'Sword' beach. Simultaneously, US parachute and glider troops landed in the marshy hinterland behind 'Utah' beach and further inland along the inundated valleys of the rivers Douve and Merderet. Due to low-level cloud the transport aircraft dropped many airborne troops in a dispersed fashion several miles off target and sometimes into the deadly marshes. Consequently, 30% of the troops landed and 50% of the equipment became immediate casualties. Despite this the US airborne troops managed to seize several of their key objectives, including the road intersection at Ste-Mère-Eglise.

By 2.15 a.m. German LXXXIV Corps in Normandy went onto full alert, although back in Paris, Field Marshal von Rundstedt remained convinced that the drops were just a diversion prior to the main Allied attack in the Pas de Calais. Amid bad weather, the D-Day landings caught the Germans by surprise, and the latter's lethargic reaction let slip their best opportunity to drive the Allies back into the sea. When at dawn Hitler finally heard about the invasion – his aides dared not wake the sleeping Führer – he agreed with von Rundstedt's conclusion. To cap these command mistakes, the bad weather had persuaded Rommel to grab some leave, and so his presence was missing during the critical first hours of the invasion.

After 4.00 a.m., 800 warships and 6,000 transport vessels of the Allied naval armada weighed anchor off the coast opposite the five invasion beaches. This vast fleet was protected overhead by 300 barrage balloons and 800 fighter aircraft. Meanwhile, between 3.00 a.m. and 5.00 a.m., 1,900 Allied planes dropped 9,000 tons of munitions on the German coastal defences, while 6 battleships, 23 cruisers, and 67 destroyers provided naval fire support.

Between 6.30 a.m. and 7.45 a.m. the Allied assault troops began landing on the invasion beaches. At 7.25 a.m. the reinforced British 3rd Infantry Division, under Lieutenant General J T Crocker's I Corps, landed on 'Sword' beach, defended by the German 716th Infantry Division (a 'static' division with little transport), with elements of 21st Panzer Division further inland. As with all the Anglo-Canadian beaches, the landing infantry were supported by commandos. Due to the bad weather, the tide at 'Sword' beach was higher than expected, which both reduced the depth of the beach and caused several landing craft to hit concealed German obstacles. By 8.00 a.m. the division's leading brigade, the reinforced 8th Infantry Brigade, had secured a number of exits from the beach. Follow-up forces, including the rest of the division, then began to disembark. By 11.00 a.m., 185th Brigade had formed up one mile inland at Hermanville, but their supporting tanks had been delayed by the huge traffic congestion on the abnormally shallow beach area. At noon the brigade began to push inland despite its lack of armour, which was ordered to catch up as best it could.

The Canadian 3rd Infantry Division commenced landing on the 6 mile-wide 'Juno' beach at 7.45 a.m. The high tide carried many of the first wave of 306 landing craft onto the half-submerged German obstacles, but many of the marooned infantrymen managed to get ashore and link up with the DD (duplex drive) amphibious tanks and assault vehicles earmarked to support them. Once ashore, the Canadians also found enemy resistance tougher than on 'Sword'. It was not until 9.30 a.m. that elements of 3rd Division began to advance inland through the coastal villages of St Aubin and Courseulles into the countryside beyond. Small German pockets of resistance continued in these coastal villages until the early evening. By noon, the Canadians had pushed up to 4 mile inland and captured the villages of Colombières and Bény sur Mer against modest opposition.

Next to I Corps sector came XXX Corps under Lieutenant General B C Bucknall, responsible for 'Gold' beach. At 7.30 a.m., British 50th (Northumbrian) Division, also of XXX Corps, began landing along the 5 mile-wide 'Gold' beach. The preliminary bombardment had missed most of the German defences around le Hamel, and the infantry of the division's 231st Brigade found themselves pinned down by murderous enemy fire. It took the division several hours to secure the beach against this stiff resistance. Nevertheless, by late morning its troops had commenced their advance inland toward Creully, 4 miles distant.

On 'Omaha' at 6.30 a.m., in advance of the British, Major General Leonard T 'Gee' Gerow's VII Corps began landing US 1st Infantry Division ('The Big Red One') and part of 29th ('Blue and Gray') Infantry Division. In terms of terrain, this sector constituted a tough assault, because the steep bluffs behind the beach channelled any Allied advance into a few obvious draws which were covered by heavy German defences. Unfortunately, due to bad weather many of the 13,000 bombs dropped by 329 US bombers fell behind these German coastal defences, while poor visibility hampered naval fire support. This deficient Allied fire support on 'Omaha' was compounded by the unexpected presence of the German 352nd Infantry Division defending the bluff. US troops disembarked into neck-deep, heavily pitching water, and struggled with heavy combat packs until they reached the beach. The Germans patiently held their fire until the first wave of assault infantry emerged out of the water into a hail of lethal bullets. The stunned survivors could manage little more than to seek shelter in shallow sand-scrapes, or behind obstacles, desperately attempting to stay alive. A few soldiers managed to reach the sea wall, where they huddled in relative safety. To make things worse, all the supporting 'DD' amphibious tanks succumbed to enemy fire or the mountainous seas, while the assault engineers – there to dismantle the underwater obstacles – also failed to make it to the beach. By noon, 1,100 US soldiers lay dead or wounded on 'Omaha', and it seemed far from clear that the Americans could even maintain their foothold on enemy-occupied French soil.

Two miles west of 'Omaha', troops from 2nd Ranger Battalion undertook a hazardous mission to capture a powerful German artillery battery located on top of the cliffs at the Point de Hoc. Equipped with grappling hooks fired by small mortars and extendable ladders, the Rangers scrambled up the cliffs, only to have their ladders pushed away by the defenders in scenes reminiscent of a medieval siege. Despite fierce enemy resistance and the adverse terrain, the Rangers managed to fight their way into the battery, only to discover that the Germans had moved their artillery pieces inland.

On 'Utah', US 4th Infantry Division, part of US VII Corps under Major General J Lawton ('Lightning Joe') Collins, began disembarking onto the beaches at 6.30 a.m., meeting relatively light resistance largely due to the modest enemy defences – the Germans believed that their deliberate inundation of the hinterland behind the beach provided a strong natural defence. Aided by accurate preliminary naval gunfire that smashed the German coastal strongpoints, US assault forces soon managed, with only modest casualties, to open exits from the beach across the marshy hinterland towards the airborne forces dropped a few hours previously.

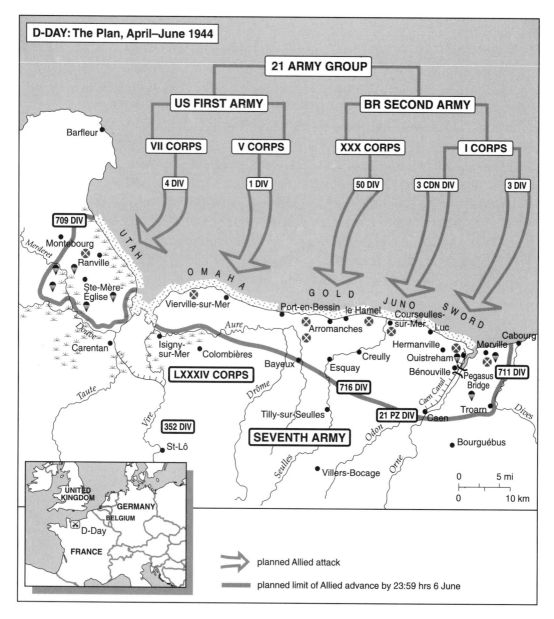

D-DAY: The Plan, April–June 1944

21 ARMY GROUP

US FIRST ARMY

BR SECOND ARMY

VII CORPS

V CORPS

XXX CORPS

I CORPS

4 DIV

1 DIV

50 DIV

3 CDN DIV

3 DIV

709 DIV

711 DIV

716 DIV

352 DIV

21 PZ DIV

LXXXIV CORPS

SEVENTH ARMY

Barfleur

Montebourg

Ranville

Ste-Mère-Église

Vierville-sur-Mer

Port-en-Bessin

le Hamel

Courseulles-sur-Mer

Luc

Cabourg

Merville

Hermanville

Ouistreham

Pegasus Bridge

Carentan

Isigny-sur-Mer

Colombières

Bayeux

Creully

Esquay

Bénouville

Arromanches

Troarn

Tilly-sur-Seulles

Caen

Bourguébus

St-Lô

Villers-Bocage

UTAH

OMAHA

GOLD

JUNO

SWORD

Merderet

Douve

Aure

Taute

Vire

Drôme

Seulles

Odon

Orne

Dives

Caen Canal

UNITED KINGDOM

GERMANY

BELGIUM

D-Day

FRANCE

0   5 mi
0   10 km

→ planned Allied attack

■ planned limit of Allied advance by 23:59 hrs 6 June

The Battle from Midday to Midnight

In the afternoon of 6 June, British 3rd Division had pushed south from 'Sword' beach toward their ultimate objective, the city of Caen. The fierce resistance offered by the 'Hillman' strongpoint north of the vital Périers ridge held up the advance, and it was only captured that evening. To the east, 185th Brigade pushed south 4 miles to Biéville, only 3 miles short of Caen, and also advanced to the Caen Canal near Bénouville, where it linked up with 6th

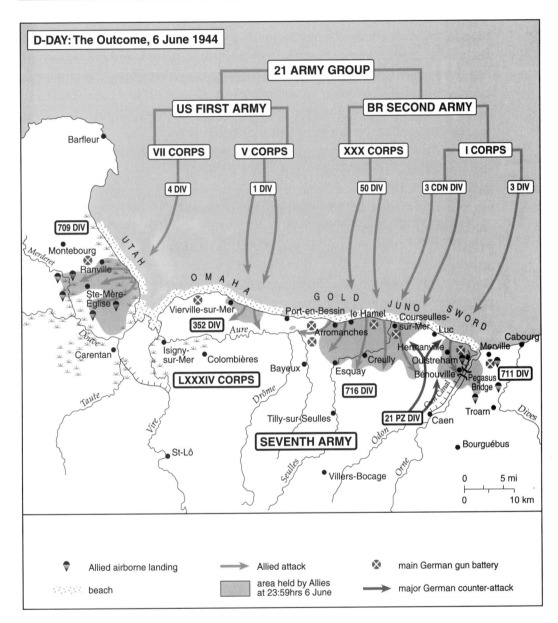

Airborne Division and 1st Special Service Brigade of commandos, who had established a 3 mile-deep bridgehead east of the River Orne.

From 'Juno' beach, Canadian 3rd Division advanced steadily during the afternoon. By evening its three brigades had pushed inland to a depth of 5 miles from Creully in the west to Anisy in the east. As on 'Sword', the main problem with exploiting the landings here was the vast congestion among the vehicles landed on the beach, which was much shallower than had been planned.

In the meantime, units of the 21st Panzer Division began to advance north toward the coast through the 4 mile-wide gap between 'Sword' and 'Gold' beaches. Heavy resistance from British tank and antitank fire on the eastern end of the Périers ridge prevented the bulk of the German force reaching the coast to establish a blocking position between the two Allied beachheads.

At 'Gold' beachhead during the afternoon, 50th (Northumbrian) Division pushed forward against fierce resistance from elements of the German 352nd Infantry Division. By dusk on 6 June, the westerly elements of 56th Brigade had advanced 5 miles, just 1 mile short of the key town of Bayeux. In the centre, 151st Brigade captured Esquay by evening, while to the east 69th Brigade first linked up with Canadian 3rd Division from 'Juno', and then pushed south 6 miles to Coulombs.

At 'Utah' that afternoon, US 4th Division continued to push inland against stiffening, but still modest, resistance. Elements of the division advanced northwest toward the Azeville battery, other units drove west to link up with the US airborne forces that had seized the Merderet bridges and Ste-Mère-Eglise, while two battalions pushed southwest toward the village of Vierville to reach the US paratroopers in the Douve valley.

By noon at 'Omaha', Lieutenant General Bradley had seriously considered ordering the re-embarkation of the assault forces, as a constant stream of reports recounting the terrible slaughter occurring ashore reached him. In desperation, US and British destroyers were pushed close into the coast to pour constant short-range fire into the German strongpoints. Although the bloodletting continued on the beach through the early afternoon, the heroism of US officers and soldiers now shifted the balance on 'Omaha' away from Allied defeat to success. Individuals and small groups, often displaying a heroic disregard for their own safety, managed to advance off the beach and up the bluffs flanking the German defences in the face of murderous enemy fire. From these positions in the bluffs, the Americans, constantly reinforced by newly landed troops, began to dislodge the enemy from their coastal strongpoints. By dusk, with 34,000 troops landed, 1st Division and 29th Division had managed to secure a tenuous foothold on Norman soil.

By midnight on 6 June the Allies had successfully landed 130,000 troops via the beaches plus another 29,000 airborne troops. Allied forces had successfully established four salients into German-occupied territory. At 'Sword' beach, 3rd Division had linked up with 6th Airborne Division in a beachhead 5 miles wide and about the same distance deep. To the west, the forces landed at 'Juno' and had linked up to form a salient 12 miles wide and 6 miles deep. Seven miles still further west at 'Omaha', US forces had carved out a precarious beachhead less than 1 mile deep across a 5 mile frontage. In the extreme west, the US forces at 'Utah' had linked up with some of the airborne troops to secure a salient 6 miles wide and 6 miles deep. Overall, the D-Day landings had been a success, and by midnight the best German opportunity to throw the Allies back into the sea had already slipped away.

The Consequences

D-Day, 6 June 1944, constituted one of the most momentous days of World War II. The lethargic German response ensured that they failed to push the Allies back into the sea on the one day of the campaign they stood a reasonable chance of doing so. If the Germans had repulsed the landings that day, this crippling blow to Allied morale would probably have delayed a repeat attempt for a year. Even if this repeat attempt had succeeded, and the Germans ultimately surrendered, so much time would have passed that the Soviet Union might have pushed even further west into Europe.

STEPHEN HART

Further Reading

Carell, P *Invasion – They're Coming*! (London, 1962)

Keegan, J *Six Armies in Normandy* (London, 1982)

Lewis, J E *Eye-witness D-Day* (London, 1994)

Ryan, C *The Longest Day* (London, 1960)

Iwo Jima
Hell in the Pacific
19 FEBRUARY – 25 MARCH 1945

Japanese Imperial Army 109th Infantry Division (reinforced)
under Lieutenant General Tadamichi Kuribayashi

VERSUS

United States Navy Fifth Fleet under Admiral Raymond Spruance
and V Amphibious Corps under Major General Harold
G Schmidt

CHRONOLOGY

15 June 1944 –	First US Navy carrier strikes against Iwo Jima
8 December 1944 –	Start of 74-day air bombardment
16 February 1945 –	Task Force 52 commences naval bombardment
19 February 1945 –	Landing operations commence
23 February 1945 –	Mount Suribachi secured
25 March 1945 –	Iwo Jima declared secure
30 June 1945 –	Last elements of Japanese resistance eliminated

"About the beach in the morning lay the dead. They died with the greatest violence. Nowhere in the Pacific have I seen such badly mangled bodies. Many were cut in half. Legs and arms 50 feet away from any body." JOURNALIST ROBERT SHERROD, DESCRIBING THE FIRST DAY ON IWO JIMA

AMPHIBIOUS ASSAULT LANDINGS are the most complex operations undertaken in war. The failure in particular of the Anglo-French landings at Gallipoli in World War I created a widespread belief that large scale amphibious landings were not possible under the conditions of modern war. Only the United States Marine Corps kept faith with the assault landing, and during the interwar years they developed techniques to overcome the principal problems. Their solutions provided the guidelines for the conduct of all British and US amphibious operations in World War II. Nowhere were the Marines' ideas more graphically vindicated than in the assault upon the seemingly impregnable Pacific island fortress of Iwo Jima in early 1945. This attack not only demonstrated how a blend of thorough planning, preparation, and organization created the conditions for a successful landing, but also how the individual courage of the officers and men of the United States Marine Corps carried the day.

The Road to Japan

On 20 November 1943, US Marine and Army forces under the strategic direction of US Admiral Chester W Nimitz, Commander-in-Chief of the Pacific Fleet and Pacific Ocean Areas, invaded the outermost point of the Japanese defensive perimeter in the Pacific: the Gilbert Islands (part of modern-day Kiribati). This was the first of the big US amphibious assaults in the Pacific. The bloody fighting on Tarawa island in particular vindicated the Marines' pre-war ideas, but also taught them a number of sobering lessons for the conduct of future landing operations.

The invasion of the Gilbert Islands was the opening blow in what became a relentless drive by US forces, an 'island hopping' campaign across the central Pacific. Each island secured provided the Americans with a new base, particularly for their long-range aircraft, each time moving closer to Japan. In January and February 1944, the Marshall Islands were secured. In June, US forces leapt forwards nearly 1,000 miles to secure Saipan, Tinian, and Guam in the Marianas, breaching the inner Japanese defence line. In October 1944, Nimitz's forces joined with General Douglas MacArthur's South West Pacific command to begin the invasion of the Philippines at Leyte Gulf. With the initial objectives in the Philippines secured, Nimitz turned his attention to the final objectives in the approach to Japan: the islands of Iwo Jima and Okinawa.

The idea of invading Iwo Jima was discussed as early as September 1943, but the need to first secure bases in the central Pacific put any plans on hold. When this task was completed with the seizure of the Marianas, the Iwo Jima operation was revived. The island was to be seized so that its airfields could provide fighter cover for long-range B-29 'Superfortress' bombers operating from the Marianas against Japanese cities. The commander of the US Army Air Force's strategic bombers based on the Marianas, Major General Curtis

LeMay, summed up the value of Iwo Jima for his operations to the naval commanders: 'Without Iwo Jima I couldn't bomb Japan effectively'.

In addition, the projected invasion of the Japanese home islands, 'Operation Olympic', required the establishment of logistic bases and airfields situated close by. The most suitable island was Okinawa in the Ryukyu Islands, 250 miles from the southernmost of the home islands, Kyushu. Iwo Jima was to be seized prior to the landings on Okinawa – which actually took place on 1 April 1945 as 'Operation Iceberg' – to protect its right flank. It was with these factors in mind that on 9 October 1944 Admiral Nimitz ordered Lieutenant General Holland M ('Howling Mad') Smith, Commander Fleet Marine Force Pacific, to prepare an assault on Iwo Jima.

The Island

Iwo Jima is a volcanic island in the Volcano Islands, some 350 miles south of Tokyo. Although the Japanese did not know that the Americans would invade there, they were aware that it presented an obvious strategic target. The island is less than 8 square miles in area and has a forbidding geography and hostile environment. About 5 miles in length, it reaches a maximum width of 2.5 miles in the north, before gradually narrowing to under a quarter of a mile in the south; its shape has often been compared to a pork chop. The beaches consist of several feet of black volcanic ash, which was difficult for infantry and tracked vehicles to traverse, and impossible for wheeled transport. When mixed with cement the ash makes high quality concrete. In the central and northern areas of the island the ground rises up from the shoreline in a series of steep terraces, reaching a small plateau averaging 350 ft in height. At the southern end, overlooking the whole island, is the 580 ft-high Mount Suribachi, which in 1945 provided excellent observation for artillery fire, particularly against the beaches and seaward approaches. Its early capture would be essential if the Marines were to establish a secure bridgehead. Vegetation in most areas is sparse, and the island has no natural water supplies. To add to the feeling of desolation, the volcanic island smells of sulphur or rotten eggs – Iwo Jima means 'sulphur island'. All of this prompted one Marine to comment, 'After God got through making the world, he must've took all the dirty ash and rubble left over and made Iwo Jima'.

Fortress Iwo Jima

The Japanese commander on Iwo Jima was Lieutenant General Tadamichi Kuribayashi, a dedicated and intelligent officer. His plan for the defence of the island differed radically from the standard Japanese practice. On other islands in the Pacific, once the Americans were ashore the Japanese forces had attempted to drive them back into the sea by mounting fanatical counter-attacks, known as *Banzai* charges, from the Japanese battle cry for 'victory'. In the face of overwhelming enemy firepower these had consistently proved futile. Kuribayashi's plan forbade any counter-attacks. Instead he intended to fortify the island heavily and then defend these positions to the death, bleeding the Americans dry in a prolonged and costly battle of attrition. He hoped that by making the cost of taking Iwo Jima as high as possible he could make the USA reluctant to invade Japan and willing to consider peace.

By February 1945 the garrison consisted of 26,000 Imperial Army and Navy personnel supported by hundreds of mortars and artillery pieces, including no fewer than 361 75-mm field guns. In the ten months prior to the attack the Japanese constructed hundreds of bunkers, which supported each other by interlocking arcs of fire. Mount Suribachi was studded with 165 bunkers, many with concrete walls 4 ft thick, while over 200 caves each concealed artillery pieces and as many as 200 troops protected behind steel doors. Across the island at Kita was another typical position, an underground command bunker 150 ft long and 75 ft wide, with surface walls 10 ft thick, entered via a 500 ft-long tunnel. The Japanese industriously burrowed tunnels throughout the whole island linking their bunkers together in order to avoid exposing themselves above ground to the devastating US firepower. Their ambition stretched to building a 17-mile circuit tunnel around the island, a sort of subterranean orbital motorway, although in the end only 11 miles were completed. Iwo Jima had become a fortress with the Pacific for a moat.

The American Plan

Clearly, only a well-organized attack could hope to succeed against the formidable Japanese defences on Iwo Jima. To carry out the invasion the Americans put together a force composed of experienced commanders and largely veteran troops. In overall command of 'Operation Detachment' was Admiral Raymond Spruance, one of the most outstanding officers in the history of the US Navy. Under his control were the naval and Marine forces responsible for capturing Iwo Jima. The commander of the amphibious force was the taciturn Vice Admiral Richmond Kelly Turner. Lieutenant General Smith was in overall charge of the troops, although direct tactical control of V Amphibious Corps was the responsibility of Major General Harold G ('Harry') Schmidt.

The plan of attack was divided into three broad phases. In the first phase, naval and air units would bombard Iwo Jima over a period of several months in order to weaken Japanese defences. In phase two, the warships of 'Task Force 52' were to carry out a three-day bombardment of enemy positions and cover the initial Marine landings. The assault would be spearheaded by the veteran 4th Marine Division and the new 5th Marine Division. These two divisions would land abreast of each other along 3,500 yards of beach on the southeastern side of Iwo Jima, between Mount Suribachi and the East Boat Basin. On the left, one regiment of 5th Marine Division would advance to the base of Suribachi, while a second would drive straight across the island to the opposite shore. At the same time, 4th Marine Division would land on the right of the beach, secure a Japanese airfield designated as 'Airfield Number 1', and then wheel right to secure the line designated '0–1'. Each division would hold one of its three regiments in tactical reserve. In the third phase, Suribachi was to be secured, and then two divisional advance northwards would clear the rest of the island. The 3rd Marine Division was to be held offshore as a reserve and committed if the attack faltered. Originally the division was to have remained far to the south on the island of Guam, but this plan was altered by Lieutenant General Smith who wanted the division close at hand. This proved a sound decision.

Final Preparations

In the early hours of 19 February the Marine assault forces joined Rear Admiral William H P Blandy's 'Task Force 52' off Iwo Jima. In all, 450 ships lay off the island. As 50,000 Marines ate a hearty breakfast, at 6.40 a.m. Blandy's support force began the final stages of a three-day preparatory bombardment of the island by 6 battleships, 4 cruisers, and 16 destroyers. As the battleships' 14-in guns crunched into suspected enemy positions throwing up rubble and spouts of flame, many observers could not fail to be impressed by the awesome display of firepower. Holland Smith and Harry Schmidt were less impressed, they had wanted a ten-day close bombardment, not three. Despite their vociferous complaints, and the memory of dead Marines floating in the lagoon at Tarawa, they had failed to persuade the US Navy of their case. The short duration, poor visibility, and refusal of the Japanese to expose their positions by opening fire meant that the preparatory bombardment was not as effective as was hoped. Iwo Jima's defenders were about to give the Marines one of their hottest welcomings of the war.

As the naval guns thundered at Iwo Jima, the Marines embarked into their assault vessels. The initial assault force comprised 8 battalions in 482 Amtracs (armoured vehicles capable of moving on land and in water) in 10 waves. The first wave was to land at 9.00 a.m., designated as 'H-Hour', two minutes later the second wave would come ashore, and the following eight other waves of assault craft were to land at five-minute intervals. This carefully organized landing plan aimed to put 9,000 men ashore in just under 45 minutes. At 8.30 a.m., with the Marine units formed up, the order was given: 'Land the landing force!' As units of the 4th Marine Division began the 2-mile approach to the beach, they went in with the prayer of their commanding officer, Major General Clifton B Cates, that as many of them as possible might be spared.

The Landings

As the lead regiments of 4th Marine Division and 5th Marine Division neared the black shoreline of Iwo Jima, the naval bombardment began to roll steadily inland still pummelling Japanese positions, while Marine Chance-Vought F4U-ID Corsair fighters streaked in low, firing rockets ahead of the troops. Apart from some sporadic fire from the island, the first waves of Marines began landing unhindered at around 9.05 a.m., but immediately things began to go wrong. The first Amtracs found that the beach terrace was too steep and too high for many of them to climb. Some managed to ram their way to the top, others retreated into the sea so that they could fire their guns over the terrace. Debouching from their vehicles the Marines, laden with equipment, sank into the black ash. Movement was slow and difficult for men and vehicles. Still, the lead regiments pushed forwards onto firmer ground unopposed.

Then 15 minutes after the first Marines came ashore, and with the beaches packed with men and vehicles, Japanese artillery and mortar fire crashed into them. The lead units of both the divisions, some 200 yards inland, came under fire from all sides as they stumbled onto concealed Japanese positions. With movement inland halted or at a crawl, congestion began to build up on the beaches. The black sand offered poor cover to the exposed troops, and foxholes filled in as fast as they were dug. Many wheeled vehicles bogged down, and even tanks found it a slow and difficult process to move inland over the terraces. As the day went on, smashed and burning vehicles, landing craft, stores, and equipment littered the beaches as Japanese fire, accurately directed from Mount Suribachi, plunged into them and the seaward approaches. The plight of the wounded was the most agonizing problem. As they lay on the beaches awaiting evacuation many were re-wounded or killed. Desperate medical corpsmen commandeered any vessel in an attempt to get their patients off the island and out to the waiting hospital ships. By midday it appeared that Lieutenant General Kuribayashi's plan was paying off.

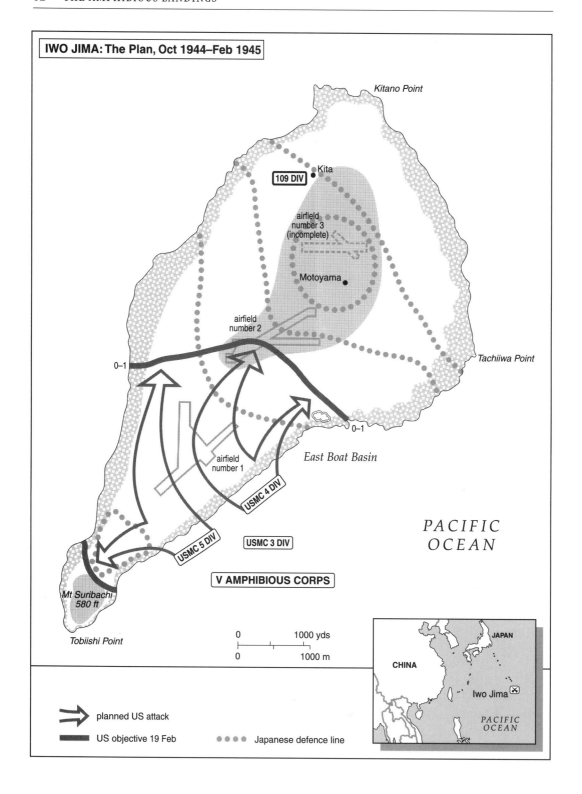

IWO JIMA: The Plan, Oct 1944–Feb 1945

Kitano Point

Kita

109 DIV

airfield
number 3
(incomplete)

Motoyama

airfield
number 2

Tachiiwa Point

0–1

0–1

East Boat Basin

airfield
number 1

USMC 4 DIV

USMC 5 DIV

USMC 3 DIV

V AMPHIBIOUS CORPS

PACIFIC
OCEAN

Mt Suribachi
580 ft

Tobiishi Point

0   1000 yds
0   1000 m

JAPAN

CHINA

Iwo Jima

PACIFIC
OCEAN

planned US attack

US objective 19 Feb   Japanese defence line

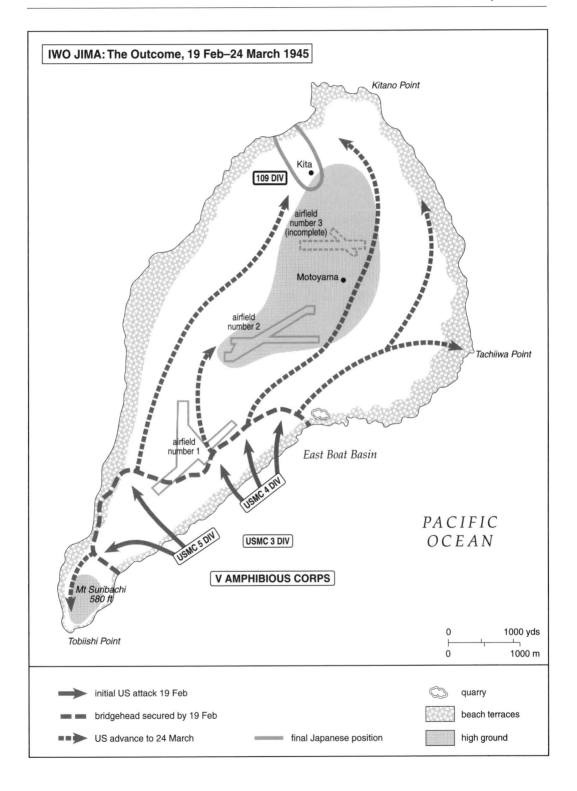

IWO JIMA: The Outcome, 19 Feb–24 March 1945

Kitano Point

Kita

109 DIV

airfield
number 3
(incomplete)

Motoyama

airfield
number 2

Tachiiwa Point

airfield
number 1

East Boat Basin

USMC 4 DIV

USMC 5 DIV

USMC 3 DIV

PACIFIC
OCEAN

V AMPHIBIOUS CORPS

Mt Suribachi
580 ft

Tobiishi Point

0   1000 yds

0   1000 m

→ initial US attack 19 Feb

▬ ▬ bridgehead secured by 19 Feb

▬▬► US advance to 24 March

▬▬ final Japanese position

quarry

beach terraces

high ground

The Drive Inland

In spite of mounting casualties and confusion on the beaches throughout the day, the Marines doggedly pushed inland towards their objectives. Typical of the fighting on that first day was the 28th Regiment, belonging to 5th Marine Division on the far left of the landing zone. This regiment had two tasks. Its 1st Battalion (or 1/28th) was to advance rapidly across the narrow isthmus to the opposite shore of Iwo Jima, while its 2nd Battalion (2/28th) was to push up to the southern slopes of Mount Suribachi in preparation for a subsequent assault.

As 1/28th pushed inland it came under mortar fire, suffering heavy casualties. About halfway across the isthmus it ran into a maze of enemy pill boxes and within minutes the advance had come to a halt in total confusion. Yet the individual courage and determination of the Marines meant that the halt was only temporary. Captain Dwayne E Mears knocked out several pillboxes armed only with a revolver before being mortally wounded. Men who became detached from their own units joined others and in small groups, heedless of their flanks, they pushed on. At around 10.35 a.m. a grand total of one lieutenant and four men reached their objective on the far shore. The rest of the battalion was strung out over the 700 yard back to the landing beaches and engaged in ferocious fighting. The 2/28th fared little better, despite receiving the support of a company of tanks and the regiment's 3rd Battalion (3/28th) from reserve. The slow progress and heavy casualties meant that 28th Regiment was short of its objectives by nightfall.

Other elements of 5th Marine Division and the entire 4th Marine Division experienced similarly fierce fighting in the centre and on the right of the landing zone. One reason for their slow progress was a lack of heavy fire support. Their own artillery could not land until late in the day because of the situation on the beaches, and shortages in mortar ammunition meant that they lost the support of many of these valuable weapons. Consequently, scarce tank support was vital for knocking out Japanese pillboxes. The tanks also tended to draw much of the Japanese fire, giving the Marines some slight respite from the whirlwind engulfing them. But even when an enemy position was cleared the Marines soon found that a new surprise awaited them. As they pressed on, the Japanese would infiltrate back into the pillbox using their extensive tunnel network, and begin firing into their backs. As one Marine commented, there were no front lines on Iwo Jima.

The heaviest fighting of the day took place on the far right, where 25th Regiment of 4th Marine Division came ashore. This landing beach was overlooked by cliffs near the East Boat Basin, and from this position the

Japanese directed a hurricane of small arms and artillery fire into the flank of the exposed Marines. Officer casualties were particularly high, one company losing eight officers by mid-afternoon. Support from mortars and artillery was denied to the Marines as the Japanese paid special attention to destroying these exposed units. Immediate tank support was delayed by enemy fire against the landing ships. Once ashore it took time for combat engineers to bulldoze a track over the terrace and clear minefields so that the armour could move inland. Only with great difficulty was the advance inland continued through to nightfall.

The Rest of the Battle

The men of V Amphibious Corps had encountered enemy defences far stronger than anticipated. Casualties at the end of the first day totalled around 2,450 troops. The heavy fighting meant that the Marines had fallen far short of their first day objectives. The 5th Marine Division had reached the opposite shore line and isolated Mount Suribachi, although little progress had been made against the defences around the base of its slope. The far shore of the island had just about been reached, but there were still pockets of Japanese resistance to mop up in front of 28th Regiment. The slowest progress had been made in the centre and on the right where the two divisions had failed to overrun 'Airfield Number 1' or reach the objective line '0–1'. The 4th Marine Division had managed to push inland for an average of barely 500 yards.

In spite of this, by nightfall 30,000 Marines with their heavy equipment and vehicles were ashore in a secure, if rather 'hot', bridgehead. In the face of fanatical Japanese resistance, the daunting terrain, and the problems encountered on that first day the Marines had achieved a great success. Now firmly established ashore, it was a question of applying overwhelming numbers and firepower in the right combination to defeat the Japanese. The subsequent weeks of fighting on Iwo Jima were every bit as fierce as on the first day. Progress was slow and the island was not declared secure until 25 March. Even after this date minor mopping-up operations continued until late June, as Japanese survivors emerged from the labyrinth of caves and tunnels. At the end, of a Japanese garrison of 26,000 troops just over 1,000 were taken prisoner, most of them too badly wounded to commit suicide. In the battle the Marines had lost a staggering 25,581 casualties, of which around 5,330 were dead.

The Aftermath

Ultimately, Iwo Jima turned out not to be essential as a fighter base to protect Le May's strategic bombers. Although P-51 Mustang fighters did operate from the island, by late Summer 1945 Japanese air power was so weak that the bombers could operate alone with relative immunity. But the island did save the lives of the crews of over 2,100 B-29 Superfortresses, which carried out emergency landings at Iwo Jima because they were too damaged to make the long trip to their bases in the Marianas. Whether this was worth the cost in dead and wounded to the Marine Corps has remained a question of debate. What is clear is that the picture of the Marines hoisting the American flag on top of Mount Suribachi on 23 February became a symbol for the courage and bravery of the men of the United States Marine Corps. Watching this event in Vice Admiral Turner's flagship, Secretary of the United States Navy James Forrestal commented, 'The raising of that flag on Suribachi means a Marine Corps for the next five hundred years'.

TIM BEAN

Further Reading
Gailey, H A *The War in the Pacific* (New York, 1995)
Wheeler, R *Iwo Jima* (New York, 1994)
Wheeler, R *A Special Valor* (New York, 1996)

THE SLOGGING
MATCHES

"There comes a time when Private Snodgrass must advance straight to his front!" GENERAL SIR ARCHIBALD WAVELL, COMMANDER-IN-CHIEF INDIA

IN WORLD WAR II, as in every other war, the planners hoped to fight battles that would overwhelm an enemy quickly, completely, and with little loss to their own side. But World War II was also industrialized global war at its most formidable. The sheer strength of the major powers on each side often meant that very often there was no chance of a quick, clean, decisive victory. The nature of the ground, or of the circumstances of the battle, often meant that there was little scope for fancy manoeuvre. Also, neither a good opposing general nor a good enemy army was likely to collapse so conveniently. Many of the war's most important battles consisted of throwing in men and firepower until one side or the other finally broke. Sometimes, as with the German assault on the Soviet Union in 1941, what was planned as a swift victory by manoeuvre turned into something quite different. By the war's middle period, many of its best generals were realistically resigned to hard fighting for apparently little gain on the ground, knowing that the damage done to the enemy would make it worthwhile in the end.

Operation Barbarossa

To the Gates of Moscow

22 JUNE – 5 DECEMBER 1941

The German Armed Forces under Führer Adolf Hitler

VERSUS

The Soviet Armed Forces under Marshal Joseph Stalin

CHRONOLOGY

22 June 1941 –	Start of the German offensive
12 August 1941–	Hitler orders the encirclement of Kiev
8 September 1941–	Start of the siege of Leningrad
1 October 1941–	Hitler orders the advance on Moscow
5 December 1941–	The German advance on Moscow is halted

"The whole structure is rotten; one kick and we can bring the building down." ADOLF HITLER IN 1940, DESCRIBING THE SOVIET UNION

THE BASIS OF the armoured blitzkrieg in World War II was always the swift and decisive victory, with the enemy defeated, crushed, and humbled in a matter of weeks or even days. But battles do not always go the way they are planned. What began as the greatest of all the German blitzkriegs, a battle of incredible speed, power, and daring that appeared to bring victory over a giant opponent within a few weeks, instead turned into the most grim and deadly of the war's slogging matches. From the failure of the German plan for Barbarossa came the horror of five years of war on the Eastern Front.

The Strategic Situation

As German troops made their triumphal march through Berlin on Saturday 6 July 1940 to celebrate the fall of France, staff officers at the headquarters of the *Oberkommando des Herres* (OKH or Army High Command) at Zossen, 20 miles south of the capital, were poring over maps of eastern Europe. The invasion of the Soviet Union was now inevitable, though the date had yet to be fixed. Hitler could see a unique window of opportunity for Germany. France had been comprehensively defeated and the Battle of Britain was about to begin. The armed forces of the Soviet Union were also in a sorry state. In November 1939, in the 'Winter War', Finland's small, under-equipped civic guard had managed to smash Soviet divisions to pieces.

One man was responsible for the rapid decline of the Soviet Army – Joseph Stalin. In 1937, with his political rivals either dead or in exile, Stalin turned to a purge of the Army, murdering more than 30,000 senior officers in one bloody year. Political commissars were given massively increased powers, and the Soviet Army reduced to a people's militia. Stalin had been more frightened of his own army than he was of the Germans. But then the blitzkriegs in Poland and France produced panic, and the winter of 1940–41 saw Soviet commanders desperately trying to put armoured formations back together, something that was easier said than done. If the *Abwehr* (German Military Intelligence) found Soviet doctrine and the structure of Soviet formations in 1941 hard to comprehend, then so did the Soviets themselves.

The Soviet Plans

Stalin expected a German attack, but erroneously assumed that its impetus would originate from aristocratic German generals, rather than a radical man of the people like Adolf Hitler. By cooperating closely with Nazi Germany he hoped to delay any attack for as long as possible. Every day from October 1939 onwards Soviet trains laden with grain, oil, and metal ores passed through Brest-Litovsk, the demarcation zone between Communist and Nazi Europe, to supply the German war effort against the western Allies.

At the same time, Stalin ordered Soviet forces westwards into eastern Poland, and also the Baltic States and the Romanian provinces of Bessarabia and Moldavia, gained by the Soviet Union through political intimidation. Surviving senior officers of the Soviet Army knew that this policy was misguided. It meant abandoning long prepared defensive positions on the Dnieper and Dvina rivers, the so-called 'Stalin Line', and exposing their forces to unnecessary risks, but no-one had the courage to tell Stalin he was wrong.

By Summer 1941 the Soviets had concentrated about 2,000,000 men, 10,000 tanks, and 12,000 aircraft all within 150 miles of the eastern border of the German Reich. Further back along the old Stalin Line were another million or so troops. And just in case more might be required, staff work was already well advanced for the transfer westward of 50 divisions and 3,000 aircraft deployed in the Far East.

The German Plans

'Führer Directive 21' of December 1940, code-named 'Operation Barbarossa' ('red-beard' from Frederick Barbarossa, a medieval warrior emperor), was the culmination of a long summer and autumn of German plans and war games. Abwehr analysts reported that the bulk of Soviet forces were being deployed along the common German-Soviet frontier, well forward of the Dnieper–Dvina line. They were split into two more or less equal groupings by the Pripyat Marshes, a vast swamp about the size of England, which saddled eastern Poland and the western Ukraine. The prognostications were almost too good to be true. Hitler decreed three separate thrusts: Army Group North led by a powerful armoured 'Panzer Group', Army Group Centre led by two 'Panzer Groups' (later renamed Panzer Armies), and Army Group South also with one Panzer Group. Thanks to the fact that the Soviets had deployed so far forward, and that the Pripyat Marshes would make Soviet north–south communication difficult, the OKH estimated the destruction of Soviet forces should take only about six to eight weeks, west of the River Dnieper. After that, the planners anticipated relatively easy advances on Leningrad, Moscow, and Kiev, approximately 600, 700, and 900 miles from the start lines, with the eventual aim of stopping on a line from Archangel to the Caspian Sea. In all, Germany deployed 3,360,000 men, 3,600 tanks, 7,500 guns, and 2,500 front-line aircraft on a front of 1,000 miles running from the Baltic to the Black Sea, the largest and most powerful army ever assembled.

The Opening Moves

At 2.40 a.m. on Saturday 21 June, Major General V E Klimovskikh, Chief of Staff to Soviet forces in eastern Poland, sent an urgent message to Moscow, reporting very suspicious large-scale German movements to his front. Back came a reassuring reply from Moscow: 'Don't panic! The boss knows all about it', which was far from true. A little over 24 hours later, at 3.15 a.m. on Sunday 22 June, the front from the Baltic to the Carpathians erupted with fire. Soviet troops on the eastern bank of the River Bug at Brest-Litovsk were astonished to see German tanks – specially adapted PzKw IVs (from *Panzerkampfwagen*, the German for tank) – emerge from the river in front of them, the first ever use of the schnorkel by land vehicles. As dawn broke, German Junkers Ju-87 Stuka dive-bombers, followed by Heinkel and Dornier bombers, swept over Soviet airfields. The Soviet machines stood wing tip to wing tip on grass fields, unprotected by early warning systems, anti-air defences, or even sandbags. Nearly half the pilots and ground crews were away on courses or on leave, while many of those remaining were sleeping off the after-effects of Saturday night's vodka. By the end of the day the Germans had struck 66 Soviet airfields, on which 70% of the entire Soviet airforce had been stationed, and had managed to destroy over 2,000 machines. Lieutenant General Kopets, the Soviet air commander, responded to the news by blowing out his brains with a pistol. But Soviet ground forces fared little better. The German panzers overran vast parks of tanks before the crews could put them into action. Many Soviet Army commanders, fearing Stalin's wrath, also committed suicide.

Stalin had in fact already received many warnings of the attack, including one from British Intelligence. The subsequent knowledge that he had been wrong forced him into denial. He blamed at first the German officer corps, claiming that all would be well if only he could make personal contact with Hitler himself. But after 36 hours Stalin realized that he been outmanoeuvred by an enemy as ruthless, cunning, and amoral as himself. He responded in characteristic fashion, drinking himself into a stupor from which he emerged only on 3 July, while his chief of secret police Lavrenti Beria took temporary charge of the Soviet Union.

The German offensive had by this time developed in two very different ways. To the north of the Pripyat Marshes, the two Panzer Groups attached to Army Group Centre, commanded respectively by General Herman Hoth and General Heinz Guderian, closed in quick succession around Brest-Litovsk, Bialystok, Minsk, and finally, on 22 July, Smolensk. Army Group North had also made rapid progress and by 18 July was only 80 miles from Leningrad. The figures involved were so extraordinary – the Germans boasted 3 million prisoners, together with 12,000 tanks and 8,000 aircraft destroyed – that even Josef Goebbels, chief of German propaganda, refused to believe them. On 3 July, Colonel General Hans Halder, the German Army Chief of Staff, wrote in his diary 'It is no exaggeration to say that the campaign in Russia has been won in 14 days'.

The Kiev Pocket

Despite these victories, the progress made by Army Group South was far slower. Although some officers blamed the elderly commander of Army Group South, Field Marshal Gerd von Rundstedt, the problems were essentially geographical. Army Group South's attack was compressed into a relatively narrow gap by the Pripyat Marshes to the north and the Carpathian Mountains to the south. In the middle of this gap it ran into the Soviet's most powerful forces, the 56 divisions of the Kiev Special Military District, which had 5,580 tanks, including 1,000 KVs and T-34s, both new types superior to the German panzers. At 50 tons the KV was the heaviest tank in the world, while the 30-ton T-34, with a 75-mm gun and sloped armour which deflected German shells, was later regarded as the best tank of the war. The advance became a grim attritional slog that came to a complete halt on 11 July, still 10 miles from Kiev.

Between 22 July and 21 August, German command on the Eastern Front was locked in bitter disagreement. Guderian and Hoth both wanted to press on to Moscow, whereas Hitler, arguing that the Soviet armed forces and not the Soviet capital were the real objective, demanded that forces be diverted from Army Group Centre towards Leningrad and Kiev. It took until 21 August for Hitler to exert his authority. Army Group Centre's panzers now began a gigantic swing south and on 12 September they linked up with German forces in the Ukraine to encircle Kiev. After six days of heavy fighting 600,000 Soviet troops surrendered – the largest number of prisoners ever taken in a single battle.

It now seemed impossible that the Germans, whose troops were being joined by smaller formations from other members of the Axis, could lose. In less than 100 days, at the cost to themselves of 400,000 casualties, they had done just what they had planned to do – they had destroyed 200 Soviet divisions west of the Dnieper, and taken over 3,500,000 prisoners. In the south German troops had occupied Kiev and were preparing to assault the eastern Ukraine, an area of enormous industrial resources vital to the Soviet war effort. In the centre the Germans were only 200 miles from Moscow, and to the north German guns were bombarding Leningrad.

The German Problem

Yet the German situation was not quite so rosy as it first appeared. They had made enormous gains at the cost of comparatively few men, but their serious loss of equipment was not being replaced fast enough through a series of

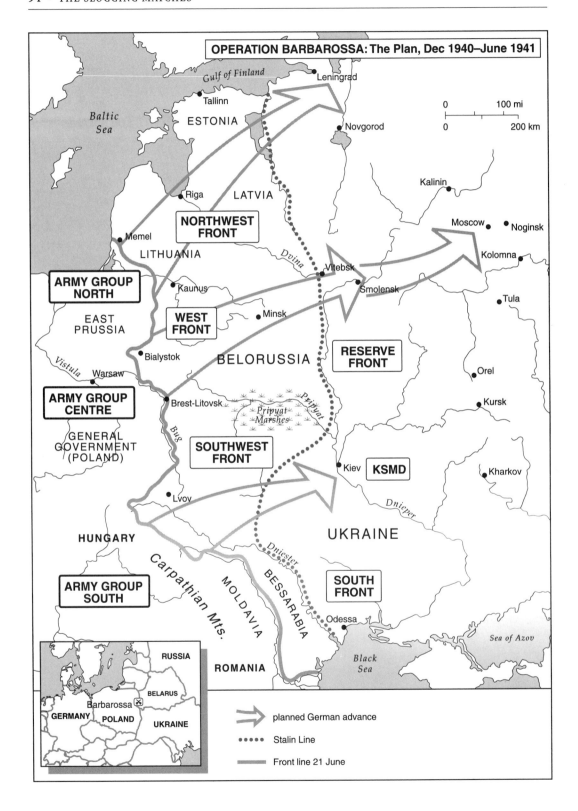

OPERATION BARBAROSSA: The Plan, Dec 1940–June 1941

Gulf of Finland

Leningrad

Tallinn

Baltic Sea

ESTONIA

Novgorod

0   100 mi
0   200 km

Kalinin

Riga

LATVIA

Moscow   Noginsk

NORTHWEST FRONT

Kolomna

Dvina

Memel

Vitebsk

LITHUANIA

Smolensk

Tula

ARMY GROUP NORTH

Kaunus

EAST PRUSSIA

WEST FRONT

Minsk

RESERVE FRONT

Orel

Vistula

Bialystok

BELORUSSIA

Warsaw

Kursk

ARMY GROUP CENTRE

Brest-Litovsk

Pripyat Marshes

Pripyat

GENERAL GOVERNMENT (POLAND)

Bug

SOUTHWEST FRONT

Kiev

KSMD

Kharkov

Lvov

Dnieper

HUNGARY

UKRAINE

Dniester

ARMY GROUP SOUTH

Carpathian Mts.

MOLDAVIA

BESSARABIA

SOUTH FRONT

ROMANIA

Odessa

Black Sea

Sea of Azov

RUSSIA

BELARUS

Barbarossa

GERMANY   POLAND

UKRAINE

planned German advance

••••• Stalin Line

Front line 21 June

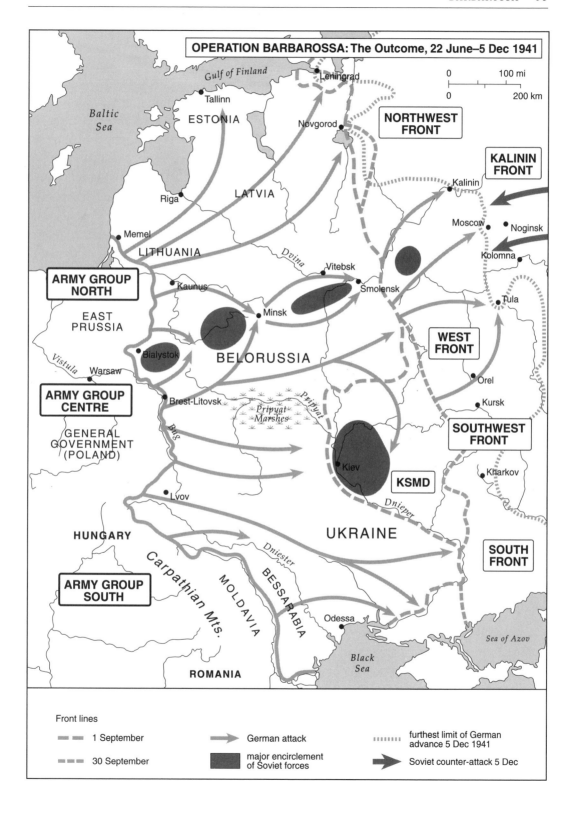

OPERATION BARBAROSSA: The Outcome, 22 June–5 Dec 1941

| 0 | 100 mi |
| 0 | 200 km |

Baltic
Sea

Gulf of Finland

Leningrad

Tallinn

ESTONIA

Novgorod

**NORTHWEST
FRONT**

**KALININ
FRONT**

Kalinin

Riga

LATVIA

Moscow • Noginsk

Kolomna

Memel

LITHUANIA

Dvina

Vitebsk

Smolensk

**ARMY GROUP
NORTH**

Kaunus

Minsk

**EAST
PRUSSIA**

**WEST
FRONT**

Vistula

Bialystok

Warsaw

BELORUSSIA

Tula

Orel

**ARMY GROUP
CENTRE**

Brest-Litovsk

Pripyat
Marshes

Pripyat

Kursk

Bug

**SOUTHWEST
FRONT**

**GENERAL
GOVERNMENT
(POLAND)**

Kiev

KSMD

Kharkov

Lvov

Dnieper

HUNGARY

Dniester

UKRAINE

**SOUTH
FRONT**

Carpathian Mts.

MOLDAVIA

BESSARABIA

**ARMY GROUP
SOUTH**

Odessa

Sea of Azov

Black
Sea

ROMANIA

Front lines

━ ━ ━ 1 September

━ ━ ━ 30 September

➤ German attack

⬛ major encirclement
of Soviet forces

┈┈┈ furthest limit of German
advance 5 Dec 1941

➤ Soviet counter-attack 5 Dec

overlapping transport and supply problems. German planners had allowed for the fact that the Soviet railway gauge was wider than the German (their railway troops were converting it as fast as possible), yet there was always a point where the line ended. Here the equipment had to be transferred to some of the Wehrmacht's 200,000 trucks, and huge logjams inevitably ensued. Only a few trucks were German – the rest had been either been bought or requisitioned from over eight different countries. With over 200 models to service, it proved almost impossible to find spares for those that broke down along the steadily deteriorating Soviet roads, which were mostly only hard earth. The 600,000 horses kept by the Wehrmacht also posed their own logistical problems, requiring regular food and water.

Tanks and other fighting vehicles also took a very long time to repair. Germany was the least motorized of any advanced industrial nation, boasting only half the number of cars of the UK and correspondingly fewer skilled mechanics. Germany's strong apprentice system, coupled with their exaltation of the 'craftsman', prevented it from mass-producing mechanics skilled in just one task, after Soviet practice. The Germans tried to compensate by centralizing their workshops, but this also meant that vehicles sent away for repair might never be seen again.

Hitler ordered the launching of 'Operation Typhoon', the renewed assault on Moscow, for 1 October. The generals were aghast at the prospect of an attack so late in the season, but German meteorologists remained convinced that the late wet spring and blazing hot summer promised a late warm autumn. If the rains held off through to late October, Moscow was theirs. It was a gamble, but Hitler had been gambling all his life. For their thrust to Moscow the Germans assembled 78 divisions, nearly 200,000 men. They still boasted substantial air superiority, but their tank strength was down by 56%, and ammunition supplies had fallen from 60 days' fighting consumption to as little as four days. While the German capacity to manoeuvre was still infinitely better than that of the Soviets, their capacity to engage in sustained attritional battle had declined substantially. If it came to another slogging match, the Germans could well be defeated.

Operation Typhoon

The attack started auspiciously. On 2 October, Guderian's panzers reached Orel to the southwest of Moscow and proceeded towards Tula, only 120 miles from the capital. Orel fell so suddenly that the trams were still running, their passengers waving at the panzers mistakenly assuming them to be Russian tanks. Two weeks later Hoth's panzers took Kalinin, 100 miles northwest of

Moscow. STAVKA (Soviet high command) realized that the Germans intended to encircle the city. If they maintained their rate of advance Moscow would be besieged by around 1 November.

On Wednesday 15 October a report that two German tanks had reached a suburb of Moscow caused stampedes at railway stations, and panic gripped the city. Party officials and secret police tried to flee in cars, leading to the first traffic jam in Soviet history. Looters raided the stalled cars and robbed the occupants, particularly those thought to be Jews. In Red Square, Lenin's mummified body was removed from its mausoleum and hidden in a still incomplete section of the Moscow Metro.

But on 6 October, Guderian noticed an ominous change in the weather. That evening he felt the first light showers of autumn. Two days later they had spread as far north as Hoth's formations. By Saturday 18 October the rain was sheeting down. German meteorologists had been wrong. The rain arrived exactly on time, heralding the Rasputiza, the 'time of mud'. As the roads disappeared into quagmires, the German advance slowed to a crawl. Knowledge that the rain had severely slowed down the German advance led to some restoration of Muscovite confidence. On 7 November, the 24th anniversary of the Revolution, Stalin addressed massed Soviet infantry from the Kremlin's balcony in Red Square. He proclaimed that 'The German invaders want a war of extermination against the peoples of the Soviet Union. Very well then! If they want a war of extermination, they shall have it!' The Soviet Union was now better placed than at any time since 22 June. The large-scale evacuation of Soviet factories continued along the still intact railway system. Over 3,000 factories had been moved from the western part of the country to east of the Urals: the vast industrial camps built around Siberian cities such as Sverdlovsk, Magnitogorsk, and Chelyabinsk would soon be in production. Meanwhile, in front of Moscow the Soviets used the breathing space afforded by the Rasputiza to increase their defences. On 10 October the formidable Marshal Georgi Zhukov, the only senior officer to have survived Stalin's purges, arrived to take command of the Moscow front. By 1 November he commanded 84 divisions with more than 1,250,000 men, 10,600 guns and mortars, 850 tanks, and 930 aircraft, all of which could be supported by the still intact Moscow rail system.

But the best news came from Tokyo, where a Soviet spy had incontrovertible evidence that Japan was about to strike south at the United States and at the British and Dutch colonial empires. This meant that Japan would not attack the eastern Soviet Union, and that the troops there could be safely moved. Long columns of Soviet trains were moving west over the Trans-Siberian railway to bring reinforcements to Moscow. In the first two weeks of

November, Zhukov's forces around Moscow received an additional 100,000 men and officers, 300 tanks, and 2,000 guns. Numerically the Soviets were once again superior to the Germans, but Zhukov and Stavka had real worries about the state of Soviet morale, so much so that reliable NKVD (secret police) troops were dug-in in the rear areas, with orders to execute soldiers suspected of desertion.

Fighting for Moscow

In mid-November the temperature dropped below freezing. As the Razputiza ended the panzers again moved forward on the frozen ground. The German plan envisaged one more envelopment and the closing of the pincers around Moscow. Guderian's Panzer Group would head northeast for Kolomna while Hoth's forces moved northeast around the capital, to then swing southeast to link up with Guderian in Noginsk, around 50 miles east of Moscow. But heavily forested terrain close to Moscow canalized their formations along obvious avenues of approach. By 27 November, Hoth's panzers had battled their way to the Volga Canal, a mere 18 miles from the Kremlin, but his divisions now mustered fewer than a dozen tanks apiece. This was very different from the fighting around Smolensk and Kiev. German divisions were designed for rapid manoeuvre, and artillery batteries had been spread out amongst semi-independent commands. Now the guns had to be brought back under central control if the Germans were to have any hope of matching Soviet barrages. But the physical business of moving guns and ammunition had become progressively more difficult as tractors broke down and horses died. By the end of November, German infantry, unwillingly assisted by long lines of starving Soviet prisoners, was dragging artillery forward. For every shell the Germans fired they got ten in return. On 1 December, Army Group Centre made a last all-out attack to take Moscow, but the balance of forces favoured the defender. On 4 December the last surviving tank of 1st Panzer Division – nicknamed 'Antony the Last' – finally broke down. A day later the advance ground to a halt. At dawn on 3 December, Zhukov's Siberian divisions crashed through the extended flanks of Army Group Centre.

The Aftermath

In the face of this onslaught the German front fragmented and fell back, then reformed and held on in a series of 'hedgehog' positions through the winter. By the fierce standards of Russian winters, with their icy blizzards, that of 1941–42 was not in fact unusually bad. But the Wehrmacht's stores of winter clothing were in depots in Poland and East Prussia. Forced to choose between sending forward ammunition or winter clothes, the Germans had gambled again by choosing the ammunition, without which they would not have got as close to Moscow as they did. The Wehrmacht very rapidly requisitioned food, clothing, shelter, and transport from the local population, of which thousands died as a result. This only increased the conviction among the Soviets that Hitler and the Wehrmacht were an unrivalled evil, and led to the formation of partisan bands throughout the occupied regions. On the night of 6 December, Hitler finally acknowledged to General Alfred Jodel, Chief of Operations at the OKW, that 'victory could no longer be achieved'.

DUNCAN ANDERSON

Further Reading

Clark, A *Barbarossa* (London, 1965)

Erickson, J *The Road To Stalingrad* (London, 1975)

Glantz, D M, and House, J *When Titans Clashed* (Lawrence, Kansas, 1995)

Overy, R *Russia's War* (London, 1997)

The Second Battle of El Alamein

Hitting Them for Six

23 OCTOBER – 4 NOVEMBER 1942

German and Italian *Panzerarmee Afrika* under
Field Marshal Erwin Rommel

VERSUS

British Eighth Army under Lieutenant General
Bernard L Montgomery

CHRONOLOGY

23 October 1942 – 'Operation Lightfoot' begins
25 October 1942 – Rommel returns to Alamein
27 October 1942 – The 'Snipe' action
2 November 1942 – 'Operation Supercharge' begins
4 November 1942 – *Panzerarmee Afrika* begins its
retreat

"*In the situation in which you find yourself there can be no other thought but to stand fast, yield not a yard of ground and throw every gun and every man into the battle ... Your enemy, despite his superiority, must also be at the end of his strength. It would not be the first time in history that a strong will has triumphed over the bigger battalions. As to your troops, you can show them no other road than that to victory or death.*" HITLER TO ROMMEL,
3 NOVEMBER 1942

THE SECOND BATTLE of Alamein is often considered a 'slogging match' won only by the superior numbers and equipment amassed by the British. The British certainly did possess the 'bigger battalions' but they could also match the Axis forces in morale and motivation. They were also commanded by a general who was determined to make Rommel 'dance to his tune'. In essence, Montgomery brought the British Army back to what it knew best – methodical set piece battles in which everything was planned and prepared in great detail. This gave the British troops the confidence they needed to beat the *Panzerarmee Afrika* in a slogging match, although Rommel and his veterans of the original *Afrika Korps* were masters of manoeuvre warfare and had out-thought and outfought the British Eighth Army many times. Alamein was a very hard-fought battle, and Montgomery's plan did not run smoothly, but he showed great skill in refashioning his offensive and keeping the pressure up on Rommel. Alamein was a slogging match, but it needed much more than just bigger battalions to ensure a British victory.

The Origins of the Battle

The 'Desert War', fought in North Africa between the Axis powers and the British (with their Allies and Empire forces), saw many changes of fortune, beginning with Lieutenant General Sir Richard O'Connor's lightning campaign of December 1940, which had almost destroyed the Italians in Libya. The German *Afrika Korps* under Erwin Rommel (who would rise to Field Marshal in the course of the Desert War) restored the situation in the Axis favour in Spring 1941 with its dramatic attack through Cyrenaica. Rommel's siege of Tobruk, the westernmost supply port for the British Eighth Army, was only lifted at the end of the bloody 'Operation Crusader' battles launched by the British in November. But Rommel's retreat was only temporary, and in May 1942 he began his attack on the Gazala line defended by the British west of Tobruk. By the end of June, Tobruk had fallen, the Eighth Army was in full retreat, and Rommel was driving his men on towards Egypt and Alexandria.

Rommel's victorious forces, now known as the *Panzerarmee Afrika*, were finally halted at the First Battle of El Alamein by a 'brave but baffled' Eighth Army (as Winston Churchill put it) under General Sir Claude Auchinleck during July 1942. In August, Lieutenant General Bernard Montgomery came out to command a revitalized and re-equipped Eighth Army, which easily halted Rommel's last, desperate attempt to reach the Nile Delta in the battle of Alam Halfa, fought at the end of August. With Egypt now finally secure, and Rommel's *Panzerarmee Afrika* in a desperate supply situation (its main supply base and port of Tripoli was over 1,000 miles away to the west), Montgomery could plan his own offensive to, as he put it, 'hit Rommel for six right out of Africa'.

Montgomery's Plan

The Alamein position was unique in the Western Desert because it had secure flanks, resting on the sea in the north and the Qattara Depression in the south. Thus the 37 miles of front could easily be held by both armies, which had concentrated their forces to hold the line. In this circumstance, the standard desert tactic of sweeping round the enemy's southern flank with mobile forces was simply inappropriate. Instead, Montgomery planned to mount a direct assault to break through Rommel's line in the north, near the coast. This would make maximum use of Montgomery's massive superiority in forces over Rommel, something which no British commander in the desert before him had ever possessed. As well as having over 1,000 guns and almost complete control of the air, Eighth Army outnumbered *Panzerarmee Afrika* by more than 2 to 1 in infantry and tanks, had generally better equipment at all levels, and was in a much better position regarding both reserves and supplies.

The Axis forces on the Alamein line had dug themselves in, and planted what they called 'Devil's Gardens' of mines and booby traps up to 5 miles deep. To cope with this, Montgomery planned to open the battle with a massive artillery bombardment, and then to use the infantry divisions of his XXX Corps, under Lieutenant General Sir Oliver Leese, to make a breach in these defences. Meanwhile, sappers would 'gap' (make gaps in) the minefields for both the infantry and armour. Once the breach was made, the infantry would continue to 'crumble' Rommel's infantry formations – which held the minefields – by which Montgomery meant wearing them down with attacks and firepower until they gave way. Meanwhile, the British armour of X Corps under Lieutenant General Herbert Lumsden (1st Armoured Division and 10th Armoured Division) would sally forth from the minefields to destroy the formidable armour of Rommel's army, contained in his German 15th Panzer Division and 21st Panzer Division, and the Italian Ariete and Littorio Divisions. This would produce what Montgomery called a 'dogfight', a fierce battle of attrition in which victory would go to the stronger side, followed by a British breakout into open desert, having blasted a hole right through the northern centre of the Axis line.

Just as importantly, given that Montgomery planned to fight a frontal battle of attrition in which the British superiority in supply and equipment would eventually tell, it was essential that Rommel was unsure of where the blow might fall. Accordingly, a sophisticated deception and misinformation plan was set in motion to persuade the Germans that the attack would be delivered in the south, with the British once more making an armoured sweep around their enemy's open desert flank, as had become almost standard for the attacking side in all previous desert battles. False radio traffic, dummy tanks and vehicles, and even a dummy fuel pipeline were all constructed in the southern sector. To add realism to these efforts, the troops of XIII Corps under Lieutenant General Brian Horrocks, including 7th Armoured Division (the famous 'Desert Rats'), were to mount a limited offensive in the southern sector in an attempt to hold both 21st Panzer and Ariete away from the main fighting.

In its essentials then, Montgomery's plan was simple enough. He estimated that the whole process, from the first break-in to crumbling, to dogfight, and then the breakout, would take 12 days.

Rommel and Stumme's Plan

Rommel was an ill and disheartened man by September 1942. He flew home to Germany for treatment early that month and left his *Panzerarmee* in the hands of General Georg Stumme, an experienced armoured commander. However, Rommel had worked out his defensive plan for the battle he knew was coming. With general supply shortages and a crippling lack of petrol, there was little Rommel could do. His army could neither advance nor retreat for lack of fuel, which meant that it had to wait and meet the British attack. Nonetheless, Rommel had disposed his infantry formations in depth, corseting the weaker Italian formations in between German ones, with outposts inside the minefields themselves. His armoured formations were held back, with 15th Panzer and Littorio in the north, and 21st Panzer and Ariete in the south, and the German 90th Light Division in reserve. Rommel's basic plan was to absorb the British blow, making any advance as difficult as possible. However, his real difficulty lay in the fact that there was only enough petrol to bring 21st Panzer and Ariete up from the south once. There was not enough fuel to send them back, so Rommel had to be certain where Montgomery's main attack was being made before he committed his armour. Once he had identified the British *Schwerpunkt* (a German term meaning 'the critical point of an attack') Rommel would concentrate his armour and counter-attack with all his might to seal off any breach. With this accomplished, Rommel could only hope that the front would bog down into stalemate once again.

The Opening Moves

The Eighth Army attack, code-named 'Operation Lightfoot', began at 9.40 p.m. on 23 October with the biggest artillery bombardment since World War I. Nearly all Montgomery's guns opened up along the front, causing great disruption and confusion to the Axis defenders. The opening of the offensive had caught *Panzerarmee Afrika* by surprise and the initial Axis response was weak and slow.

Like many British armies of history, Montgomery's Eighth Army was an amalgam of troops from many parts of the world, with contingents from the British Empire and various Allies. Initially, the soldiers of the 9th Australian Division, 51st (Highland) Division, 2nd New Zealand Division, and 1st South African Division, each attacking on a two-brigade front, made good progress through the enemy positions and minefields. However, once the Germans and Italians began to recover from the shock, the fighting became bitter and confused all along the front. Advancing in darkness and with huge clouds of dust obscuring their vision, it became increasingly difficult for the attacking troops to keep direction, and mines and booby traps caused considerable casualties. While the Australians and New Zealanders were able to capture their final objectives, the Highlanders were stopped short of their objective, known as the Oxalic Line, except on the extreme left flank, and the South Africans were halted quickly and suffered heavy casualties. Nonetheless, the infantry attack had bitten deeply into the Axis lines and caused considerable disruption.

While the infantry attack was proceeding, the sappers and pioneers tasked with minefield gapping were working hard to make the required number of gaps. For the first time the sappers had a number of gadgets to help them in their job, including new mine detectors supplied by Polish troops, and flail tanks known as Scorpions. However, the mine detectors were found to be too sensitive to be useful, and the Scorpion tanks threw up such choking clouds of dust – as well as exploding mines – that they soon broke down. Ultimately, most of the mine clearing had to be done in the traditional manner by prodding with the bayonet, and this slowed the operation down considerably. The Axis minefields were also found to be deeper than expected, which meant that by dawn on 24 October there were fewer gaps through the minefields than had been expected. On 1st Armoured Division front only one gap was made, but on 10th Armoured Division front with the New Zealanders four gaps had been made, up to the Miteirya Ridge but not beyond.

The men of the armoured regiments had spent a distinctly unpleasant night on 23 October, moving up nose to tail along tracks that were feet-deep in dust.

Delays due to dust, traffic jams, and misdirection meant that 10th Armoured Division did not get forward as quickly as had been hoped, although units of the 9th Armoured Brigade, which had been attached to 2nd New Zealand Division, did manage to reach the Miteirya Ridge. At dawn on 24 October, the elements of 10th Armoured Division that had managed to get through the minefield gaps attempted to advance off the Miteirya Ridge and found themselves exposed to the full weight of the Axis anti-tank gunners and artillery. Meanwhile, many other tanks were stuck in traffic jams in the minefields themselves or further back. It was an impossible situation for armour. Major General A H Gatehouse, the 10th Armoured Division commander, expressed these views to Montgomery in a heated exchange over the telephone early on 25 October but Montgomery flatly ordered him to push on with his armour regardless of casualties. Nonetheless, after a day of battle where the exhausted infantry had to crouch in their hastily dug foxholes as an armoured battle raged around them, Gatehouse ordered his tanks to withdraw back to the ridgeline. Montgomery's planned breakout had failed. After the event, it was clear that the minefields were too deep to be penetrated in a one-night attack, and that the armour would be left penned in to face the teeth of the Axis defence.

On 25 October feint attacks were mounted by 7th Armoured Division, supported by 50th (Northumbrian) Division on the southern sectors of the front. However, rough terrain, extensive minefields, and the spirited defence by the Italian Folgore Parachute Brigade meant that 7th Armoured Division suffered heavy casualties for little gain. Montgomery wished to keep this division as 'a force in being' and the attack was called off on 27 October. Nonetheless, these efforts had done their job: unsure of the main thrust, 21st Panzer and Ariete were still held in the south, away from the main battle.

Axis uncertainty was compounded by confusion in their chain of command. When the battle began, General Stumme was in command of the *Panzerarmee*. His most controversial decision was to forbid retaliatory artillery fire when the British barrage opened. However, on 24 October, he decided to go to the front lines to see what was happening. Unfortunately, his car was caught in an artillery barrage and Stumme, who was about to climb out, had a heart attack and was flung from the car as the driver sped off. Stumme's fate was not learnt until the next day, and in the meantime, General Wilhelm Ritter von Thoma took command and Rommel was recalled from Germany. Rommel arrived with his forces at Alamein late on 25 October, but it took time for him to understand the confused situation, thus delaying the Axis reaction still further.

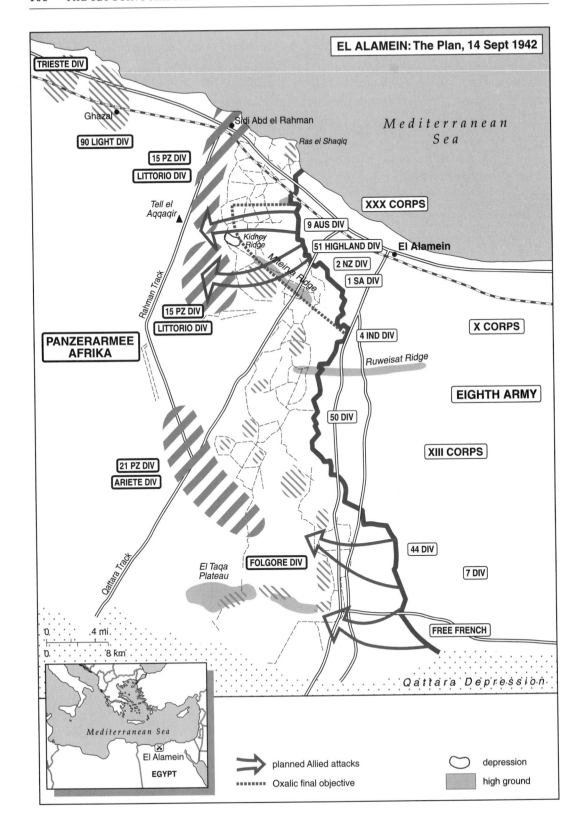

EL ALAMEIN: The Plan, 14 Sept 1942

TRIESTE DIV

Ghazal

Sidi Abd el Rahman

Mediterranean Sea

90 LIGHT DIV

Ras el Shaqiq

15 PZ DIV

LITTORIO DIV

Tell el Aqqaqir ▲

XXX CORPS

9 AUS DIV

Kidney Ridge

51 HIGHLAND DIV   **El Alamein**

2 NZ DIV

Miteirya Ridge

1 SA DIV

Rahman Track

15 PZ DIV

LITTORIO DIV

X CORPS

PANZERARMEE AFRIKA

4 IND DIV

Ruweisat Ridge

EIGHTH ARMY

50 DIV

XIII CORPS

21 PZ DIV

ARIETE DIV

44 DIV

Qattara Track

El Taqa Plateau

FOLGORE DIV

7 DIV

0   4 mi.

0   8 km

FREE FRENCH

Qattara Depression

Mediterranean Sea

El Alamein

EGYPT

⟹ planned Allied attacks   ⌣ depression

▪▪▪▪▪▪▪ Oxalic final objective   ▨ high ground

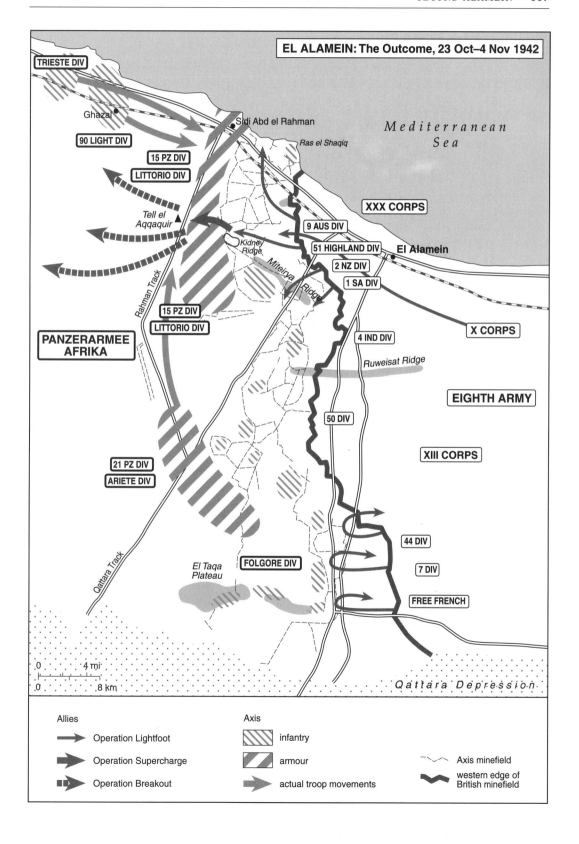

EL ALAMEIN: The Outcome, 23 Oct–4 Nov 1942

TRIESTE DIV

Ghazal

Sidi Abd el Rahman

Mediterranean Sea

90 LIGHT DIV

Ras el Shaqiq

15 PZ DIV

LITTORIO DIV

Tell el Aqqaquir

Kidney Ridge

XXX CORPS

9 AUS DIV

51 HIGHLAND DIV

El Alamein

Miteirya Ridge

2 NZ DIV

Rahman Track

1 SA DIV

X CORPS

15 PZ DIV

LITTORIO DIV

4 IND DIV

PANZERARMEE AFRIKA

Ruweisat Ridge

EIGHTH ARMY

50 DIV

XIII CORPS

21 PZ DIV

ARIETE DIV

44 DIV

7 DIV

Qattara Track

El Taqa Plateau

FOLGORE DIV

FREE FRENCH

0   4 mi

0   8 km

Qattara Depression

Allies

→ Operation Lightfoot

➡ Operation Supercharge

▪▪▪▶ Operation Breakout

Axis

▨ infantry

▨ armour

➡ actual troop movements

〰 Axis minefield

〰 western edge of British minefield

The Dogfight

Montgomery's initial breakout plan had not succeeded, and on 25 October he cancelled any further attacks by 2nd New Zealand Division, and pulled out 10th Armoured Division to rest and refit near El Alamein station. Instead, Montgomery ordered an attack northwards by 9th Australian Division, supported by 1st Armoured Division. This attack began that night, and met with initial success, threatening to cut off elements of the German 164th Light Division around Ras el Shaqiq. While this northern attack got underway, Montgomery continued his ruthless application of superior numbers and weight of firepower in a dogged slogging match. Heavy artillery bombardments, air attacks, and limited infantry attacks were all thrown at the Axis defenders during the next few days in an attempt to wear down their strength. These crumbling attacks, while expensive for the British, were successful in 'writing down' Rommel's strength (to use Montgomery's phrase) and pinning his main forces. Perhaps the best example of these operations was the action around the location code-named 'Snipe', fought near the feature known as Kidney Ridge (one of the 51st (Highland) Division's objectives for 'Lightfoot') on 27 October by the 2nd Battalion of the Rifle Brigade (commanded by Colonel 'Vic' Turner) and 239th Anti-Tank Battery of the Royal Artillery. During the night, this small force had advanced right into the Axis positions. Next day, the men of the Rifle Brigade and Royal Artillery struggled to man their 19 6-pounder anti-tank guns in the face of numerous German and Italian tank attacks, as Rommel pushed his armoured divisions in a counter-attack aimed at sealing the breach in his line. By evening on the 27 October, Turner and his battalion were forced to withdraw due to lack of ammunition, but during the day his men had managed to knock out over 34 Axis tanks and armoured vehicles, a significant proportion of Rommel's remaining tank strength.

On the night of 30–31 October the Australians launched another attack towards the coast. Although they were met with heavy fire, particularly from a strongpoint known as Thompson's Post and a blockhouse near the railway line, the Australians managed to get across the railway and coast road, thus endangering the 164th Light Division. Rommel's attention was drawn to the sector and he personally supervised an attack by 90th Light Division and elements of 21st Panzer Division on 31 October in an attempt to stabilize the situation. Constantly hammered by Axis artillery and forced to repel numerous German attacks, the Australians suffered enormous casualties but were able to hang on in the face of daunting odds and bitter attacks.

Operation Supercharge

While the Australians were drawing Rommel and his *Afrika Korps* onto themselves, Montgomery again changed the direction of his main thrust by planning 'Operation Supercharge'. This was to be the final breakout, using a modified version of 'Operation Lightfoot'. An initial infantry attack would be supported by an enormous concentration of guns, which would then make a breach around Tell el Aqqaquir, about 15 miles west of Alamein station on the Rahman Track, for the armour to pass through and complete the destruction of the *Panzerarmee Afrika*. Montgomery entrusted the task to Major General Bernard Freyberg, commander of the 2nd New Zealand Division, although the infantry for the attack actually came from two British brigades. Postponed for 24 hours due to the complexity of the planning and practical difficulties, 'Operation Supercharge' opened in the early hours of 2 November 1942. At 1.05 a.m. shells from over 800 guns crashed out on a frontage of only 4,000 yards. With this huge weight of artillery support, the attack of the two infantry brigades went like a drill, and they achieved their objectives deep within the Axis positions without too much difficulty. Montgomery had informed Brigadier John Currie, commander of 9th Armoured Brigade, that he was prepared to accept 100% losses in his formation in order to achieve success. Currie's job was far from enviable. His brigade was to assault the German artillery and anti-tank gun screen just before dawn and thus create a breach, which the regiments of 1st Armoured Division could then exploit. Unfortunately, Currie's attack was delayed by half an hour, so that although his tanks did reach the German gun line and manage to destroy over 30 guns, his tanks were then caught silhouetted by first light, and thus became perfect targets for the German anti-tank gunners. Literally in minutes Currie's brigade was eliminated, and by the end of the day he had lost 75 out of 94 tanks.

The 1st Armoured Division was also delayed in its approach march, which meant that it was unable to exploit the confusion caused by the sacrifice of 9th Armoured Brigade. But using the gap in the German gun screen, its regiments took up defensive positions under the protection of the British artillery. Rommel's instinctive reaction to counter-attack the penetration followed, and 1st Armoured Division was attacked by both the 15th Panzer Division and 21st Panzer Division, and 90th Light Division, as well as elements of the Italian Littorio Division and motorized Trento Division. Desperate Axis counter-attacks went on for the rest of the day, and the confusion and carnage of this tank battle was enormous. 'For hours', one survivor described, 'the whack of AP [armour piercing] shot on armour plate was unceasing.' The British armour stood its ground and inflicted heavy losses on the Germans;

117 Axis tanks were destroyed during the battle. The grim reality of the situation dawned on Rommel that evening, when von Thoma reported that his German forces had been reduced to one third of their initial strength and had only 35 serviceable tanks for 3 November. The British breakout had been held but at enormous cost. However, that night Rommel ordered a withdrawal along the coast to Fuka, 60 miles to the west of Alamein.

The End of the Battle

3 November was a frustrating day for the British as, seeing that Rommel's troops were visibly thinning out behind a powerful rearguard, they tried without success to push through the battered *Panzerarmee*. But as this withdrawal got under way, Rommel received a shocking order from Hitler, who insisted that not a yard of ground was to be given up. Astounded but obedient, Rommel countermanded as many of the retreat orders as possible. This caused enormous confusion among the Axis units, and, in particular, condemned the Italian infantry units in the south to destruction and capture.

On 4 November, British armoured cars of the 9th Royal Lancers finally squeezed past Axis units and broke out into the open desert, quickly followed by other units of the Eighth Army. Field Marshal Albert Kesselring, German Commander-in-Chief South, personally countermanded Hitler's orders and allowed Rommel to retreat once more. But as Rommel desperately attempted to save as much of his army as possible, the Eighth Army was able to bag large numbers of Axis prisoners in a series of sharp actions. The battle of El Alamein was over.

Montgomery's plan had not gone as predicted, but the battle had lasted for 12 days. Eighth Army had suffered 13,560 casualties and lost 500 tanks (300 of which were recoverable) but Rommel's *Panzerarmee Afrika* had been smashed and over 35,000 Axis prisoners were captured. When the Anglo-American landings in Morocco and Algeria, code-named 'Operation Torch', took place on 8 November, the Axis position in North Africa was doomed. While Montgomery has been criticized for his conduct of the pursuit of Rommel's fleeing troops, by 23 January 1943 Tripoli, the last city of the Italian Empire, had fallen, and the race into Tunisia continued. The Desert War was finally over, and in Churchill's words 'it might almost be said that before Alamein we never had a victory, while after Alamein we never had a defeat'.

NIALL BARR

Further Reading

Barnett, C *The Desert Generals* (London, 1960)

Carver, M *El Alamein* (London, 1962)

Hamilton, N *Monty, The Making of a General* (London, 1981)

Macksey, K *Rommel, Battles and Campaigns* (London, 1997)

Kursk

Cauldron of Armour

5 – 23 JULY 1943

German Ninth Army under Colonel General Walther Model
and Army Group South under Field Marshal Erich von Manstein
VERSUS
Soviet Central Front under General K K Rokossovsky,
Voronezh Front under General N F Vatutin,
and Steppe Front under General I S Konev

CHRONOLOGY

15 April 1943 –	German planning starts for 'Operation Citadel'
1 July 1943 –	Hitler authorizes 'Operation Citadel'
5 July 1943 –	German offensive starts
13 July 1943 –	Hitler orders the end of the operation
23 July 1943 –	German withdrawal to original positions complete

"This offensive is of decisive significance. It must end in a quick and decisive success… The victory at Kursk must have the effect of a beacon seen round the world." ADOLF HITLER

THE 19TH-CENTURY Prussian military philosopher Carl von Clausewitz wrote that of all the methods of fighting the defence was the strongest. If a commander could discern his opponents' main point of attack then he could prepare strong defences to meet it. Once the attacking forces were exhausted the defender could counter-attack with his relatively fresh troops to win a decisive victory. In the following battle it will be seen how 'Operation Citadel', aimed at the city of Kursk in central Russia near the Ukrainian border, was thwarted by formidable Red Army defences, which paved the way for a series of massive counterstrokes. This was the last major German offensive on the Eastern Front, and it failed.

The Strategic Background

In November 1942 the Red Army had achieved the unthinkable. In just 4 days it had encircled 250,000 of the German Army's best troops in the city of Stalingrad. In a series of successive operations throughout December and into early 1943, the Red Army exploited the gaping hole it had created in the German front line. As Soviet forces swept into eastern Ukraine, STAVKA (the Soviet high command) unleashed further attacks widening the breach in the front. By mid-February the Germans had been pushed back over 300 miles at enormous cost. In light of their continued success, the Soviets were confident of overwhelming the German forces in the Ukraine, but their hopes were soon dashed. After conducting a fighting retreat of great skill throughout the winter, Field Marshal Erich von Manstein, the commander of Army Group Don, unleashed a powerful counter-attack in late February and March. His reserve panzer forces pushed back the overstretched and exposed Soviet armoured spearheads with great loss. The shock of the German riposte, the exhaustion of many Red Army units, and the beginning of the spring thaw (*rasputitsa*, 'time without roads'), which turned the ground into a quagmire, persuaded STAVKA to halt its advance. By late March, the Eastern Front had descended into relative quiet as both sides rebuilt their shattered forces and considered what moves to make in the Spring.

German Strategic Options

In early 1943 Germany confronted an unfavourable strategic situation. The German armed forces had only managed to replace the losses suffered during the bitter fighting at Stalingrad and in southern Russia by transferring forces from the much quieter west. This could only be a short-term solution to the problem of the growing superiority of the Allies in men and equipment, and the increasing threat of the British and Americans to southern or western Europe. If Germany was to have any chance of avoiding defeat, it was essential that one of the Allies should be crippled by a decisive blow early in 1943. Because the Red Army was the most immediate threat to Germany, the Eastern Front was the obvious place for an attack.

But although the Germans had substantial panzer reserves for an offensive, their overall strength on the Eastern Front was not enough to mount an attack capable of defeating the Soviet Union outright. The most that might be achieved was the destruction of a large number of Soviet forces, which would severely reduce their ability to undertake large-scale offensives in 1943. The growing power of the Red Army and probable Anglo-American operations in the Mediterranean meant the Germans had only a brief period of time to use their reserves, before they lost the initiative and the war swung against them decisively. Hitler also needed a military triumph to steady his wavering Finnish, Hungarian, Romanian, and Italian allies.

Although Hitler and his senior commanders agreed on the basic strategic plan for the Eastern Front, strong differences of opinion existed over the method by which the intended blow was to be struck. The two basic options were either to conduct a mobile defence, which aimed to repeat the success of von Manstein's earlier counterstroke, or to seize the initiative and attack first. In early April the decision was made to attack.

The German Plan

The German high command decided to mount its spring offensive in the area of Kursk, in the centre of the Eastern Front. At this point a large salient jutted into the German front line, offering the possibility of easily cutting off and encircling a substantial number of Soviet troops. This was to be achieved by two powerful pincers of armour striking from the north and south into the Soviet rear, and linking up east of the city of Kursk itself. The northern spearhead comprised Ninth Army under Colonel General Walther Model. In the south, under the supervision of von Manstein, was Colonel General Hermann Hoth's Fourth Panzer Army, including II SS Corps of three SS panzergrenadier (armour and motorized infantry) divisions, the first use of SS armoured troops on such a scale, and also Army Detachment Kempf. These forces would consist of over 2,700 tanks and assault guns; altogether 63% of the German armoured forces in Russia.

Speed was critical to the success of the German assault. Once the Soviets discerned the scale and intention of 'Operation Citadel', they would quickly transfer large numbers of reserves to the Kursk area. If this happened before the two pincers linked up, then the Germans would be subjected to powerful counter-attacks and drawn into an unfavourable battle of attrition. It was vital that the operation was completed in five or six days before the Soviet reserves arrived.

But in spite of the need for urgency to catch the Soviets unprepared, Ninth Army's lack of readiness, Hitler's insistence on reinforcing many units, and deployment of the new PzKw V 'Panther' tank postponed the attack from

April to July. The delay led Field Marshal von Manstein and Colonel General Heinz Guderian – the Inspector General of Armoured Forces – to oppose the operation on the grounds that the Soviets had been given time to strengthen their defences and prevent a quick victory. Although Hitler stated that the thought of the operation made his stomach churn, on 1 July he gave the order for the attack to start four days later.

The Soviet Plan

The delays in mounting 'Citadel' gave Soviet military intelligence time to identify the build-up of enemy armoured forces north and south of the Kursk salient. Additional information from a spy ring, code-named 'Lucy', informed Joseph Stalin on 2 July that the attack would commence within the next four days, and further information was obtained from the British 'Ultra' codebreakers. Consequently, the Germans lacked any element of surprise: one of the most important factors for success in war.

The question facing STAVKA was how to deal with the German offensive. Initially, Stalin insisted on mounting a pre-emptive attack to seize the initiative and destroy enemy forces around Kursk. But after much debate Stalin's now trusted adviser at STAVKA, Marshal G K Zhukov, persuaded him that more could be gained by remaining on the defensive. Zhukov's plan was for the Red Army to prepare strong defensive positions to absorb the German assault. Once the panzer divisions had been worn down by protracted, attritional fighting, the Soviets would be free to launch a series of offensives designed to liberate most of southern Russia in the second half of 1943.

The Kursk salient was defended by two Soviet 'Fronts' (broadly the Soviet equivalent of a German Army Group, but smaller). To the north was General K K Rokossovsky's Central Front, and to the south General N F Vatutin's Voronezh Front. Their combined strength came to 900,000 troops, 5,700 anti-tank guns, 19,500 field guns and mortars, and over 3,100 tanks and self-propelled guns. Throughout the spring months the two Fronts, aided by Soviet civilians, constructed eight defence lines around Kursk to a depth of 110 miles. The three principal lines were divided into main, second, and rear defence zones. Each zone consisted of a series of strongpoints laid out in a checkerboard pattern to provide mutual support and defence in depth. The strongpoints each held up to a company of infantry, supported by tanks, artillery, mortars, and anti-tank guns. Extensive use was made of minefields to slow the German advance and canalize it into pre-arranged killing areas: on average there were 2,400 anti-tank, and 2,700 anti-personnel mines per mile, and over half a million mines in total.

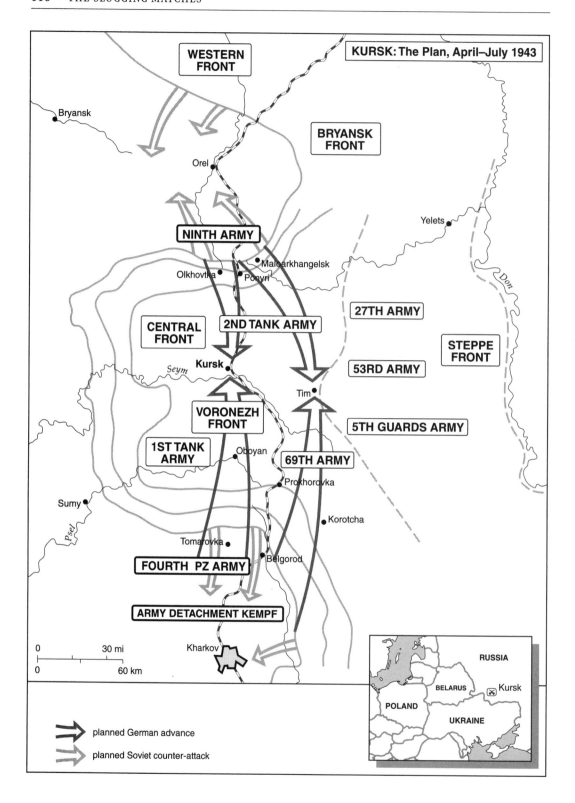

KURSK: The Plan, April–July 1943

WESTERN FRONT

Bryansk

BRYANSK FRONT

Orel

Yelets

NINTH ARMY

Maloarkhangelsk

Olkhovka

Ponyri

27TH ARMY

CENTRAL FRONT

2ND TANK ARMY

STEPPE FRONT

53RD ARMY

Kursk

Seym

Tim

VORONEZH FRONT

5TH GUARDS ARMY

1ST TANK ARMY

Oboyan

69TH ARMY

Sumy

Prokhorovka

Psel

Korotcha

Tomarovka

FOURTH PZ ARMY

Belgorod

ARMY DETACHMENT KEMPF

0   30 mi
0   60 km

Kharkov

Don

RUSSIA

BELARUS

Kursk

POLAND

UKRAINE

planned German advance

planned Soviet counter-attack

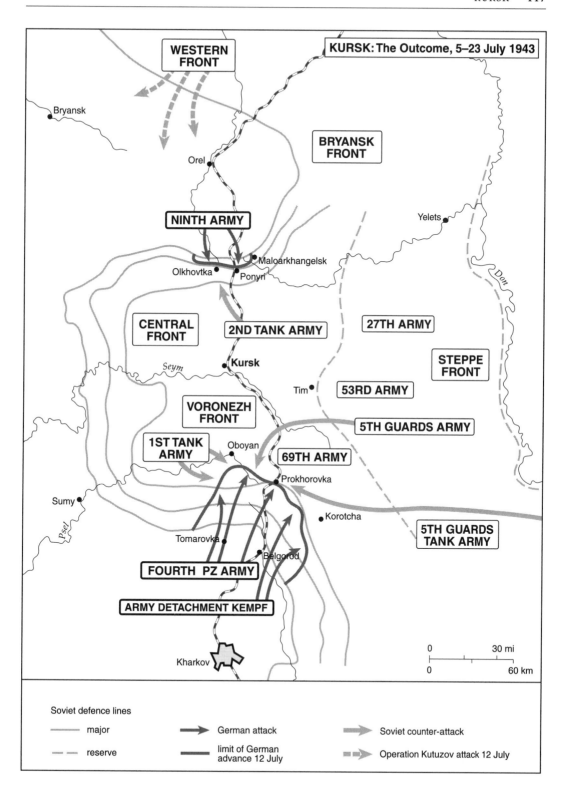

KURSK: The Outcome, 5–23 July 1943

WESTERN FRONT

Bryansk

BRYANSK FRONT

Orel

NINTH ARMY

Yelets

Maloarkhangelsk

Olkhovtka • Ponyri

CENTRAL FRONT

2ND TANK ARMY

27TH ARMY

Kursk

Seym

STEPPE FRONT

Tim

53RD ARMY

VORONEZH FRONT

5TH GUARDS ARMY

1ST TANK ARMY

Oboyan

69TH ARMY

Prokhorovka

Sumy

Korotcha

Psel

5TH GUARDS TANK ARMY

Tomarovka

FOURTH PZ ARMY

Belgorod

ARMY DETACHMENT KEMPF

0	30 mi
0	60 km

Kharkov

Soviet defence lines

——— major

German attack

Soviet counter-attack

- - - reserve

limit of German advance 12 July

Operation Kutuzov attack 12 July

The scale of Soviet defences meant that to complete the operation in the few days allowed by the German high command, the panzers had to overwhelm the first of these defence lines by early afternoon, in order to have time to close up to the next line and prepare an attack for the following morning. Any disruption to this timetable would give the Soviets time to reinforce the front line with strategic reserves from other parts of the Eastern Front. What the Germans did not know was that the Soviets already had strong reserves near Kursk, in the form of the 500,000 men of General I S Konev's Steppe Front. From the outset, Citadel's chances of success were remote.

Operation Citadel

Late on 4 July, General Rokossovsky obtained intelligence from a German prisoner that the attack would begin at 3.30 a.m. the following day. With the approval of Zhukov – who had come from STAVKA to take overall command of the Kursk area – around 2.20 a.m. the two Soviet Fronts began a pre-emptive artillery bombardment designed to inflict heavy casualties on the German infantry packed into their jumping off positions. Although it caused some disruption, the barrage was less effective than intended. The German attack was not scheduled until 5.30 a.m. and most of their units were safe in their dugouts. Even so, it was a clear indication that the Soviets were expecting an attack.

Once their attack started, the rate of advance on 5 July was much slower than the Germans had anticipated. The depth and strength of Soviet defences and density of their minefields surprised the Germans, making progress difficult. In the north, Model initially held all but one of his six panzer divisions in reserve, preferring to let the infantry create a breach through which the armour would subsequently advance. Slow progress saw two additional panzer divisions committed late in the afternoon.

By evening, Ninth Army had penetrated only between 4 and 6 miiles along a 25-mile front held by Soviet 13th Army and 70th Army. Most of the first Soviet line had been overcome, but fierce fighting and enemy counter-attacks meant that Model's forces were not in position to attack the second line next morning. During the night, Rokossovsky moved up his armoured reserves, including the powerful 2nd Guards Tank Army, to reinforce the second line at those points where the main German attacks were expected.

In the south, the brunt of Hoth's Fourth Panzer Army's attack fell upon Lieutenant General I M Chistyakov's 6th Guards Army. This unit had hurriedly deployed to the Kursk area and lacked sufficient equipment and training to halt the ferocious attack by 700 tanks of XLVIII Panzer Corps and

II SS Corps. The German tanks attacked in a *Panzerkeil* ('armoured wedge') led by heavy PzKw VI Tiger tanks, whose thick armour and long range 88-mm gun allowed them to knock out enemy anti-tank guns with relative impunity. Once the Soviet guns were silenced, medium PzKw IV and PzKwV Panther tanks with infantry moved in to clear up the remaining enemy positions. Although Hoth's forces succeeded in overwhelming most of Vatutin's first line by noon, Soviet troops continued to fight tenaciously, mounting vigorous counter-attacks which slowed the panzers' advance in several areas. By nightfall, only 1st SS Panzergrenadier Division 'Leibstandarte Adolf Hitler', and 2nd SS Panzergrenadier Division 'Das Reich' of II SS Corps had managed to close up to the second Soviet defence line. The rest of Fourth Panzer Army was only halfway to its first day objective, and heavily engaged.

On Hoth's right flank, Army Detachment Kempf's attack (under General Franz Werner Kempf) failed to penetrate the first Soviet defence line. The time consumed establishing bridgeheads across the River Dnieper for its III Panzer Corps, together with heavy Soviet resistance, meant that German forces were still embroiled in the midst of the Soviet defences. In spite of considerable success against the first Soviet line on both sectors of the salient, the German attack was seriously behind schedule.

Halting Model

During fierce fighting 6–11 July, Model's Ninth Army tried to breach Rokossovsky's second line of defence. The Germans concentrated their attacks against the Olkhovtka ridge and the town of Ponyri. Convinced that the capture of the ridge would open the way for an advance into open terrain, on 6 July, Model attacked with 2nd Panzer Division 'Vienna' and 9th Panzer Division. Supported by artillery and aircraft, these two divisions penetrated defences on the high ground either side of Olkhovtka village by evening, but Soviet forces continued to resist. At Ponyri, the fighting swept back and forth, the tanks of XLI Panzer Corps gained some ground, but failed to break through the enemy positions. The fighting continued along the front in much the same manner 7–8 July as Rokossovsky and Model fed in reserves.

On 9 July, Model staged one last attempt to break through at Ponyri. Rokossovsky was ready for him. Soviet infantry divisions were transferred from quieter sectors of the front, tanks dug in for protection, and large numbers of field guns and *Katuysha* ('Little Katie') multi-barrelled rocket launchers, nicknamed 'Stalin's Organ' by the Germans, concentrated around Ponyri. After a bitter struggle the Germans managed to occupy part of the town, but the Soviet line remained unbroken. Fighting continued 10–11 July as the Soviets counter-attacked. Although Model's forces managed to hold their positions, the heavy losses sustained since 5 July and the appearance of fresh Soviet divisions ended any hope of success. In six days of fighting Ninth Army had advanced just 8 miles, failing to breach the enemy's second line of defence. Even if the front had broken at Ponyri and Olkhovtka, Rokossovsky had a heavily manned third line to fall back on.

Battle in the South

Although Vatutin's troops had managed to retire in good order on 5 July and continue fighting, the threat to 6th Guards Army was serious enough for Stalin to divert 27th Army from Central Front's reserve to the south. On 6 July, XLVIII Panzer Corps attacked into 6th Guards Army's positions in the direction of Oboyan. Soviet counter-attacks slowed the German advance, but by evening fighting was taking place in Voronezh Front's second defence line. On the left, *SS-Obergruppenfuhrer* (Lieutenant General) Paul Hausser's II SS Corps, with heavy air support, punched deep into Chistyakov's 6th Guards Army's front, creating a serious breach in the line. Vatutin shifted his reserves to counter the threat while STAVKA released its 2nd Tank Corps and 10th Tank Corps to his command.

Through 7–10 July the Germans ground their way through the Soviet defences in the direction of Oboyan. Hausser continued to push forward with two panzer divisions, inflicting heavy losses on Soviet defenders. But the failure of Army Detachment Kempf to keep up with the II SS Panzer's advance forced Hausser to use his 3rd SS Panzergrenadier Division 'Totenkopf' for flank protection, weakening his assault. To remedy this situation, Kempf's III Panzer Corps abandoned its attack eastward to Korotcha and swung north. Initially good progress was made against weak Soviet defences, but lack of infantry to secure III Panzer Corps' flanks against counter-attacks forced it on to the defensive.

On 7 July, Vatutin ordered Lieutenant General M E Katukov's 1st Tank Army to deploy south of Oboyan, and block Hoth's advance. During 8–9 July, Katukov was forced to gradually retreat in the face of a combined onslaught from German armour and aircraft. However, the progress of Lieutenant General Otto von Knobelsdorff's XLVIII Panzer Corps was slow, and Soviet forces counter-attacked vigorously whenever possible. By 10 July, Vatutin correctly discerned that the fighting along the Oboyan-Belgorod road was intended to distract attention from preparations for an attack by II SS Corps in the direction of the little rail station village of Prokhorovka.

The Climax of the Battle

Late on 10 July, 3rd SS Panzergrenadier Division 'Totenkopf', released from its flank duties, had succeeded in crossing the river Psel and breaking into the third Soviet defence line. On its right, 1st SS Panzergrenadier Division 'Leibstandarte Adolf Hitler' repeated this in front of Prokhorovka. To the south on 11 July, Detachment Kempf's III Panzer Corps, having resumed its offensive a day earlier, broke into open country. Sensing the opportunity to move through the enemy defences and then wheel into the flank of Soviet forces in front of Oboyan, von Manstein ordered the two panzer corps to attack along a 13-mile front between the river Psel and to the south of Prokhorovka on 11 July.

STAVKA had been following the German advance closely. On 6 July it ordered Konev's Steppe Front to transfer Colonel General A S Zhadov's 5th Guards Army and Lieutenant General P A Rotmistrov's 5th Guards Tank Army to Vatutin. Two days later both armies arrived undetected by the Germans just north of Prokhorovka. It had been intended that these new formations would join 1st Tank Army and 6th Guards Army in a counter-attack against the German bulge in the Soviet line. But in response to II SS Corps' advance near Prokhorovka, it was decided to attack with just 5th Guards Army and 5th Guards Tank Army on 12 July to forestall a German breakthrough.

At 8.30 a.m. on 12 July, Rotmistrov gave the codeword 'Steel' and 5th Guards Tank Army began its attack. The day was overcast with occasional heavy rain, which restricted close air support. Soon afterwards Hausser's three SS panzergrenadier divisions renewed the previous days' attack, pushing doggedly through 5th Guards Army's positions. As II SS Corps and III Panzer Corps met 5th Guards Tank Army at Prokhorovka, 800 Soviet and 450 German tanks crashed into one another, and a series of vicious engagements developed. In some areas Soviet tanks charged straight at the Germans in order to engage at point-blank range where their lighter guns would be effective against the stronger armour of some German tanks.

In the centre, 1st SS Panzergrenadier Division 'Leibstandarte Adolf Hitler' broke into Prokhorovka, but, subjected to strong counter-attacks from elements of 2nd Tank Corps, it was driven out by nightfall. To the east of the town, 2nd SS Panzergrenadier Division 'Das Reich' became locked in a chaotic mêlée with other elements of 2nd Tank Corps. Soviet units broke into the German rear overrunning their artillery, while one SS tank unit crashed through two lines of Soviet anti-tank guns inflicting heavy casualties. Meanwhile 3rd SS Panzergrenadier Division 'Totenkopf's attempt to outflank

Prokhorovka to the west was halted when two reserve Soviet tank corps were committed. Further south, III Panzer Corps became embroiled in equally bitter fighting as Rotmistrov threw in his 5th Mechanized Corps to stop it. By nightfall the German attack had been halted at a cost of 450 tanks to the Soviets. Germans losses were considerably less at 110 tanks, but their attack had been driven back.

The End for Citadel

Fighting continued near Prokhorovka until 15 July, but the failure at Prokhorovka and the heavy casualties incurred since 5 July had convinced the German High command that 'Citadel' could not succeed, and on 13 July Hitler had cancelled the operation. Even if events had gone more favourably for the Germans on 12 July, STAVKA still had plenty of strategic reserves to block any breakthrough. But it was in the north that the real death blows were dealt to 'Citadel'. The failure of Model's Ninth Army ended the possibility of a double pincer attack to encircle Soviet forces. Then on 12 July, General V D Sokolovsky's Western Front attacked the northern part of the German salient around Orel, more than 100 miles to the north of Kursk in 'Operation Kutuzov', intended to encircle Model's forces tied down fighting the Central Front. Intelligence forewarned the Germans, and despite heavy casualties Ninth Army managed to avoid the trap, but with the northern pincer destroyed 'Citadel' was clearly finished. Hoth and Kempf's forces conducted an orderly withdrawal to their original front line by 23 July. But Zhukov's planned counteroffensives were now waiting to start, and the initiative on the Eastern Front was firmly in the Red Army's grasp.

TIM BEAN

Further Reading
Dunn, W S *Kursk: Hitler's Gamble, 1943* (Westport, 1997)
Glantz, D M *The Battle for Kursk 1943* (London, 1999)
Healy, M *Kursk, 1943* (London, 1992)
Jukes, G *Kursk: The Clash of Armour* (London, 1968)

THE AIR POWER FACTOR

"On 17th December 1903, at Kill Devil Hill, Kitty Hawk, North Carolina, Orville Wright flew for twelve seconds, and thereby added a third dimension to war." Colonel J F C Fuller

IT WAS ALREADY obvious by the start of World War II that air power, the use of aircraft in warfare, had transformed the nature of battles both on land and at sea. From its fragile beginnings, the aircraft had by 1918 already shown what it could do, and what it might do. The argument that stretched from the interwar years, through World War II, and beyond was exactly what form the most effective application of air power might take. The need for control or command of the air in order to conduct successful battles on land or at sea was perhaps the most obvious value of air power. Certainly, the need for command of the air when launching any kind of amphibious attack was self-evident. Aircraft of all kinds were also used as a form of 'flying artillery' in support of land campaigns, in order to provide the extra strength sometimes needed to bring victory. But air power enthusiasts also made much greater claims of a revolution in warfare, arguing that fleets of heavy bombers attacking enemy cities directly could remove the need for battle on land or at sea altogether. These ideas were tested in particular in the great Allied air offensives against Germany. The resulting battles were carefully planned and desperately fought on both sides.

The Battle of Britain

Spitfire Summer

10 JULY – 31 OCTOBER 1940

The German Luftwaffe under Reichs Marshal Hermann Goering

VERSUS

Royal Air Force Fighter Command under Air Chief Marshal
Sir Hugh Dowding

CHRONOLOGY

10 July 1940 –	First phase of battle begins
16 July 1940 –	Hitler Directive for 'Operation Sea Lion'
13 August 1940 –	'Eagle Day', second phase of battle begins
7 September 1940–	Third phase of battle begins with attacks on London
6 October 1940 –	Fourth phase of battle begins with night attacks
12 October 1940 –	Hitler formally cancels 'Operation Sea Lion'
31 October 1940 –	Official end of battle

"We must regard the next week or so as a very important period in our history. It ranks with the days when the Spanish Armada was approaching the Channel… We have read about this in our history books; but what is happening now is on a far greater scale and of far more consequence to the life and future of the world and its civilisation than those brave old days."

WINSTON CHURCHILL, 11 SEPTEMBER 1940

THE DEBATE OVER the military application of aircraft had been vigorous ever since the first manned flight in 1903. For a large part of World War I, aircraft were used primarily in a reconnaissance role and as the eyes of the artillery. But in 1918 the 'air flank' of armies and was exploited more fully, and demanded a reassessment of what military aviation could successfully achieve. The interwar years saw the rapid development of aircraft, and by the late 1920s they were being used not only for reconnaissance and spotting, but also in support of ground troops, for battlefield interdiction, transportation, and bombing. The bombing role, in particular, caught the imagination of the military. Air warfare theorists did not think that aircraft were mere adjuncts to ground warfare, but war-winning weapons in their own right. In the 1930s the idea that 'the bomber will always get through' struck fear into the hearts of many who recognized the new-found potency of Germany's Luftwaffe in particular.

The Battle of Britain, fought during the Summer and Autumn of 1940, put all these theories, and the capabilities of the bomber, to a severe test. It was the first decisive air battle in history. Indeed, so unusual and specific to the time were the circumstances under which it was fought, that it is possible that never again will air power alone decide an issue that is so important. It was a battle of machines, of men (and women also, particularly on the British side), and, above all, of plans and theories of how aircraft could and should be used.

The Origins of the Battle

After their rapid victory over France and the Low Countries in May and June 1940, German morale was high. Few observers believed that Britain could hold out for long against a determined German offensive. What became known as the Battle of Britain was the air battle fought in order for the Germans to attain the air superiority that they required to launch 'Operation Seelowe' ('Sea Lion'), an amphibious invasion of southern England across the English Channel. Adolf Hitler had such confidence in the newly promoted Reichs Marshal Hermann Goering's Luftwaffe that he also believed a sustained attack might make the new British prime minister, Winston Churchill, recognize the strength of Germany and sue for peace. On 16 July 1940, a directive from Hitler ordered preparations for the invasion of England to begin. The Führer anticipated that these preparations would be completed by mid-August.

Such optimism was not well founded – the German plans both for 'Sea Lion' and for the Battle of Britain itself were severely flawed. To undertake an amphibious invasion across the English Channel the Germans needed command of the air, particularly in the face of the formidable Royal Navy. In broad terms, their plan for the Battle of Britain was to send waves of bombers by daylight, escorted by fighters, to attack high-value targets along the English Channel coast and in southeastern England. This would force the Royal Air Force (RAF) to commit its fighters to defend these targets, so that over a few weeks Fighter Command would be worn away to nothing in fighter versus fighter combats. But the Luftwaffe had been optimized for the tactical support of the German Army, not independent bombing. It lacked a long-range heavy bomber, and its main single-engined fighter, the Messerschmidt Bf 109 (later known as the Me 109), had such a limited range that its combat time over England as far north as London was just a few minutes. As was so often the case in World War II, the hopes of the German leadership clouded the reality of the situation that faced them.

Britain, on the other hand, was extremely realistic about the danger that was faced. Since 1936, the RAF had been preparing for defence under the guidance of the perceptive commander-in-chief of Fighter Command, Air Chief Marshal Sir Hugh ('Stuffy') Dowding, working tirelessly to ensure that Britain was in the best possible position to ward off German air raids. Dowding and Fighter Command were quick to see the importance of Radio Directional Finding (RDF), which later came to be known as radar. The ability to track the course and altitude of enemy aircraft 150 miles away allowed the squadrons of Fighter Command to be in position at the right time to intercept them. This advantage was crucial, for Fighter Command could boast no superiority over the Germans in pilot training and fighting ability, or in the quantity and quality of their fighter aircraft. While many of the Luftwaffe's pilots had combat experience, Fighter Command was desperately short of pilots, working hard to train new squadrons, to re-equip escaped pilots from countries already under German occupation, and to take volunteers from almost all over the world. The best of the British fighters, the Supermarine Spitfire, was broadly equal and in some ways superior to the Bf 109, but the most numerous, the Hawker Hurricane, was not.

At the beginning of the battle the Luftwaffe, organized into 3 *Luftflotten* ('air fleets'), assigned 2,500 serviceable aircraft to the attack, including 656 Bf 109s, but the RAF had only 609 fighters. Dowding's plan depended on a highly integrated command system based on RAF 'sector stations', subordinate airfields all over southern England receiving information from the Observer Corps, from RDF, and from aircraft, and so directing the fighters to intercept. By husbanding his squadrons and feeding them into the battle in small numbers, Dowding hoped to prevent the great losses which the

Luftwaffe hoped to inflict and to drag the battle out to the point at which bad Autumn weather would make 'Sea Lion' unfeasible. Dowding's front line consisted of Fighter Command's Number 11 Group under the New Zealander, Air Marshal Sir Keith Park, responsible for southeastern England. To the north of London, and in direct support of Park, was Number 12 Group under Air Marshal Sir Trafford Leigh-Mallory.

The First Phase – The *Kanalkampf*

On 10 July 1940, the first phase of the battle began with the German attempt to gain air superiority over the English Channel – the *Kanalkampf* ('Channel Battle'). In the month of fighting that followed, both shipping and coastal towns were targeted and a great deal was learned by the combatants. These lessons concerned not only the pilots but also the ground crews, the British air defences, and both sets of commanders. The intensity of the fighting was remarkable, and both sides suffered some heavy losses, but it was the Germans who claimed success in early August when Goering announced that the Luftwaffe had established air superiority over the Strait of Dover during daylight hours. This was not far from the truth, but what he had not taken into consideration was the fact that German aircraft losses in July were double those of the British – 180 against 70 aircraft.

The Germans were massively exaggerating British losses and playing down their own to bolster morale at home. Although it was true that the RAF was struggling to replace lost pilots, Goering had deceived himself into thinking that he was winning the battle of aircraft numbers. In fact, far from winning this attritional battle, he was losing it. Britain was replacing its lost aircraft faster than Germany; in July alone British industrial workers produced 496 fighters. By the end of August, when Goering was convinced that Fighter Command was on the brink of collapse, it had 1,081 front-line fighters available and another 500 undergoing repair.

The Second Phase – The Finest Hour

Having, so Goering believed, secured control of the English Channel at its narrowest point, the Luftwaffe changed tactics for what was expected to be a short week or so finishing off Fighter Command's last reserves before the invasion. The second phase of the Battle of Britain began on 13 August, *Aldertag* ('Eagle Day'), when the Luftwaffe conducted 1,486 sorties against various targets across the southeast of England, emphasizing Fighter Command airfields and sector stations. Although Eagle Day itself was not the great success that Goering had hoped, he was satisfied that by concentrating his attacks on fighter stations, the British would be drawn into a battle in which Dowding's remaining squadrons would be wiped out. On 15 August the Luftwaffe, in their most concerted effort of the campaign, flew 1,786 sorties involving all three *Luftflotten*. Once again the fighting was exhausting and torrid, and once again the day ended without the Luftwaffe attaining the great victory that they had hoped. German losses were heavy with the RAF shooting down 75 aircraft for the loss of 34 fighters. Indeed, *Luftflotte 5*, mounting raids across the North Sea from Norway, suffered such great damage on 15 August that it took no further part in the battle. Only *Luftflotte 3* and *Luftflotte 2*, based in France and Belgium respectively, carried on.

Fighter Command was hanging on, and for every day that it survived, the invasion of England looked less likely. The RAF were doing an outstanding job, as Churchill's famous speech in the House of Commons on 20 August acknowledged: 'The gratitude of every home in our island, in our Empire, and indeed throughout the world, except in the abodes of the guilty, goes out to the British airmen who, undaunted by odds, unwearied by their constant challenge and mortal danger, are turning the tide of the World War, by their prowess and their devotion. Never in the field of human conflict was so much owed by so many to so few.'

Yet it was far too early to celebrate. Although the RAF was thwarting the Luftwaffe at nearly every turn, they were also suffering increased pilot and aircraft losses. New German tactics of delivering feint attacks across the Channel confused the British defences, and as 11 Group found out, increased Luftwaffe fighter escorts for bombers meant greater RAF losses. In the week before 6 September, the Luftwaffe lost 225 aircraft and the British 185 fighters. As bombers accounted for about half of the German figure, the British were clearly beginning to lose more fighters than the Germans. These were aircraft which, despite the high production rate, they could not replace quickly enough. In just two weeks Dowding had also lost a quarter of his pilots.

During this second phase of the battle the Luftwaffe began to exert intolerable pressure on Fighter Command. Airfield damage together with aircraft and pilot losses meant that the Luftwaffe was close to attaining air superiority over Kent and Sussex in early September, and there was little that the British could do about it. The battle was reaching its critical period. Had the Germans maintained this pressure on the RAF into September then it was probable that Fighter Command would have been defeated. But instead, the Luftwaffe changed its plans. Although it was clear to Dowding that Fighter Command was stretched to its limits, the Germans did not recognize this and

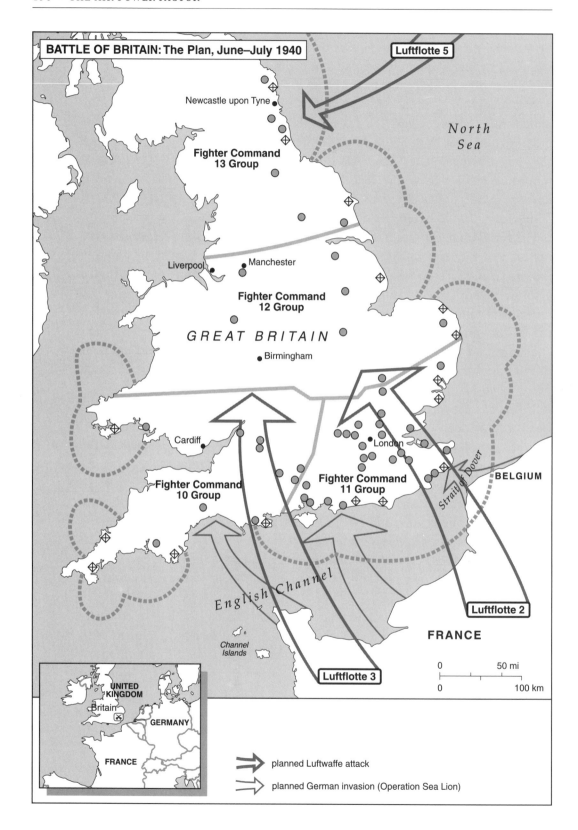

BATTLE OF BRITAIN: The Plan, June–July 1940

Luftflotte 5

Newcastle upon Tyne

North Sea

Fighter Command 13 Group

Liverpool Manchester

Fighter Command 12 Group

GREAT BRITAIN

Birmingham

Cardiff

Fighter Command 10 Group

London

Fighter Command 11 Group

Strait of Dover

BELGIUM

Luftflotte 2

English Channel

Channel Islands

FRANCE

| 0 | | 50 mi |
| 0 | | 100 km |

Luftflotte 3

UNITED KINGDOM

Britain

GERMANY

FRANCE

planned Luftwaffe attack

planned German invasion (Operation Sea Lion)

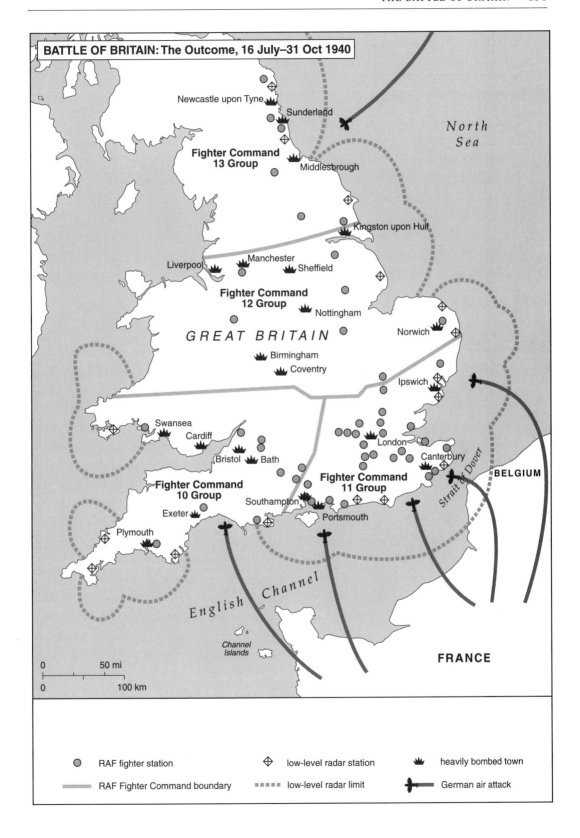

BATTLE OF BRITAIN: The Outcome, 16 July–31 Oct 1940

North Sea

Newcastle upon Tyne
Sunderland

Fighter Command 13 Group

Middlesbrough

Kingston upon Hull

Liverpool
Manchester
Sheffield

Fighter Command 12 Group

Nottingham

Norwich

GREAT BRITAIN

Birmingham
Coventry

Ipswich

Swansea
Cardiff

London

Bristol Bath

Canterbury

Strait of Dover

BELGIUM

Fighter Command 10 Group

Southampton

Fighter Command 11 Group

Exeter

Portsmouth

Plymouth

English Channel

Channel
Islands

FRANCE

0   50 mi

0   100 km

RAF fighter station

low-level radar station

heavily bombed town

RAF Fighter Command boundary

low-level radar limit

German air attack

were not in a position to find out. Inaccurate intelligence, poor staff work, and Goering's inadequacies combined to make the Luftwaffe strategically blind and operationally unfocused. So bad were these problems that the Luftwaffe had no priority of targets. Its dithering leaders continued to be bemused by the fact that Fighter Command could put fighters into the air; 'here come the last 50 Spitfires' one German commander remarked sourly in the face of yet another Fighter Command attack on his formation. They also totally underestimated the importance of radar to their enemy. From 18 August the RDF stations were left unmolested, as Goering had decided that they did not deserve the resources that were being used against them.

With so many weaknesses undermining their own plans in early September, the Germans did not know just how close they were to defeating Fighter Command and winning the air superiority over England that they desired. Thus, in a mistaken attempt to force Dowding's hand, they changed their strategy and began to bomb London.

The Third Phase – London

This change in German strategy to bombing London came about almost by accident. Although a number of Hitler's military advisers had been suggesting an attack on London for some time, the Führer thought that attacks on the British capital would make it less likely that Churchill would be drawn to the negotiating table, and feared reprisal attacks on Berlin. On the night of 24 August, 170 Heinkel He 111s on a mission to bomb oil installations at Thameshaven and an aircraft factory at Rochester, become lost and jettisoned their bombs over London in error. The reaction of the British was as Hitler had feared, and on the night of 25 August the RAF bombed Berlin in a raid that the Nazi leadership had vowed would never happen.

The bombing of London, although clearly a mistake, did mean that another option was now open to German planners as they struggled with the problem of how to vanquish Fighter Command. Hitler eventually decided upon a sustained attack on the capital after being convinced that the population of London would be so terrified by bombing that Dowding would be forced to commit his few remaining fighters, and Churchill would be more likely to negotiate for peace. The first raid on London took place during the afternoon of 7 September, when over 300 bombers escorted by some 600 fighters targeted the capital and dropped bombs and incendiaries on the East End and the docks. This new strategy caught Fighter Command by surprise, and Luftwaffe losses were light, as the bombers set about their work with little RAF attention to distract them. The fires burnt late into the night, and from the smouldering ruins of warehouses, shops, and homes were pulled 1,337 seriously wounded civilians and 360 dead. The attack did terrify Londoners, but it never did lead to widespread panic on that day or any other. Whole streets were razed to the ground by the raids and many families suffered at the hands of the Luftwaffe, but rather than eroding their will to resist, it actually hardened the resolve of the whole nation to defeat Germany.

As it became clear that the Germans had shifted their focus of attention wholly to London, so Fighter Command became better prepared to meet and defeat the raiders. Having to come so far, the escorting German fighters were severely restricted by fuel limitations, while for the first time the full strength of 12 Group could also be used to greatest effect. With their airfields now left untouched by the Luftwaffe, RAF fighters began to turn the tide of the battle.

On 15 September, which was destined to become 'Battle of Britain Day', the fighting came to a climax. On that day Churchill was told that the RAF had shot down 183 German aircraft for the cost of 26 of their own fighters. RAF policy was to report their own losses truthfully and enemy losses according to the claims of their pilots, and the German loss figure was greatly exaggerated – but the importance of the day was not. Having thrown everything at Fighter Command, the Germans had still failed to attain the air superiority that they sought. They now watched as the RAF went on the offensive to destroy German invasion preparations, with Bomber Command attacking their forces in the invasion ports. Already, plans were being drawn up for a new German offensive in the east against the Soviet Union. In a little over two weeks, the Germans had gone from the brink of victory to the brink of defeat. On 17 September, although the raids on London continued, Hitler postponed 'Sea Lion' indefinitely.

The Fourth Phase – The Blitz

The original purpose for the Battle of Britain had vanished. On 6 October, with the raids on London not having the decisive impact that had been anticipated and with the Luftwaffe suffering increasing losses, daylight attacks came to an end and were replaced with night attacks, known to the British as 'the Blitz', which would last through the winter. This move was a tacit acknowledgement by the Germans that the Battle of Britain had been lost, and that Hitler was no longer interested in the raids as a precursor to an invasion. 'Sea Lion' was formally cancelled on 12 October, but attacks on London continued for another 76 consecutive nights (except for the single night of 2 November), before coming to an end in 1941.

Conclusion

The Luftwaffe lost the Battle of Britain not because it was outfought in the skies over the English Channel and southeastern England, but because it was out-thought. The Luftwaffe was not as awesome as recent campaigns might have suggested, and the many weaknesses within the German command structure were readily apparent even during this early phase of the war. The Germans lost the Battle of Britain due to an unfocused strategy, which did little to aid the Luftwaffe in a task for which it was ill suited; an inability to appraise crucial situations properly; staff work which lacked precision; and a misplaced overconfidence on the part of its leadership which led to dithering when decisive action was required. Set against this the British were highly motivated, well led, realistic, and flexible. Under Dowding, Fighter Command remained operationally and tactically astute throughout the campaign.

The result of the Battle of Britain had consequences that reached much farther than just the cancellation of their invasion of England. The campaign against Britain was the first great defeat suffered by the Germans in the war, and marked the beginning of the decline of the Luftwaffe. Having lost 1,733 aircraft in the campaign, it took the Germans until Spring 1941 to replace them, just at a time when vital production capacity was required for the coming campaign against the Soviet Union. The Battle of Britain thwarted Hitler's invasion hopes, revealed many deep-seated German military and economic weaknesses, and proved to the world not only that the Luftwaffe was far from invincible, but also that the bomber would not always get through.

LLOYD CLARK

Further Reading

Collier, B *The Battle of Britain* (New York, 1962)

Cooper, M *The German Air Force, 1933–1945 – An Anatomy of Failure* (London, 1981)

Deighton, L *Fighter – The True Story of the Battle of Britain* (London, 1977)

Wykeham, P *Fighter Command* (London, 1962)

The Schweinfurt Raid
America's Worst Day
14 OCTOBER 1943

US Army Eighth Air Force under Lieutenant General Ira C Eaker

VERSUS

Luftwaffe Fighter Command under Lieutenant General
Adolf Galland

CHRONOLOGY
21 January 1943 – The 'Casablanca Directive'
10 June 1943 –   The 'Point Blank Directive'
17 August 1943 – The first Schweinfurt and
                  Regensburg Raid
14 October 1943 – The second Schweinfurt Raid

"The mission of October 14th had demonstrated that the cost of such deep penetrations by daylight without fighter escort was too high … the Eighth Air Force was in no position to make further penetrations either to Schweinfurt or to any other objectives deep in German territory." US OFFICIAL REPORT ON THE SCHWEINFURT RAID

IT IS A great tragedy of war that commanders can blindly persist with plans which have been repeatedly proven to be dangerously misguided. After World War I, visionary young officers in a number of countries argued that in the future wars would be won not by armies or navies but by fleets of aircraft bombing enemy cities, in what became known as 'strategic' bombing. World War II saw the creation of such strategic bombing fleets, chiefly by the British and Americans, of which perhaps the strongest and the most famous was 'The Mighty Eighth', the USAAF (US Army Air Force) Eighth Air Force.

This was air war in what had always been seen by its advocates as its most pure and effective form. But the practical problems of carrying out long-range strategic bombing were immense. One issue in particular came to dominate the argument: in the absence of an effective fighter escort with enough range, was it possible for heavy bombers to fly unescorted over the heart of Germany in daylight? After heavy losses sustained in the first attacks on German cities after May 1940, the Royal Air Force (RAF) Bomber Command concluded that it was not, and switched to night bombing. The USAAF persisted in unescorted daylight bombing. On 14 October 1943 it launched an air armada against Schweinfurt, one of the most heavily defended industrial towns of the Third Reich.

The Strategic Context

On 21 January 1943 the Anglo-American Combined Chiefs of Staff (CCS) issued the 'Casablanca Directive' in support of a plan from Lieutenant General Ira C Eaker, commander of Eighth Air Force, to start a Combined Bombing Offensive (CBO) against Germany, with the British bombing at night and the Americans by day. This confirmed that the primary objective of the CBO was 'the progressive destruction and dislocation of the German military industrial and economic system, and the undermining of the morale of the German people to a point where their capacity for armed resistance is fatally weakened'.

Planned in four phases between April 1943 and April 1944, the CBO only reached its full significance when the 'Point Blank Directive', which amended the 'Casablanca Directive', was issued by the CCS on 10 June 1943. While listing various categories of targets, it gave absolute priority to the destruction of German fighters and the factories where they were built, as it was realized that 'Operation Overlord', the projected liberation of France in 1944, could not be launched until air supremacy had been achieved. The directive reflected also the express wish of the US bomber commanders, who, during the first 14 operations of the CBO, had sustained virtually all their losses from enemy fighters as opposed to Flak (German anti-aircraft fire). Eaker concluded that only once he had annihilated the German fighter air arm would it be safe to penetrate into the heart of Germany.

Behind this rationalization of objectives lay the prolonged, often bitter Anglo-US debate over the merits of daylight strategic bombing. While General Henry H ('Hap') Arnold, commander of the USAAF, had been greatly impressed by the British theory of strategic bombing, neither he nor his subordinates approved of the costly results of RAF night bombing. Daylight bombing, the Americans argued, would enable them to hit pinpoint targets, such as oil installations and aircraft factories. The main US heavy bombers, the B-17 'Flying Fortress' and B-24 'Liberator', were also less suited to night flying.

The American Plan

A draft version of 'Point Blank' issued on 14 May had already noted the critical importance of ball bearings to the German war effort. The 'concentration of that industry', it pointed out, made 76% of German ball-bearing production 'outstandingly vulnerable to air attacks'. US strategic planners prioritized the five ball-bearing plants located at Schweinfurt – which between them supplied 52.2% of all German ball-bearing production, and 39.1% of ball bearings obtained from all sources – for their increasingly ambitious daylight bombing offensives. RAF Bomber Command declined to take part in an offensive against such small, remote targets.

The first major USAAF raid on Schweinfurt, and subsequent raids on Germany, had already demonstrated the immense problems in planning and executing such deep penetration operations, especially when the limit of US fighter cover was 250 miles out from England, barely reaching the westernmost towns of Germany. A double mission of 376 Flying Fortresses had been despatched to Schweinfurt and Regensburg on 17 August, unescorted for most of the way. In the consequent ferocious air battles, 60 US bombers were shot down, mostly by the Luftwaffe fighter command, a loss rate of 16%. Since each crew flew 25 missions before a rest, a loss rate above 4% for each mission made death almost a statistical certainty.

Despite these losses and the evident problem of lacking long-range fighter aircraft protection, US commanders stubbornly persevered with plans for a second raid on Schweinfurt. Lieutenant General Eaker remained convinced of the strategic and economic necessity of completely eliminating ball-bearing production at these key plants, which had only been partially destroyed during the first raid. Eaker also remained confident of the merits of precision bombing, so recently improved by the invention of the Norden bombsight, and new electronic and radar navigation systems. Despite the recent heavy losses, US commanders remained convinced of the high survivability of their self-defending bomber force, provided they strictly adopted the correct tactical formation. By 1943 US bombardment groups had developed the 'combat box', a new staggered formation comprising three squadron formations, each covering the other at different heights and with complementary arcs of fire. Within this box, it was theorized, the recently increased armament of the B-17s and B-24s (up to twelve .50-calibre machine guns, mostly situated within power-driven plexiglass turrets), could successfully protect them from all angles. Given such an extremely tight formation, it was contended that the B-17s and the B-24s, carrying 5,000-lb and 8,000-lb bomb loads respectively, could fend off any serious German attacks.

The second Schweinfurt raid was scheduled by Eaker and his staff for Thursday, 14 October 1943. Three simultaneous penetrations were initially planned. Eighth Air Force's 1st and 3rd Bombardment Divisions, comprising 360 B-17s, were to cross the Netherlands in two task forces 30 miles apart. Meanwhile 60 B-24s of 2nd Bombardment Division would form a third task force to fly further south. As the B-17s' routes would take them beyond normal maximum endurance, it was planned that those without long-range 'Tokio' fuel tanks would carry an extra fuel tank in the bomb bay, reducing their bomb-load capacity. One group of short-range P-47 Thunderbolt fighters was to escort each of the penetrating task forces as far as possible, and an additional group was to provide cover from about half-way across the English Channel. To protect stragglers, two squadrons of RAF Spitfire IXs would sweep the assembly area five minutes after the last of the attacking forces had left, and other RAF squadrons would be held in readiness for action if required.

The German Plan

The US plans had been conducted against the background of several ominous developments in German ground and fighter defensive organization. During 1943 the emphasis had shifted increasingly to concerted action against daylight raiders. Even though the British raids over Germany were still more numerous, the US precision raids were of much greater potential consequence for the German war industry. The first raid on Schweinfurt had come as a particular shock to the German high command, who regarded the ball-bearing industry as their Achilles' heel. After this first raid, Albert Speer, the armaments minister, had predicted that if the raids continued at such levels the German armaments industry would come to a standstill in four months.

The major reorganization required to meet these new mass precision raids was no easy task. There was an overall shortage of trained and experienced Luftwaffe pilots, with many of them increasingly diverted to the beleaguered Eastern Front. During 1943, as the tide of war slowly turned against Germany, Luftwaffe fighter defences were further undermined by direct political interference by Adolf Hitler himself, who ordered a reduction in fighter construction in favour of ground-level attack aircraft and bombers. Consequently, of the 7,477 single-engined fighters produced in the first eight months of 1943, only a small proportion were allocated to home defence units.

Despite these crises, by August 1943 German defensive plans had created a formidable network. This consisted basically of two elements – anti-aircraft guns and fighters. In the course of 1943 the number of Flak guns deployed in Germany significantly rose from 14,949 to 20,625, chiefly light guns of 20–40 mm calibre and heavier guns of 88–128 mm calibre. New 'Flak towers' and associated guns were reorganized to provide arcs of predicted fire, to engage bombers from the start of their level bombing run with box barrages put up at their approximate height just short of their anticipated bomb release point.

Of far greater significance in German defence planning against future US daylight raids were its interceptor fighters, of which the most common were the Messerschmidt Me 109G, with a speed in excess of 380 mph, and the even faster Foche-Wulf FW 190A, compared to 200 mph for the US bombers. The basic Luftwaffe operational unit for defensive purposes continued to be the *Jagdgeschwader* ('fighter group' or JG) of about 120 aircraft.

German methods and plans for attacking the improved US bomber formations increased in variety and efficiency during 1943. The main objective was for fighters to continually break up the bomber formations so that individual aircraft could be finished off as they fell away damaged. German fighter pilots soon realized that the new US box formations produced far less fire from the front than from any other angle. Consequently, the Luftwaffe developed several different methods of head-on attack, which varied from *Schwarm* ('swarm' of 4 aircraft) to *Staffel* ('squadron' of about 12 aircraft) strength. Often flying parallel and in front of US bombers, on a signal from their coordinator (frequently in a converted Junkers Ju 88 light bomber) the fighters would sweep into their attack, either half rolling away in front of the bombers or pulling up over the top of them, and then flying back to attack from the front. By early August 1943, the increased firepower of the FW 190s also encouraged Schwarm-strength attacks in line abreast from the rear. During deep penetration missions such as Schweinfurt, fighters would refuel and each attack the bombers two or three more times.

Other methods of breaking up offensive bomber formations included using twin-engined aircraft, such as the Messerschmidt Me 110 and Me 410s, to fly above the tightly packed bombers and drop fragmentation bombs. Explosive rocket projectiles, carried by FW 190s and Me 109s, could also cause immense damage when lobbed into tightly packed bomber formations at between 1,000 and 1,700 yard range.

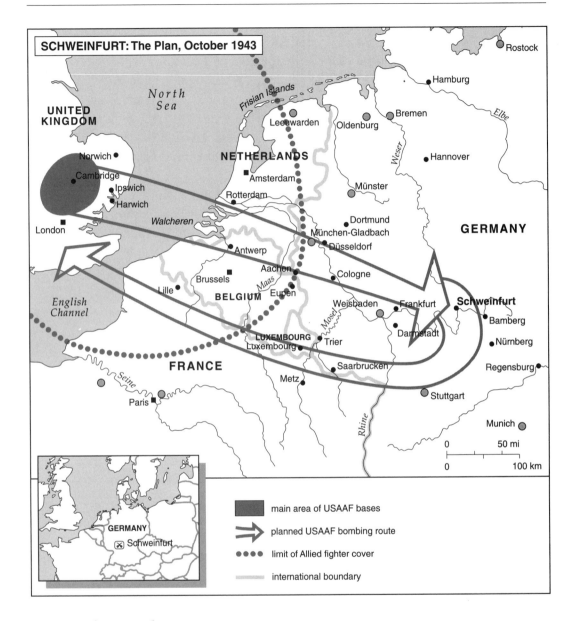

SCHWEINFURT: The Plan, October 1943

main area of USAAF bases

planned USAAF bombing route

limit of Allied fighter cover

international boundary

The Early Stages

From the very start, the massive bombing raid launched against Schweinfurt on 14 October 1943 was significantly compromised by the one uncontrollable factor in any battle plan: inclement weather. The heavily overcast conditions caused chaos at designated rendezvous points. This problem, combined with the heavy losses of the previous week over Münster and elsewhere, meant that it was impossible to muster the projected 360 battle-worthy B-17s. The B-24s of 2nd Bombardment Division were also particularly badly affected. With

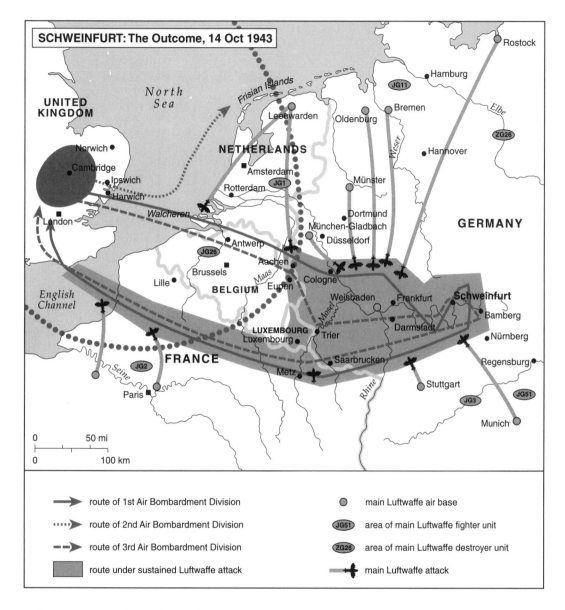

SCHWEINFURT: The Outcome, 14 Oct 1943

route of 1st Air Bombardment Division

route of 2nd Air Bombardment Division

route of 3rd Air Bombardment Division

route under sustained Luftwaffe attack

main Luftwaffe air base

JG51 area of main Luftwaffe fighter unit

ZG26 area of main Luftwaffe destroyer unit

main Luftwaffe attack

only two units of 29 planes finally joining together, numbers were insufficient for any deep penetration raid, and they were forced to fly an uneventful diversionary feint across the North Sea towards the Frisian Islands.

Vivid memories of the first costly August raid meant that morale among many bomber crews was unusually low. A medical officer present at the final briefing noted how the first mention of Schweinfurt, 'shocked the crews completely... it was obvious many doubted that they would return'. Over Walcheren Island, the escorting P-47 fighters managed to repel the first

German attacks, made by single-engined fighters from JG26. It was a deceptively easy start. As on the first Schweinfurt raid, the Luftwaffe made its appearance in force at around 1.00 p.m., immediately after the P-47 escorts had turned back near Aachen.

The Main Battle

Between Aachen and Frankfurt the now unprotected 1st Bombardment Division faced a relentless onslaught, mainly from FW 190s and Me 109s. For three solid hours the unescorted bombers were exposed to the full fury of the German flak and fighters. Wave after wave of fighters closed in for the kill. Most of the tactics used by the German fighters that horrendous day had been used before – formation attacks, the use of rockets and heavy-calibre cannon, air-to-air bombing, concentration on one group at a time and on stragglers. But never before had the enemy made such full and expertly coordinated use of these tactics. As Lieutenant General Eaker later privately confessed to his superior General Arnold, the Luftwaffe 'turned in a performance unprecedented in its magnitude, in the cleverness with which it was planned, and in the severity with which it was executed'. Most alarming for the US aircrews was the sheer scale of the enemy attacks. General Adolf Galland recalled that he 'managed to send up almost all the fighters and destroyers [Me 110s and Me 410s] available for the defence of the Reich, and, in addition to this, some fighters of the Third Air Fleet (*Luftflotte 3*) in France. Altogether some 300 day fighters and 40 destroyers took part in the battle which for us was the most successful of the year'.

One unpleasant variation of the Luftwaffe's normal tactics was the use of single-engined fighters as a screen for twin-engined aircraft to close in for rocket attacks. These rockets, which travelled slowly enough to be clearly visible, presented an especially chilling sight. One US bomber pilot recalled watching in horror as one rocket arched through his formation heading straight for a nearby B-17. Striking the fuselage just to the rear of the cockpit it tore open the side of the plane and blew one wing completely off. The pilot briefly glimpsed the men in the cockpit still sitting at their controls, then they were engulfed in flames.

The German fighters systematically concentrated on one formation at a time, breaking it up with rocket attacks and then finishing off cripples with gunfire. In a further comment upon this desperate period after the P-47s had turned back, another pilot remembered how 'all hell was let loose... the scene [was] similar to a parachute invasion, there were so many crews bailing out'. It was a sadly mauled 1st Bombardment Division that finally reached the target from Frankfurt. Its leading element, 40th Combat Bombardment Wing, lost 27 aircraft before Schweinfurt was even reached – its 350th Group losing all but three out of 15 aircraft.

By contrast, 3rd Bombardment Division escaped far more lightly. Departing the English coast about 10 miles south of Harwich at 12.25 p.m., five minutes after the 1st Bombardment Division, it picked up its escort of 53 P-47s 30 minutes later after crossing the Belgian coast. At Eupen, just after the escorting P-47s had turned back, a sharp southward turn took the B-17s away from the route of 1st Division towards Trier and Mosel. Flying to the east of Luxembourg, the bombers avoided the Ruhr Flak concentrations. At 2.05 p.m., 3rd Division again turned east towards the 'Initial Point' of the bombing run, near Darmstadt. Only between Mosel and Darmstadt did the air battle intensify, and the first serious pass was made around the Trier area. By the time they reached Schweinfurt their leading formation, 96th Combat Bombardment Group, had lost only one aircraft.

The Bombing Run

The US bombing over the target itself was unusually effective. A sudden change of course near the 'Initial Point' confused enemy fighters, and the air attacks diminished significantly as the B-17s turned into their bomb run. For once the weather was kind, and good visibility allowed 1st Division to drop a high concentration of bombs on all its Schweinfurt target areas. Even the crippled 40th Group put over half its bombs within 1,000 feet of the aiming point. The thick smoke from 1st Division's attack meant that 3rd Division was less successful. In all, 228 surviving B-17s dropped some 395 tons of high explosive bombs and 88 tons of incendiary bombs on and about all three of the big ball-bearing plants. Of 1,222 high explosive bombs dropped, 143 fell within the factory area, 88 of which were direct hits on the factory buildings.

After the final bombing run, 1st Division turned south and then west below Schweinfurt, but there was no let-up in the Luftwaffe attacks. Fighters from JG3 and JG51 attacked the trailing 41st Wing, while FW 190s shot down three B-17s of the leading 379th Group. Around Metz and Stuttgart, twin-engined night fighters joined the attack, continuing as the bombers flew across France. By the time of its return to England, 1st Division had lost a further 10 aircraft, making a total of 45 for the mission, not counting crew losses in damaged aircraft.

Having reached the target with relatively few losses, 3rd Division suffered much more heavily on the homeward journey. Immediately after leaving Schweinfurt a very intense attack took place by about 160 single-engined aircraft, backed by twin-engined Me 110s, Me 210s, and Ju-88s, with the lower flying bomber groups as the main focus. Particularly badly hit again was 96th Group; 14 aircraft were lost in the return.

Poor weather again played a critical role on the final return leg as thick fog, reducing visibility to 100 yards, closed airfields in England. This prevented Allied fighters from escorting either division to their home bases, while German fighters from JG2 were able to pursue and inflict even more casualties on the dismayed and weary bomber crews as they limped across the normally friendly English Channel waters.

The Aftermath

The battle had been an unmitigated triumph for German defensive plans and a huge blow to US air power. Eaker's doctrine of unescorted daylight precision bombing had been shattered beyond repair. Out of 260 bombers which pressed the attack, 60 B-17s had been shot down – an appalling loss rate of almost 25%. A further 12 aircraft which made it home were fit only for scrap, and 121 needed repairs. Only 62 out of 260 aircraft were left relatively unscathed. Over 600 men, many of them experienced crewmen, were missing either as prisoners or dead. Wild US claims of first 288, and then 186, enemy fighters destroyed were soon disproved – the Germans lost 38 fighters destroyed in combat and 20 damaged.

The attack on 14 October remained the most important and successful of the 16 Allied bombing raids on Schweinfurt in the course of the war. Albert Speer later suggested that 67% of the plants' ball-bearing production had been lost – a possibly exaggerated figure. German reorganization and redeployment of factories was so rapid and thorough that further attacks – the next now delayed by four months due to the terrible US losses – were far less successful.

Forever known as 'Black Thursday' in US air force history, the Schweinfurt raid represented the highest percentage loss to any major USAAF task force during the whole wartime campaign. Only with the development of the long-range P-51 Mustang fighter, capable, with its extra fuel tanks, of escorting heavy bombers all the way to such distant targets, did deep penetration daylight precision bombing become a feasible way of waging the war in the air.

EDMUND YORKE

Further Reading

Coffey, T *Decision over Schweinfurt* (New York, 1978)

Craven, W F, and Cate, L J *The Army Air Forces in World War Two* (Chicago 1949)

Galland, A *The First and the Last* (London, 1952)

Sweetman, J *Schweinfurt: Disaster in the Skies* (London, 1971)

Monte Cassino
Victory through Air Power?
17 JANUARY – 25 MAY 1944

German Army Group C under Field Marshal Albert Kesselring

VERSUS

Allied 15th Army Group under Field Marshal Sir
Harold Alexander

CHRONOLOGY

17 January 1944 –	The Fourth Battle of Monte Cassino opens
15 February 1944 –	Allied bombing of the monastery
19 March 1944 –	'Operation Strangle' begins
11 May 1944 –	'Operation Diadem' begins
5 June 1944 –	Allies liberate Rome

"It just had to be bombed. Oh, it was malignant. It was evil somehow. I don't know how a monastery can be evil, but it was looking at you. It was all-devouring if you like – a sun-bleached colour, grim. It had a terrible hold on us soldiers."
SERGEANT EVANS OF THE 2ND LONDON IRISH REGIMENT

BEFORE WORLD WAR II, air power theorists had believed that aircraft alone could win the next war. Some never gave up this view. But as the war progressed, so senior airmen on the Allied side began to argue that while – perhaps – ground troops or ships might be of some value, it was air power that really won the battles for the generals and admirals, and that they should recognize this. One highly controversial test came in a hard-fought battle in Italy. In December 1943, Allied troops approached the town of Cassino, 60 miles southeast of Rome. Dominated by the mountain of Monte

Cassino, with its historic Benedictine monastery, Cassino formed an integral part of the German defensive position called the Gustav Line. Here the Allies would stay, despite fighting three battles for Cassino. But in spring 1944, the Fourth Battle of Monte Cassino, a major ground offensive in conjunction with a major air offensive, broke the Gustav Line and opened the road to Rome.

The Origins of the Battle

Following their landings in southern Italy, by the end of September 1943 after a tough fight the Allies had progressed inland, Mussolini had been overthrown, and Italy had surrendered. But the Germans used the mountainous and river-strewn terrain of central Italy to conduct a fighting withdrawal, forcing the Allies to grind forward in bitter attritional struggles. On 17 January 1944, the Allies launched their first attempt to break the Gustav Line in the region of Cassino, but, after initial progress, were firmly rebuffed. In February they tried again to no avail. In the course of this battle the monastery, the general area of which was occupied by German troops, was destroyed by Allied heavy bombers on 15 February. The rubble, however, continued to provide an excellent defensive position for the Germans. In March the Allies demolished the town with an enormous bombardment from the air and artillery during 'Operation Dickens'. But German troops led by 1st Parachute Division continued to hold out.

The German Plan

German strategy concentrated on buying time to equip and man the Gustav Line. Here Field Marshal Albert Kesselring, an outstanding defensive commander himself belonging to the Luftwaffe, intended to stand and fight using his Tenth Army commanded by General Heinrich Scheel von Vietinghoff, to prevent the Allies driving up the Liri valley. Dominated by Monte Cassino, this represented the most direct route to Rome, courtesy of 'Highway 6'.

The Gustav Line itself ran the width of Italy and incorporated formidable natural terrain. The part confronted by the main Allied forces ran from Monte Cifalco to Monte Cairo, passing through Colle San Angelo and Monte Cassino before crossing the Liri valley, through the Aurunci Mountains and Castelforte to Minturno. Eight miles to the rear lay a second defensive line, the 'Hitler Line'. The 1st Parachute Division held Monte Cassino, and 44th 'Reichsgrenadier Hoch und Deutschmeister' Infantry Division held the Liri valley; on the other side of the valley, 71st Infantry Division was dug-in, with

94th Infantry Division on its right. These were battle-hardened formations; however, their formidable defences did lack depth. Tenth Army was also short of manpower, and if the Allies attacked the whole German position simultaneously it would struggle to hold the line.

The Allied Plan

By the end of March, the Allies appeared bereft of ideas on how to break the Gustav Line. The task of resolving this strategic impasse fell to the British Lieutenant General A F ('John') Harding, who had become the Chief of Staff to 15th Army Group under Field Marshal Sir Harold Alexander in January. Harding presented his findings to Alexander on 22 February, an analysis which formed the bedrock of 'Operation Diadem', which finally cracked the Gustav Line in May.

Harding believed the key issue was not taking ground but the destruction of German troops. His 'Diadem' conception envisaged trapping the Germans in the Liri valley rather than driving them out. He was sure the Germans would continue their protracted defence: the Gustav Line was strong, they had invested considerable resources in it, and Hitler was disinclined to concede ground. This presented more opportunities than difficulties. If Kesselring stood his ground and the Gustav Line was broken, German troops risked being trapped and annihilated. At the very least, a composed fighting withdrawal similar to that of October 1943 to January 1944 would not be possible.

The Allied advantage lay in armour, artillery, and – air power. Harding concluded the main effort must be the Liri valley. Monte Cassino's formidable defences cast a grim physical and psychological shadow, but the valley was the only place where armour and artillery could be used en masse because of the mountainous terrain. It was also a bottleneck but it had to be held if the right and left wings of German Tenth Army were to remain in touch and hold the Gustav Line.

The key to Harding's plan was that all the Allied forces from the Cassino region to Italy's Tyrrhenian coast must attack simultaneously. This would disperse German troops, maximizing the chances of a breakthrough in the Liri valley. On the right, Polish II Corps, part of British Eighth Army, would attack Monte Cassino, while the main body of Eighth Army would cross the River Rapido and drive up the Liri valley. The French Expeditionary Corps, part of US Fifth Army, would attack 71st Division from Castelforte through the Aurunci Mountains to the left of Eighth Army. On the left flank, US II Corps would attack and fix German 94th Division, while advancing up the coast.

'Operation Diadem' also envisaged a critical role for US Sixth Corps at Anzio. If the cork of the Liri bottleneck could be blown, Harding saw a breakout from Anzio to Valmontone at the northwest end of the Liri valley as the anvil upon which the Allies would annihilate Tenth Army.

A key role was given to deception. The Allies exploited German fears about more amphibious landings, following Salerno in September 1943 and Anzio in January 1944. Kesselring was prone to overestimate the Allies' ability to launch such operations. Allied intelligence successfully simulated an amphibious force in the Salerno region, persuading Kesselring to divert reserves to deal with a potential Allied landing at Civitavecchia.

Operation Strangle

As part of the plan to break the Gustav Line, on 19 March US Major General John K Channon, Commander of the Mediterranean Allied Tactical Air Force, issued his 'Directive Number 2', governing 'Operation Strangle'. Through this operation, which lasted until 11 May, Allied air power sought to destroy German rail, road, and sea communications, thus undermining the ability of German Army Group C to supply Tenth Army on the Gustav Line. Allied airmen had been critical of what they saw as the misuse of their heavy bombers in a direct role, bombing Cassino town and Monte Cassino monastery. They believed that bombing German communications could by itself induce a withdrawal by Tenth Army from the Gustav Line.

The Italian rail system appeared vulnerable to air attack, as the mountainous terrain ensured there were numerous bridges, viaducts, tunnels, and cuttings. The directive classified marshalling yards and repair facilities as primary targets, while 'interdiction' targets such as bridges, viaducts, tunnels, and track were designated of secondary importance. During 'Strangle', medium bombers tended to concentrate on interdiction targets, while Allied fighter-bombers focussed on marshalling yards, moving trains, railtrack, and road vehicles. Allied air tactical commanders exercised considerable discretion in executing 'Strangle' as it became clear that hitting 'interdiction' targets made a greater impact upon German supply and communications.

In total, in the course of 'Strangle' 15,239 sorties were flown, with 1,136 tons of bombs and other ordnance dropped on marshalling yards, 1,692 tons on interdiction targets, and 200 tons were dropped on roads and vehicles. Rail targets were chosen at least 100 miles from the Gustav Line, to create the impression this was an independent air offensive. The Germans fought an incessant battle to repair track damage as quickly as it was inflicted. On 11 April, Kesselring made his subordinate Major General Wenninger 'General with special responsibility for the maintenance of rail communication in Italy'.

For all its power, 'Strangle' failed in its ambitious aim of entirely destroying German road and rail communications, so inducing a German withdrawal from the Gustav Line. However, as Wenninger's appointment indicates, a great deal was achieved: rail transit became virtually impossible for the Germans, and track repair became a major military operation. They were forced into a vulnerable road dependence, consuming sparse fuel they needed for defensive mobility. But the full impact of 'Strangle' was not felt until the major Allied ground offensive, 'Operation Diadem', in May 1944. Once the Gustav Line was breached, German troops lacked the mobility and ammunition to cope with the speed and firepower of the Allies' multiple thrusts.

Operation Diadem

In the plan for 'Diadem', British XIII Corps was to be Eighth Army's strike force. But before it could advance up the Liri valley, the River Rapido had to be crossed – 60 ft wide and 6 ft deep, with a swift current, steep banks, and German defences of strongpoints connected by trenches, wire, and mines. The rapid bridging of the river was the key to success. The British attack began at 11.00 p.m. on 11 May, but by the following evening, with only four battalions across, the Rapido crossing had fallen well behind schedule and the Allied bridges remained incomplete. As the Germans poured down artillery and mortar fire, XIII Corps was ordered to bridge the Rapido that night, regardless of cost. By 5.30 a.m. on 13 May, 4th Infantry Division had thrown a bridge across the river and secured a bridgehead. To the south, XIII Corps' other division, 8th Indian Division, had also crossed the river and moved inland. However, they had not broken through into the open and German 44th Infantry Division was far from defeated.

The battlefield for Polish II Corps lay between Monte Castellone and Monte Cassino, about 5,000 yard away. This was a tiny but deadly battlefield of some 6 square miles, disfigured by a tangled mass of rock, ravines, and cliffs. The ground was made up of two parallel ridges forming the rim of a saddle-shaped valley, and the German defences, manned by 1st Parachute Division, were anchored by strongpoints on the western ridge. On the eastern side the German positions ran along Snakeshead Ridge to the foot of the ruined abbey, where the circle of interlinked positions were united.

At 1.00 a.m. on 12 May, the Poles led by General Wladislaw Anders, began their attack with 5th Kresowa Division on the right, and 3rd Carpathian Division on the left. The assault was met with a hail of fire, and communications between the two divisions broke down. By midnight on

12 May, the Poles were no closer to the monastery and had incurred severe casualties. General Anders suspended operations.

While the British and Poles hammered away at the Germans, the French Expeditionary Corps (FEC) attacked German 71st Infantry Division. Although senior Allied leaders neglected its mountain warfare prowess, the FEC, under General Alphonse Juin's inspirational leadership and containing specialist Algerian and Moroccan colonial mountain troops, would distinguish itself during 'Diadem'. However, on 12 May, the French were unsuccessful as 71st Division acquitted itself in style. General Juin went forward to reassess the attack and ordered his commanders on, encouraged by 3rd Algerian Division's success in taking Castelforte. At 3.15 a.m. next day, the French began their assault on Monte Girafano. After 12 hours of fierce fighting, 2nd Moroccan Division stormed the German positions, while to their right French 1st Infantry Division successfully advanced towards San Ambrogio and San Apollinare. In the mountains of the Castelforte region, 4th Moroccan Mountain Division infiltrated and outflanked German positions.

By the end of 13 May the French had broken the Gustav Line, and Juin ordered a daring exploitation. The results were spectacular: by the evening of 14 May they had swept through the 71st Division to a depth of 7 miles on a front of 16 miles, capturing the pivotal mountain town of Ausonia. Major General Raapke, commanding 71st Division, reported to General von Vietinghoff that his division's strength had been reduced by 70% and that four-fifths of his officers had been wounded. The Gustav Line was cracking: while the Germans defeated the Poles and contained the British, the French had taken the prize.

Breaking the Gustav Line

The US II Corps, commanded by Major General Geoffrey Keyes, also began its attack on 12 May, led by 85th Infantry Division and 88th Infantry Division, which succeeded in taking Ventosa but not its main objective of San Maria Infante. However, the retreat of German 71st Division before the French forced German 94th Division to withdraw also. The fast-learning US units harried them all the way, and by 15 May, US II Corps had destroyed 60% of 94th Division's fighting power, speeding the French Expeditionary Corps on their way.

By 15 May, German Tenth Army's right flank had been broken asunder. Meanwhile in the Liri valley, Eighth Army was beginning to turn the screw. Having won a footing across the Rapido, XIII Corps set about capitalizing on its tactical triumph by breaking through German 44th Division. General Sir

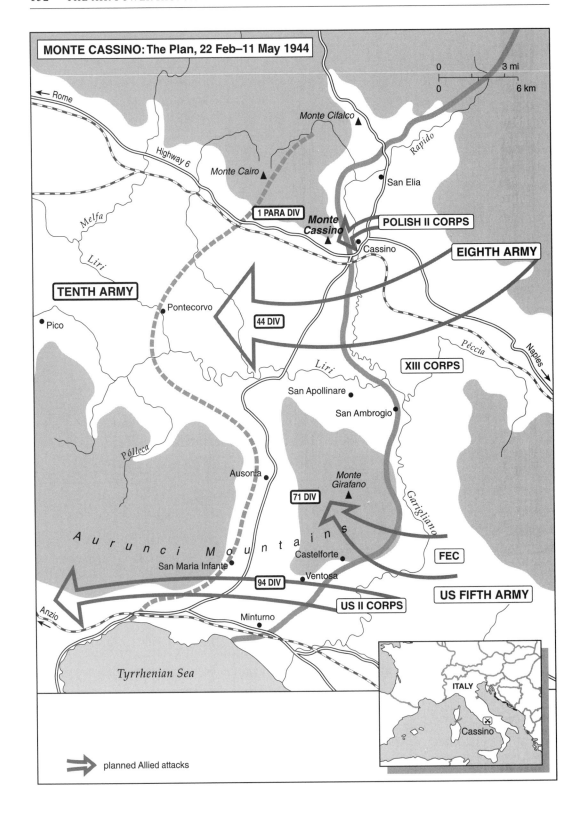

MONTE CASSINO: The Plan, 22 Feb–11 May 1944

0   3 mi
0   6 km

← Rome

Monte Cifalco ▲

Rapido

Highway 6

Monte Cairo ▲

San Elia •

Melfa

1 PARA DIV

Monte Cassino ▲

POLISH II CORPS

Liri

Cassino •

EIGHTH ARMY

TENTH ARMY

Pontecorvo •

44 DIV

• Pico

Péccia

Naples →

Liri

XIII CORPS

San Apollinare •

San Ambrogio •

Pólleca

Ausonia •

Monte Girafano ▲

71 DIV

A u r u n c i   M o u n t a i n s

Garigliano

Castelforte •

FEC

San Maria Infante •

94 DIV

Ventosa •

US II CORPS

US FIFTH ARMY

← Anzio

Minturno •

Tyrrhenian Sea

ITALY

⊠ Cassino

⇒ planned Allied attacks

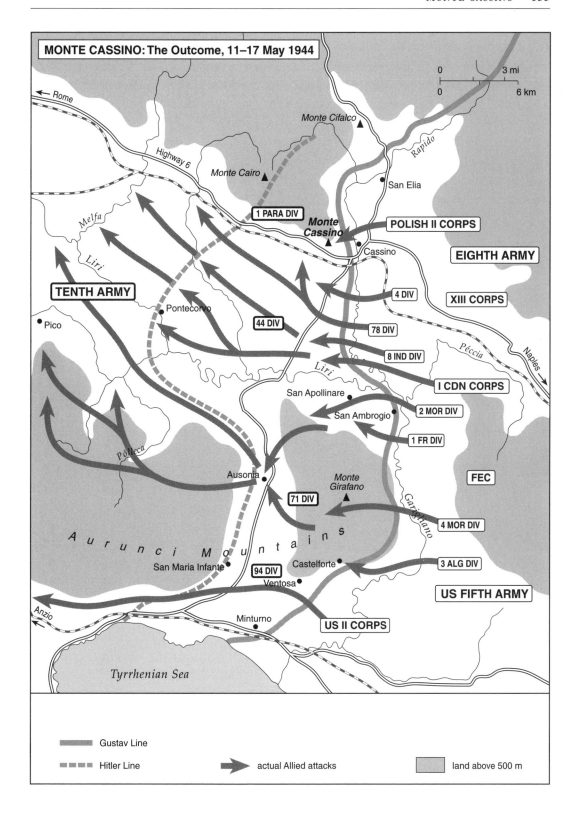

MONTE CASSINO: The Outcome, 11–17 May 1944

← Rome

0   3 mi
0   6 km

Monte Cifalco ▲

Rapido

Highway 6

Monte Cairo ▲

San Elia •

1 PARA DIV

Monte Cassino ▲

POLISH II CORPS

EIGHTH ARMY

Cassino •

Melfa

TENTH ARMY

Liri

4 DIV

XIII CORPS

Pontecorvo •

44 DIV

78 DIV

• Pico

8 IND DIV

Péccia

Naples →

Liri

San Apollinare •

I CDN CORPS

San Ambrogio •

2 MOR DIV

Póllea

1 FR DIV

Ausonia •

Monte
Girafano ▲

FEC

71 DIV

Garigliano

4 MOR DIV

A u r u n c i   M o u n t a i n s

San Maria Infante •

94 DIV

Castelforte •

3 ALG DIV

Ventosa •

US FIFTH ARMY

← Anzio

Minturno •

US II CORPS

Tyrrhenian Sea

Gustav Line

Hitler Line   ➤ actual Allied attacks   land above 500 m

Oliver Leese commanding Eighth Army, conscious of the FEC success to his left, committed both his British 78th Infantry Division and the whole of Canadian I Corps to the battle on 14 May, at the northern and southern ends of the Liri valley. By 16 May, 78th Division had won a bridgehead 3 miles deep, at a cost of 4,000 casualties, and by next day they and the Canadians had extended this to 5 miles. However, Eighth Army had still not broken through, and as it advanced its commanders grew frustrated at the lack of room for manoeuvre.

As the French dashed through the mountains, and Eighth Army ground its way up the valley, on Monastery Hill General Anders' Poles prepared to renew their struggle with 1st Parachute Division. There could not be anything sophisticated about the plan: it had to be to storm the enemy's ramparts. The attack began at night on 16 May, and at their first attempt the Poles made a brilliant silent attack, only to be driven back by a German counter-attack. On 17 May the Poles again crept forward but made no substantial advance. At 9.00 p.m. Anders instructed the troops to dig in and attack again at dawn on 18 May.

However, as the Poles advanced towards the monastery the next day they found it deserted: on orders from Kesselring, given the advance of Eighth Army in the valley and the French in the mountains, 1st Parachute Division had reluctantly withdrawn from the positions they held against all comers. At 10.20 a.m. on 18 May, a patrol of 12th Podolski Reconnaissance Regiment cautiously entered the monastery and raised the Polish flag. At 4.00 p.m. a Polish patrol linked up with 78th Division on Highway 6, and the agony of Monte Cassino had ended.

The German Position

Kesselring and Vietinghoff agreed on 16 May to abandon the Gustav Line. British Eighth Army was advancing relentlessly, while their own Tenth Army's right flank was being mauled by the Americans and French. It was essential to withdraw to the Hitler Line while it could be defended and before the rampaging French cut off those German troops in the valley who had tried valiantly but unsuccessfully to hold the Gustav Line. Monte Cassino was no longer the main concern: the objective now was to prevent a complete Allied breakout.

The Hitler Line was a formidable obstacle, and British attempts to 'bounce' it were frustrated by a strong defence and difficult terrain. The valley floor was wooded and studded with irrigation ditches made all the more awkward by the narrowness of the valley. In ferocious fighting 18–20 May, Eighth Army failed to break the Hitler Line. General Leese ordered a set-piece assault in the

Canadian sector. The attack, 'Operation Chesterfield', was launched on 23 May to coincide with 'Operation Buffalo', the breakout from Anzio by Major General Lucian K Truscott's US VI Corps. On 23 May, Canadian 1st Division finally smashed its way through the Hitler Line, while in the mountains the French marched on.

The victory was nearly won. Harding's conception had been brought to life, but it called for the *coup de grâce* to be administered on the ground by US VI Corps advancing from Anzio to Valmontone, so trapping German Tenth Army. 'Operation Buffalo' was no elaborate Allied scheme of manoeuvre: VI Corps would simply have to blast its way out of the bridgehead into open country, and after two days hard fighting it had escaped from Anzio. Meanwhile, Allied intelligence detected the powerful 'Hermann Goering' Parachute Panzer Division moving south with the objective of Valmontone, to secure an escape route for Tenth Army.

The race was on: VI Corps must beat the Herman Goering Division to Valmontone. However on 25 May, General Mark W Clark commanding US Fifth Army issued VI Corps new orders, to wheel left and implement Clark's preferred design of 'Operation Turtle', a direct advance to Rome. The remaining US troops committed to 'Buffalo', a division and a brigade, continued to advance on Valmontone. At 11.00 p.m. on 27 May, US 3rd Infantry Division and Herman Goering Division clashed 2 miles west of Highway 6, and the Germans had won the race. Kesselring, much to the relief of his beleaguered commanders, ordered a general but orderly withdrawal. Army Group C was defeated but it was intact.

The Aftermath

The Gustav Line was broken, the spectre of Monte Cassino left behind, but it should have been more. The biggest controversy was Clark's decision to abandon 'Operation Buffalo' in favour of Rome. There is little doubt that he did this to ensure that he and not British Eighth Army entered the Eternal City. The final irony is that Clark's triumphal progress into Rome on 5 June was completely overshadowed by the launch next day of 'Operation Overlord', the Normandy landings. The second major controversy was the extent that 'Operation Strangle' had played in the Allied victory, and whether the bombing of Monte Cassino monastery had helped the Allied advance. Although no-one doubted the importance of air power to the eventual success of 'Operation Diadem', in this as in many other battles it was hard to make a case that bombing and not ground fighting had decided victory.

STEPHEN WALSH

Further Reading

Ellis, J *Cassino: The Hollow Victory* (London, 1984)

Graham, D, and Bidwell, S *Tug of War* (London, 1986)

Kesselring, A *The Memoirs of Field Marshal Kesselring* (Novato, CA, 1988)

THE WAR AT SEA

"My education and experience in the First World War has all been base on roads, rivers, and railroads. During the past two years, however, I have been acquiring an education based on oceans and I've had to learn all over again." GENERAL GEORGE C MARSHALL, US ARMY CHIEF OF STAFF, 1943

WORLD WAR II was above all else a global war, and that meant a war based on sea power, since the oceans cover more than half the world's surface. The British Empire, with a fleet that had dominated the world until the 1920s and still represented one of the most powerful and deadly weapons ever devised, confronted its enemies at sea throughout the world. The Soviet Union could rely on the other Allies for sea communications and convoy supplies, often of a critical nature. For the Japanese and the USA, whose conflict was fought out on the fringes of the Pacific Ocean, where distances are measured in thousands of miles, the sea was the principal factor in the way the war could be fought. Only for Nazi Germany, with its territorial ambitions lying within the heartlands of Europe, was control of the sea a secondary issue. In particular Adolf Hitler, who had lived all his life in Austria and southern Germany, never seemed to understand the importance of a navy to every successful – and above all long-lived – empire in history, often to the despair of his admirals. These are three examples of important naval battles from the war, each very different but each in its own way decisive. As each of them shows, victory at sea in World War II was often the forerunner to even greater success.

Sink the *Bismarck*!
Battle in the Atlantic
18 – 27 MAY 1941

German battleship *Bismarck* and heavy cruiser
Prinz Eugen under Admiral Gunther Lutjens

VERSUS

British Royal Navy forces including the Home Fleet
under Vice Admiral Sir John Tovey
and Force 'H' under Vice Admiral Sir James Somerville

CHRONOLOGY

19 May – *Bismarck* and *Prinz Eugen* leave Kiel

21 May – *Bismarck* and *Prinz Eugen* leave Korsfjord,
south of Bergen

24 May – *Hood* and *Prince of Wales* engage *Bismarck*
and *Prinz Eugen*

26 May – *Ark Royal* torpedo planes attack *Bismarck*

27 May – *Rodney* and *King George V* sink *Bismarck*

"It shows what a long arm the British Navy has." VICE ADMIRAL
SIR JAMES SOMERVILLE

SINCE THE INTRODUCTION of heavy artillery into ocean-going warships, the 'battleship' had been the supreme instrument of sea power, the one that could give and receive the heaviest blows and, in sufficient force, secure control of the sea for the smaller craft to exploit. Normally battleships were collected into fleets and engaged each other in fleet actions, with control of the sea going to the winner. In World War I the German fleet, inferior in number, and badly positioned, was reluctant to take the risk of battle, and despite escaping destruction at Jutland on 31 May 1916, shifted its war effort to submarines (*Unterseebooten* or U-boats) that would attack British merchant shipping. This campaign was ultimately defeated by the introduction of convoys. By 1941 the battleship had assumed a different role in German strategy, and the British had, perforce, to counter that shift. Twentieth-century battleships used heavy artillery of enormous range and destructive power, to attack the ever stronger alloy steel armour carried by other battleships. However, the rise of alternative weapons systems and delivery vehicles, notably the air-launched torpedo, would call into question the old assumptions. The *Bismarck* sortie came at the hinge of change from the old order to the new, and exploited elements of both.

The Strategic Situation

Although the Battle of the Atlantic, the longest running and most complex campaign of World War II, was largely fought by U-boats and small escort vessels, the Germans had always seen the submarine campaign as one option in their strategy to cut Britain's oceanic lifeline. Grand Admiral Eric Raeder, head of the *Kriegsmarine* (German Navy), recognized that after the experience of the submarine campaign of 1917–18 in any future war, Britain would convoy its merchant shipping. This would greatly increase the problems for attacking submarines. However, Raeder was a 'big ship' admiral, and recognized that a large, slow-moving merchant ship convoy escorted by small antisubmarine vessels would be desperately vulnerable to the attack of a fast battleship. While the submarines could subject convoys to attrition, a surface battlegroup would be able to wipe them out, destroying the whole convoy strategy on which British survival was based.

Pre-war naval planning in Germany had been based on avoiding war until at least 1942, so when war came in 1939 the Germans were far from ready. Their largest warships were two 35,000-ton fast battleships, the sister ships *Scharnhorst* and *Gneisenau*, which were only armed with 11-in guns. After the fall of France several German warships were able to sortie into the Atlantic, including the two *Scharnhorst* class ships, which operated together. However, they were not permitted to engage British battleships, and therefore had to leave the most valuable convoys. Despite this disadvantage, the success of German surface raiders, in addition to the work of the U-boats and the Luftwaffe, had inflicted serious damage on British oceanic communications by spring 1941.

The German Plan

'Operation Barbarossa' (the German attack on the Soviet Union), about to be launched in June 1941, would necessarily remove much of the air, and some of the naval strength from the Atlantic theatre. Yet there was time for one last effort. After lengthy periods of work up in the Baltic two brand new German ships, the 45,000-ton battleship *Bismarck* with eight 15-in guns and a speed of 30 knots, and the 17,000-ton heavy cruiser *Prinz Eugen* with eight 8-in guns and a speed of 32 knots, were in excellent order. However, they were both deeply flawed ships, as time would tell.

The aim of the *Bismarck* sortie was to secure command of the sea in the mid-Atlantic, if only temporarily, to break up the convoys. This would greatly enhance the ability of the U-boats to sink merchant ships. The sortie can be seen as Hitler's last gamble to win the war in the west before he attacked the Soviet Union. If the *Bismarck* could operate effectively in the Atlantic, with six supply ships already in place, she would be followed by her sister the *Tirpitz*, soon to be completed, and by the refitted *Scharnhorsts*, posing an insuperable problem for the British fleet, which simply did not have enough battleships to meet the threat.

The British Response

Fortunately, the breaking by the British of the German Enigma ciphers at this time provided just enough intelligence to enable the British to meet the threat, while the Royal Navy, stretched as it was by the war with Germany and Italy, was still powerful enough to defeat the challenge. As the *Bismarck* and *Prinz Eugen* passed out of the Baltic and through the Kattegat on 19 May they were observed by aircraft from the neutral Swedish cruiser *Gotland*. Her report reached the British naval attaché in Stockholm, and arrived in London late on 20 May.

The British were already on the alert because of unusual German reconnaissance over Scapa Flow, and FW 200 'Condor' aircraft sorties to report on the ice between Jan Mayen Island and Greenland. This led to increased cruiser patrols, directing the heavy cruiser HMS *Suffolk* to pay particular attention to the edge of the ice sheet. Two photograph reconnaissance Spitfires were sent to the Norwegian coast, and, at 1 p.m. on 21 May, located the German ships in the Bergen Fjord, less than two hours after their arrival. At this time the decryption of older German signals left the Admiralty in no doubt that the German ships were going to attack Atlantic trade.

On this basis Vice Admiral Sir John Tovey, commanding the British Home Fleet, with his flag in the battleship *King George V*, made his dispositions. Tactically Enigma traffic was of no use, as the delay in reading it at this time was between three and seven days.

The Opening Moves

After *Prinz Eugen* refuelled, the German ships left Bergen at 7.45 p.m. on 21 May. Lutjens had departed without refuelling *Bismarck* because he had been informed that weather conditions in the Denmark Strait, with a heavy overcast, were ideal for evading the British patrols, but would not last long. The British finally learnt that the Germans had left at around midnight on 22 May. They had headed north, leaving their escorting destroyers at Trondheim, before heading west to pass round the north of Iceland.

British cruisers were already on station north and south of Iceland. On 21 May they were reinforced from Scapa Flow by the Home Fleet battlecruiser squadron, consisting of the battlecruiser HMS *Hood*, the brand new battleship *Prince of Wales*, and six destroyers under Vice Admiral Sir Lancelot Holland. The Home Fleet, commanded by Tovey in the *King George V*, with the battlecruiser *Repulse* and the aircraft carrier *Victorious*, put to sea from Scapa on 22 May to cover the Iceland–UK gap. The British were in position to intercept the Germans on either side of Iceland.

At 7.22 p.m. on 23 May the heavy cruisers *Norfolk* and *Suffolk*, both 10,000 tons with eight 8-in guns and 32 knots, under Rear Admiral Frederick Wake-Walker, intercepted the Germans in the Denmark Strait, north of Iceland. When *Norfolk* strayed into range *Bismarck* opened fire with her 15-in guns, but the shock disabled her gunnery radar. Thereafter, relying on *Suffolk's* superior radar, the two cruisers shadowed the Germans from outside the range of *Bismarck's* guns.

The First Battle

Meanwhile, Admiral Holland hurried to engage. He would appear to have sought tactical surprise, expecting that the Germans would avoid action if they had a chance. After a period out of radar contact, in which Holland spread his forces to locate the enemy, losing touch with his destroyers and impairing his angle of interception, he came into visual contact with the Germans at extreme range at around 5.30 a.m. on 24 May.

Holland steered to engage. He chose to approach at a relatively steep angle as he wished to close the range to about 15,000 yards as soon as possible. This would minimize the danger to his elderly flagship, which had thin deck armour, and was vulnerable to long-range hits. Unfortunately he did not send the *Prince of Wales*, which was brand new and much better protected, to lead the formation. Nor did he give Captain John Leach, commanding the *Prince of Wales*, permission to fight in open order.

At 5.53 a.m. on 24 May (celebrated by the British as 'Empire Day') the two squadrons opened fire at approximately 25,000 yards. *Hood* initially opened fire on the *Prinz Eugen*, which had the same profile as *Bismarck* and was leading the German line, without causing any damage. The *Prince of Wales* opened fire on *Bismarck*. However, because of the fine approach, and the failure of one of *Prince of Wales's* guns, the British began the action firing only five 14-in guns at *Bismarck*, out of a potential total of eight 15-in and nine 14-in guns. This was unfortunate, and was exacerbated by the failure to bring the two heavy cruisers into action to engage the *Prinz Eugen*. As no British shells hit the ship to disturb her gunnery control team, *Bismarck's* opening salvoes were remarkably accurate, despite being directed by optical rangefinders, rather than her inoperable radar. Her second or third salvo, and possibly one from *Prinz Eugen*, hit *Hood*, causing a large ammunition fire on her upper deck, among the anti-aircraft rocket and gun ammunition.

Then, just as Holland was turning his squadron to bring their after turrets into action, *Hood* was hit again, by one or more 15-in shells. The shell struck the engine room, sending red hot splinters into the after 4-in powder magazine, which ignited and set off the after 15-in cordite magazines. The ships' X-Turret (the superfiring after-mounting) was blown overboard, and small debris, mostly rivet heads, rained down on *Prince of Wales* half a mile astern. A catastrophic deflagration in the magazines broke the back of the ship, and she capsized to port, sinking within three minutes, taking with her all but three of her 1,400-man crew. *Hood*, the largest and most impressive warship in the world, had been the visible symbol of the Empire for 20 years.

By this stage the range had closed to 18,000 yards, and the Germans shifted their fire to *Prince of Wales*, which was hit by four 15-in and three 8-in shells. One 15-in shell devastated the compass platform, disabling almost all the control personnel. To make matters worse, *Prince of Wales* was suffering mechanical problems in two of her three main turrets, where shipyard engineers were struggling to keep her systems functioning. Captain Leach wisely broke off the action at 6.13 a.m., but not before *Prince of Wales* had hit *Bismarck* three times – a creditable performance for a ship so far short of full combat efficiency, that reflected well on her use of radar for accurate ranging. The second hit penetrated *Bismarck's* side armour, flooded the port generator room, and began to flood the forward port boiler room. This reduced power and cut her speed to 28 knots. The third shell smashed right through the bow without exploding, but flooded two compartments with oil and water, deprived the ship of access to 1,000 tons of fuel, opened up a large hole in the bow below the waterline, and caused a serious fuel leak. This left her bow low in the water, created a pronounced oil slick in her wake, and contaminated other fuel tanks. This last, when combined with Lutjens's failure to fill his tanks to the maximum at Bergen, forced him to abandon the commerce-destroying cruise and head for France. The damage could not be repaired without docking the ship, and flooding continued, albeit slowly. Operating as fugitives on an ocean under British control the Germans were acutely aware of their vulnerability to any loss of speed.

Losing Touch

The British ships under Admiral Wake-Walker now resumed shadowing, while Tovey hurried to intercept. A brave carrier strike by nine Swordfish torpedo planes flown from *Victorious* in appalling weather that night scored one hit amidships on *Bismarck*. The shock effect of this hit, exacerbated by gunfire and rapid changes of course, wrecked the original damage control measures, increased the damage to the area of the second shell hit, where welds were failing, and tore away the sailcloth patch on the bow, causing further flooding and reducing speed.

That evening Lutjens suddenly turned towards the British ships and opened fire, which created an opportunity for *Prinz Eugen* to break off and escape into the Atlantic. Shortly after 3 a.m. on 25 May the British lost contact with *Bismarck*, which had been zigzagging, and then suddenly shifted course. At this time Tovey was only 100 miles away, and closing fast, but his hopes of an early action were dashed. By now the *Prince of Wales*, *Victorious*, and *Repulse* were running low on fuel, and had to break off. *King George V* was also low on fuel, but was able to continue. Unless *Bismarck* was quickly located and dramatically slowed down she would get to France before Tovey could catch her.

Despite his victory, Lutjens was depressed and fatalistic, feeling trapped by the superior performance of the British radar, which he could detect out to 35,000 yards. He did not realize that the British could not receive their radar echoes at that range. Consequently he made excessive use of radio communications with Germany. While none of his signals were decrypted before the *Bismarck* was sunk, they did betray his location to British High Frequency Direction Finding stations (HF/DF). Possibly unaware that he had escaped, Lutjens sent three more signals early on 25 May. These enabled the

British to work out that *Bismarck* was heading for France, rather than doubling back to Norway or proceeding on into the Atlantic. Critically they allowed the Admiralty to move the battleship *Rodney*, which had just left the North West Approaches heading for the USA, into position to meet *Bismarck* in the Bay of Biscay. It also enabled the battlegroup Force 'H' under Vice Admiral Sir James Somerville, based at Gibraltar, to intercept *Bismarck* late on 23 May. However, Somerville's battlecruiser, the *Renown*, was too weakly protected to engage *Bismarck*. His main weapon would be the aircraft carrier *Ark Royal's* efficient air group of Swordfish torpedo strike planes.

By this stage the Admiralty in London was directing 20 major warships from all sides of the North Atlantic theatre to converge on *Bismarck*, and positioning them to deal with her possible movements. British forces included the Home Fleet and Force 'H' from Gibraltar, with other units in the Atlantic theatre including seven battleships and battlecruisers, two aircraft carriers, cruisers, and destroyers. Lutjens was proceeding at 20 knots to conserve fuel for a battle, and to reduce the serious yawing effect produced by the Force 9 winds and the heavy swell that were running at right angles to his course.

Regaining Contact

On the evening of 25 May, Luftwaffe Enigma, a much easier target for British cryptanalysts than Naval Enigma, had revealed that the *Bismarck* was heading for France, and at 6.12 p.m. the Home Fleet was advised accordingly. The following morning, *Bismarck* was sighted by an RAF Coastal Command Catalina flying boat, about 130 miles south of the Home Fleet. But the Home Fleet would not be able to catch her, unless she could be damaged. On the afternoon of 26 May, *Ark Royal* flew off a strike, but the planes mistakenly attacked their squadron mate the cruiser *Sheffield*, then 20 miles north of *Bismarck*, although she looked nothing like the German ship. Fortunately for *Sheffield* the magnetic torpedo pistols failed to detonate. Fifteen more aircraft, armed with torpedoes with contact pistols then flew off.

In the gathering gloom of the evening, the Swordfish put in a near perfect attack, catching *Bismarck* between two lines of torpedoes at an angle of 90°. Two hits were scored, and despite the small warheads of the 18-in torpedo (surface ships used 21-in weapons), the *Bismarck* was crippled. The first hit merely added to the damage below the waterline, but the second doomed the ship. In that one attack the Royal Navy's interwar thinking about the use of aircraft at sea was thoroughly vindicated, unlike the design work of the German naval architects. The second torpedo hit the *Bismarck* in the stern, just above the rudders. Due to poor design, inferior welding, and the whiplash

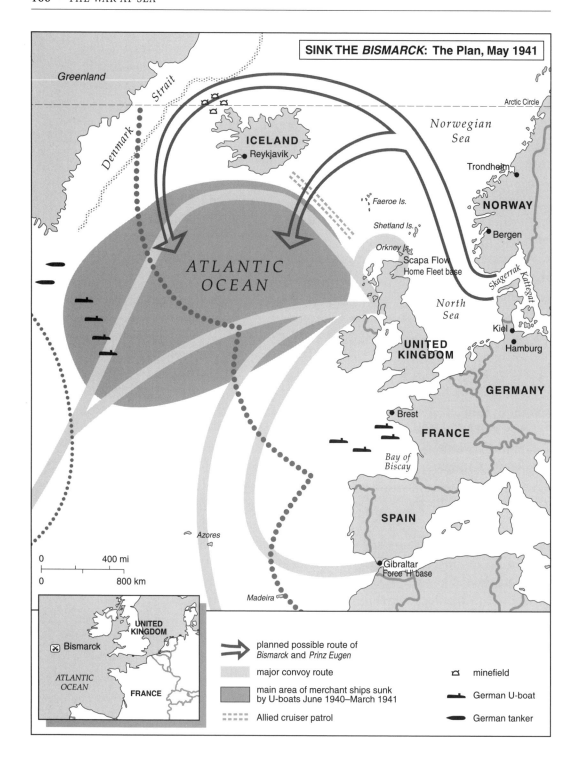

SINK THE *BISMARCK*: The Plan, May 1941

Greenland

Denmark Strait

Arctic Circle

Norwegian Sea

ICELAND
Reykjavik

Trondheim

Faeroe Is.

ATLANTIC OCEAN

Shetland Is.

NORWAY

Bergen

Orkney Is.
Scapa Flow
Home Fleet base

North Sea

Skagerrak

Kattegat

Kiel

Hamburg

UNITED KINGDOM

GERMANY

Brest

FRANCE

Bay of Biscay

SPAIN

Azores

Gibraltar
Force 'H' base

Madeira

0 ____ 400 mi
0 ____ 800 km

UNITED KINGDOM

⊠ Bismarck

ATLANTIC OCEAN

FRANCE

⟹ planned possible route of
Bismarck and *Prinz Eugen*

major convoy route

main area of merchant ships sunk
by U-boats June 1940–March 1941

Allied cruiser patrol

⌗ minefield

⊢ German U-boat

▬ German tanker

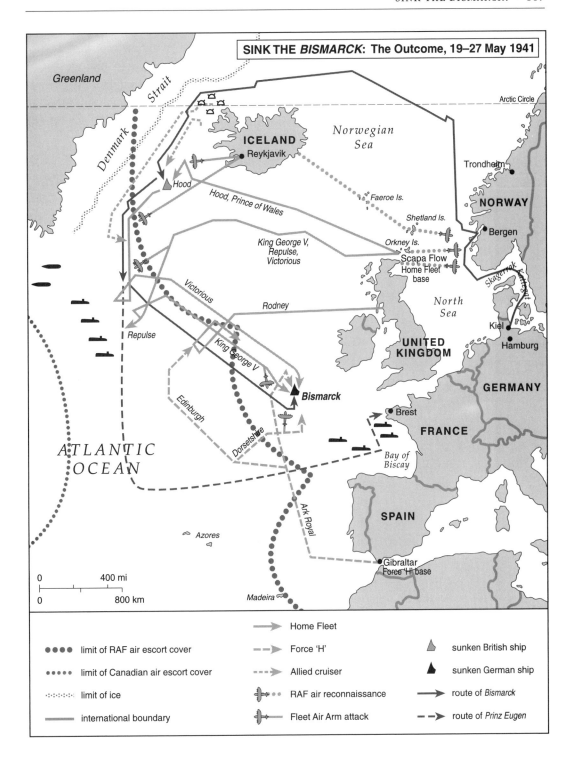

SINK THE *BISMARCK*: The Outcome, 19–27 May 1941

Greenland

Denmark Strait

Arctic Circle

Norwegian Sea

ICELAND
Reykjavik

Trondheim

Hood

Hood, Prince of Wales

Faeroe Is.

Shetland Is.

NORWAY

Bergen

King George V, Repulse, Victorious

Orkney Is.

Scapa Flow
Home Fleet base

Skagerrak

Kattegat

Victorious

Rodney

North Sea

Kiel

Repulse

King George V

UNITED KINGDOM

Hamburg

GERMANY

Edinburgh

Dorsetshire

Bismarck

Brest

FRANCE

ATLANTIC OCEAN

Bay of Biscay

SPAIN

Ark Royal

Azores

Gibraltar
Force 'H' base

0   400 mi
0   800 km

Madeira

●●●● limit of RAF air escort cover	Home Fleet
●●●●● limit of Canadian air escort cover	Force 'H'
⋯⋯⋯ limit of ice	Allied cruiser
── international boundary	RAF air reconnaissance
	Fleet Air Arm attack

▲ sunken British ship

▲ sunken German ship

→ route of *Bismarck*

⇢ route of *Prinz Eugen*

effect of the blow at one end of the ship, the stern section suffered an almost complete structural failure, falling onto the rudders, which were then at 12° to port, for a violent manoeuvre attempting to avoid the torpedoes. With 1,000 tons of steel sitting on her rudders, the *Bismarck* was left to go round and round in circles. There was no possibility of reaching the damaged areas without docking the ship, and before the Germans had time to think about their problems their attention was drawn to other threats.

Although originally ordered to provide an antisubmarine screen for the Home Fleet, the brilliant destroyer leader Captain Philip Vian, in the Tribal class destroyer HMS *Cossack*, followed the old maxim of steering to the sound of guns. His Fourth Destroyer Flotilla of five destroyers closed on *Bismarck*, and reported her erratic movements. Vian quickly recognized that she was no longer under control. During the night he conducted a series of skilful and determined torpedo attacks that kept the Germans busy until daybreak, although they did not score any hits. *Sheffield* lay close at hand, to direct the Home Fleet in for the kill.

The End of the Battle

Bismarck was now trapped, 400 miles from Brest and outside the range of Luftwaffe aircraft. The only U-boat in the area had no torpedoes. Tovey elected not to fight at night, as there were so many friendly ships in the area, and the enemy was now unable to escape. Early on 27 May, *King George V* and the 1920s vintage battleship *Rodney* (nine 16-in guns and 22 knots) under Captain F G H Dalrymple-Hamilton caught up with *Bismarck*. *Renown* was left in reserve, in case the battleships were damaged. *Rodney* was permitted to engage in open order, to make maximum use of her powerful gun battery. The three ships opened fire at 8.47 a.m. at a range of 20,000 yards. Although *Bismarck's* opening salvoes were impressive, falling close to *Rodney*, the accuracy of her fire quickly fell away as *Rodney* scored hits with her fourth salvo and quickly disabled *Bismarck's* A-Turret. By 9.00 a.m. *Bismarck's* rate and accuracy of fire had appreciably diminished, so *Rodney* and *King George V* closed to 11,000 yards. The two British ships then systematically knocked *Bismarck* to pieces, destroying her armament, control systems, and superstructure. After 9.30 a.m. the *Bismarck* was unable to reply, and the British closed in for the kill. It was an entirely one-sided battle, there were no hits on the British ships. *Bismarck* was devastated by a rain of 16-in, 14-in, and 8-in projectiles, the latter from the cruisers *Dorsetshire* and *Norfolk*. After 9.30 a.m. *Rodney* closed to less than 4,000 yards. At this range her 2,048-pound shells would penetrate any armour on the German ship, wrecking even the gun turrets and conning tower.

All told the British battleships fired 719 rounds of heavy ammunition, scoring around 70 hits. However, the range was so close that all the damage to *Bismarck* was above water, rather than in her magazines, or the underwater hull; and this type of short range action was exactly what *Bismarck* had been designed to resist. *Rodney* fired her torpedoes, but missed. At 10.15 a.m. *Bismarck* was dead in the water, blazing furiously, and Tovey broke off the action. The *Dorsetshire* closed and torpedoed the devastated ship, first on the starboard side and then on the port side, which was already listing 15°. After a further damage, including scuttling by her crew, the *Bismarck* sank at 10.36 a.m. Of her 2,000-man crew, 110 were rescued by *Dorsetshire* and the destroyer *Maori* before a submarine alert forced them to break off, and a few more were picked up by U-boats. Tovey did not wait for the end, being concerned to leave the area before U-boats arrived, and desperately short of fuel for the return leg. On the way home the destroyer *Mashona* was sunk by the Luftwaffe.

The Aftermath

Prinz Eugen spent a fruitless week in the North Atlantic before scuttling into Brest with engine trouble, which remained the Achilles heel of the German cruisers, on 1 June. In the interval the steady work on Enigma had revealed the location of four of the eight German supply ships sent out to support the sortie. Six would be intercepted as a direct result of Enigma intelligence, and another was intercepted and sunk by good cruiser work. A further seven German supply and weather ships were also captured or sunk, having been located by Enigma intelligence, but the Admiralty had deliberately left them after sinking the others, in order not to make the Germans suspicious. In fact, the Germans were astonishingly complacent about their supposedly 'perfect' machine encryption, and attributed their problems to other intelligence systems.

The *Bismarck* action demonstrated that a superior fleet with good intelligence should be able to deal with isolated raiders. Had the Germans waited to release all their heavy surface units at the same time, as they could easily have done, the results might have been very different. Command of the sea had been used, and maintained, to defeat the boldest stroke the Germans ever tried on the broad oceans, in either world war. The crisis of the Battle of the Atlantic had passed, and the pride of the German Fleet now lay miles below on the floor of the Atlantic.

Although wartime mythology transformed her into the 'unsinkable' battleship, the *Bismarck* was actually a rather old-fashioned design, clearly based on the Imperial German Navy's *Baden* of 1916, and no stronger than other modern battleships of her era, except that her additional size, some 10,000 tons more than the contemporary British ships, was of benefit. In her final action she did not score a single hit on her enemies. As in World War I, German gunnery was excellent under ideal conditions, but rapidly deteriorated once the enemy found the range and began to hit. *Bismarck's* complex optical systems only worked when the crew were calm; the stress of battle impaired their performance.

ANDREW LAMBERT

Further Reading

Ballard, R *Discovery of the Bismarck* (Toronto, 1990)

Hinsley, H et al. *British Intelligence in the Second World War Vol. I* (London, 1979)

Roskill, S W *The War at Sea: Vol. I* (London, 1954)

Pearl Harbor
Strike from the Sea
7 DECEMBER 1941

Japanese Imperial Navy First Air Fleet under
Vice Admiral Chuichi Nagumo
VERSUS
United States Navy Pacific Fleet under
Admiral Husband E Kimmel

CHRONOLOGY
26 November 1941– First Air Fleet leaves Japan
2 December 1941 – The Japanese attack order is given
7 December 1941 – The attack on Pearl Harbor
8 December 1941 – The United States declares war on
Japan

*"Yesterday, December 7, 1941 – a date that will live in infamy – the
United States of America was suddenly and deliberately attacked by
naval and air forces of the Empire of Japan. Always will we
remember the character of the onslaught against us. With confidence
in our armed forces – with the unbounded determination of our
people – we will gain the inevitable triumph – so help us God."*
FRANKLIN D ROOSEVELT'S ADDRESS TO CONGRESS

ONE OF THE great threats of sea power is the massed surprise attack on
coastline positions or islands, or on other fleets in harbour. The
ability of warships to bring their formidable firepower perhaps
undetected across the high seas, apparently posing no threat to anyone, and
then suddenly to strike with devastating effect on a weak or isolated garrison
has been one of the main weapons of surprise attack throughout the history

of naval warfare. In keeping with its traditions and philosophies of war, there was perhaps no greater exponent of the surprise strike from the sea than the Japanese Imperial Navy. The development in the course of World War I of the aircraft carrier greatly increased both the range and power of such a surprise attack. Long before World War II, naval theorists wondered what such an attack might look like, how it might work, and whether it would succeed. One thing was clear: such a surprise attack would only be launched by a country willing to risk opening a war by attacking first against a stronger opponent.

The Strategic Situation

In Tokyo in December 1941 a pre-emptive strike on US naval power in the Pacific made much military and political sense. A history of rivalry in Asia between Japan and the USA had, for nearly half a century, made conflict between the two a real possibility. By the middle of 1941 that conflict appeared inevitable. The war in Europe had polarized respective positions: Japan, aligned with the Axis Powers and having a neutrality pact with Russia, was clearly pursuing her expansionist aims in the Far East. The USA, her avowed isolationism already severely tested, and with important interests in Asia, could not ignore Japanese expansion.

Japan's occupation of French Indochina on 24 July 1941 was tangible evidence of these expansionist intentions. President Franklin D Roosevelt responded by demanding that Indochina be declared neutral, and froze all Japanese assets in the USA. But more importantly, on 1 August the President declared an embargo on all petrol and crude oil exports to Japan; the British and the colonial government of the Dutch East Indies followed suit (the Netherlands, like France, was under German occupation). To the Japanese, Roosevelt's embargo was tantamount to an act of war – Japan had no oil resources of its own. Without access to oil and oil-derived products, it would be paralysed economically and militarily.

Thus it was clear to the Japanese leadership that a war with the USA in the Pacific was unavoidable, and it was in this context that they turned to Admiral Isoroku Yamamoto, Commander-in-Chief of the Combined Fleet. Yamamoto's plan to attack Pearl Harbor promised a unique opportunity to immediately seize the initiative in this war, striking a blow at what the Japanese leadership perceived to be an arrogant enemy who had meddled in the affairs of the Far East too long.

The Rival Plans

Pearl Harbor, roughly halfway between the US West Coast and key Japanese bases in the Marshall Islands, was the strategic centre of the USA's naval operations in the Pacific. As such, it would be an obvious target in the event of war – a fact long appreciated by both US and Japanese commanders. US Navy exercise in the 1930s had practised responses to just such an attack. Lieutenant Commander Rysunosuke Kusaka, Yamamoto's Chief of Staff, had written a paper on how to attack Pearl Harbor from the air in 1935. Yamamoto himself had become convinced that an air attack on Pearl Harbor was viable after studying the success of the British air attack on the Italian Fleet anchored in the harbour of Taranto on 12 November 1940.

Yamamoto's plan was designed to hit the US Pacific Fleet, based at Pearl Harbor, at the same time as simultaneous strikes took place against US, British, and Dutch forces in Southeast Asia. By crippling the US threat in the Pacific, Japan could then concentrate on controlling resource-rich territory in Asia without rendering its home territory vulnerable. Yamamoto also believed that such a devastating blow could dissuade the as yet untested US superpower from entering World War II. It was well known that US public opinion was divided on the subject of war, and many among the Japanese leadership believed that a pre-emptive strike could serve to keep the Americans out.

There were several key elements in Yamamoto's plan. First, he insisted that the attack take place in daylight and with total surprise. This would be difficult given the distance the naval task force would need to cover, and timing the actual declaration of war would be crucial in allowing the Americans little or no time to raise the alarm before the attack. In terms of specific objectives, Yamamoto rightly identified the Pacific Fleet's aircraft carriers as the prized targets. He believed that air supremacy was vital in any war in the Pacific, and thus to degrade the US capability in this area would hand Japan a significant advantage. In addition to the rest of the Pacific Fleet including its battleships at Pearl Harbor, there were many aircraft based on Oahu island belonging to the US Army Air Corps, the US Navy, and the US Marines, and damage inflicted on these would make it still more difficult for the Americans to challenge Japan in the air. Yamamoto demanded that all types of attack be used – dive and level bombers as well as torpedo bombers and fighters.

Although, if surprise was achieved, the Americans at Pearl Harbor would present something of a 'sitting duck', there were a number of technical problems that had to be resolved before the attack became feasible. Intense pilot training and the innovative work of Japanese ordnance specialists was key to the success of the attack. Training began in July, a full six months before the raid itself. In a period of intense training – 10–12 hours a day was not unusual – the pilots were able to improve their accuracy significantly. The horizontal bomber pilots, flying Nakajima B5N2 Type 97s (known as 'Kates' to the Americans, who gave Japanese bombers women's names), raised their accuracy at 10–15,000 ft from 10% to 50%, while the dive-bombers, Aichi D3A1 Type 99s ('Vals'), went from 50% to 60% accuracy. This training was in part the result of the conditions they would encounter at Pearl Harbor. The remaining Nakajima 'Kates' configured as torpedo bombers would have to approach their targets as low as 150 ft, because of the shallow harbour water into which their torpedoes would drop.

The Japanese ordnance specialists were busy too. The usual Model II torpedo had to be modified to work in the shallow waters of Pearl Harbor. The modifications necessary were major and all stops had to be pulled out in order for the requisite number of torpedoes to be available in time. There was also a lack of bombs with an armour-piercing capability. The well-protected decks of the US warships meant that the Japanese would need heavy calibre bombs, and the race was on to produce enough of the 400-mm, 800 kilogram armour-piercing projectiles that were specially designed for the task.

In addition to forming the First Air Fleet under Vice Admiral Chuichi Nagumo in order to carry out the air strike, Yamamoto also arranged for 25 fleet submarines to proceed independently to Pearl Harbor. After the attack these submarines would intercept any US reinforcements and attack any warships attempting to sortie. Five midget submarines, formidable weapons in themselves, would enter the harbour and target any ships missed by the air attack. Each midget submarine carried one officer and one crewman. Able to achieve a speed of 24 knots submerged and equipped with torpedoes that could inflict twice as much damage as those used by conventional submarines, they were more than up to the task. However the chances of the midget submarine crews surviving the aftermath of the raid were slim – it was highly unlikely that they would be able to escape through the narrow opening to Pearl Harbor.

First Air Fleet itself consisted of six large aircraft carriers – the *Akagi*, *Hiryu*, *Kaga*, *Shokaku*, *Soryu*, and *Zuikaku* – plus two battleships – the *Hiei* and *Kirishima* – two heavy cruisers, one light cruiser, and nine destroyers. In addition, eight tankers accompanied the task force to provide refuelling, while three submarines acted as scouts ahead of the convoy.

Since the Americans did not know definitely that Pearl Harbor was to be attacked, their planning for defence was only limited. But the USA had become convinced that Japanese aggression was imminent. The US codebreaking system 'Magic' allowed Roosevelt and his advisers to keep closely abreast of Japanese diplomatic developments. However the feeling in Washington was that the Philippines and the British and Dutch colonies in Southeast Asia would be the first to feel the force of the Japanese war machine. Despite several incidents that in retrospect identify Pearl Harbor as the Japanese target, the Americans failed to take the threat of an air attack seriously.

Indeed, the main threat to the US Army posts and installations on Oahu, as well as to the ships at Pearl Harbor, was believed to be sabotage. As well as measures taken to raise internal security, the US Army and US Navy also devised an inter-service plan to protect the Hawaiian Islands against external attack. In such an event the Army would provide anti-aircraft fire and fighter interception, while the Navy would carry out both long- and short-range patrols which would alert the island to any hostile forces in the vicinity. When tested in battle the plan would fail dramatically. Much of the reason for this lay in the lack of communication between the Army and Navy. As well as disagreements about particular tactics, there was some confusion as to what each specific role was to be, and where their responsibilities lay. In addition, both Navy and Army were largely ignorant of the other service's contribution or capabilities.

The Attack

On Sunday 7 December, at 7.49 a.m. Hawaiian time, the first wave of Japanese fighters, bombers, and torpedo planes swooped down upon the US Pacific Fleet anchored in Pearl Harbor. Despite having to cover over 3,000 nautical miles since leaving its base at Kure on 29 November, First Air Fleet had struck with complete surprise.

To avoid detection, the Japanese had sailed east across the Pacific by a northerly route, thereby avoiding both the busy sea lanes and the airborne patrols from the US bases on Wake Island and on Midway Island. The armada then stood-to at a point roughly 1,000 nautical miles north of the Hawaiian Islands. On receipt of the code signal 'Climb Mount Niikata' on 2 December, First Air Fleet sailed south towards Oahu, with poor weather screening its progress.

The fleet refuelled for the last time 500 miles north of Oahu. The tankers returned home. The fleet assumed battle formation – the carriers aligned in parallel, the battleships and heavy cruisers providing defence on the flanks. Nagumo ordered their speed to increase to 24 knots, and the fleet headed towards the launch point 300 miles north of the islands. Once at the launch

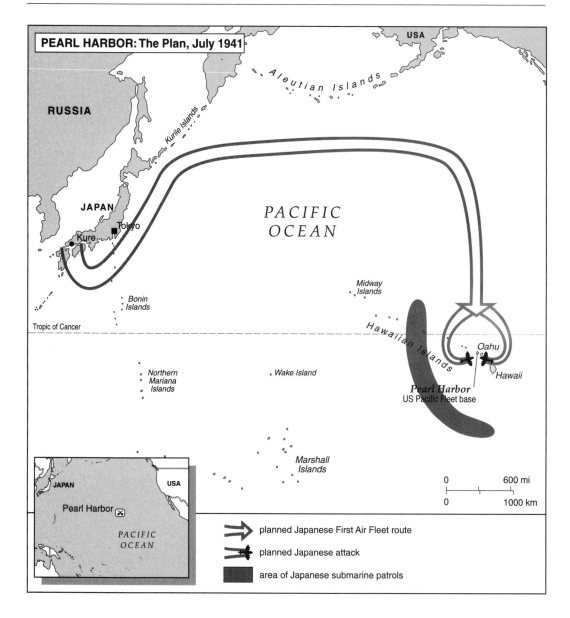

point the excitement aboard the fleet was tangible. Once satisfied that all was in order, Nagumo ordered the air attack to begin.

Japanese scouting aircraft reported that 9 battleships, 7 light cruisers, 20 destroyers, and 3 seaplane tenders were anchored in Pearl Harbor. In fact, there were 8 battleships – the USS *Arizona*, USS *California*, USS *Maryland*, USS *Nevada*, USS *Oklahoma*, USS *Pennsylvania*, USS *Tennessee*, and USS *West Virginia*. In addition there were 2 heavy cruisers, 29 destroyers, and 5 submarines. The aircraft carriers of the Pacific Fleet were out on patrol,

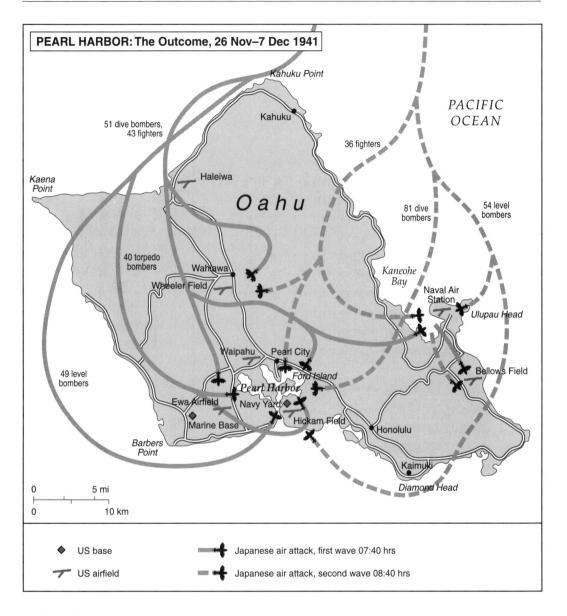

PEARL HARBOR: The Outcome, 26 Nov–7 Dec 1941

Kahuku Point

PACIFIC
OCEAN

51 dive bombers,
43 fighters

Kahuku

36 fighters

Kaena
Point

Haleiwa

Oahu

81 dive
bombers

54 level
bombers

40 torpedo
bombers

Wahiawa

Wheeler Field

Kaneohe
Bay

Naval Air
Station

Ulupau Head

Waipahu   Pearl City

Ford Island

Bellows Field

49 level
bombers

Pearl Harbor

Ewa Airfield

Navy Yard

Marine Base

Hickam Field

Honolulu

Barbers
Point

Kaimuki

Diamond Head

0   5 mi

0   10 km

◆   US base   Japanese air attack, first wave 07:40 hrs

⊥   US airfield   Japanese air attack, second wave 08:40 hrs

looking for a possible Japanese threat.

At 6.00 a.m. the first wave of 183 torpedo planes, dive-bombers, level bombers, and fighters took off from the Japanese carriers. Although the US Army mobile army radar set at Opana near Kahuka Point reported incoming planes approximately 140 miles to the north, it was decided that this was only a flight of US B-17 bombers expected from the mainland, and no alarm was raised. Three quarters of an hour later, the US destroyer *Ward* sank a Japanese midget submarine trying to enter Pearl Harbor, but still no general alert was given while confirmation of the *Ward's* actions was sought.

So, at 7.49 a.m., 40 torpedo bombers led by Lieutenant Commander Shigerharu Murata began the attack on the US battleships anchored side by side in 'battleship row' next to Ford Island in the middle of Pearl Harbor. Meanwhile, the fighter escort of 43 Zeros swept over Oahu in search of US planes, 51 dive-bombers climbed to 12,000 ft to commence their attack, and 49 torpedo bombers turned towards Barbers Point to begin their run. At 7.53 a.m. Fuchida radioed the Akagi with the codeword 'Tora Tora Tora' (the Japanese for 'Tiger' three times) meaning that there were no US planes to be seen: the attack was a complete surprise.

In minutes the Japanese bombers and fighters destroyed on the ground the majority of Army Air Corps planes based at Wheeler, Bellows, and Hickam Fields on Oahu; their task was made the easier by the wing-tip to wing-tip formation of the aircraft, another antisabotage measure. The attacks on naval patrol planes and fighters of Ford Wing at Ewa Airfield were equally successful. Meanwhile, the torpedo bombers split into two groups. One of 16 aircraft headed for the west side of Pearl Harbor; the remaining 24 flew southeast before turning north over Hickam Field, then northwest to attack Battleship Row, where the US warships were lined up like bowling skittles.

The *West Virginia* and *Oklahoma* were hit repeatedly – both were sunk. The *California* took two torpedo hits and sank too. The *Nevada* managed to get underway despite being hit by torpedoes and two bombs, and headed for the mouth of the harbour. But fearing that another hit on her might block the harbour, the *Nevada's* captain was ordered to bring her back in. After being hit by three more bombs, she was finally run aground.

By 7.15 a.m. the second wave of 171 strike planes had left their carriers, and arrived over Oahu at 8.55 a.m. Of these, 54 'Kate' bombers concentrated on the airfields, and 81 'Vals' sought out those ships that had survived the first onslaught. Despite the considerable barrage thrown up by ship and shore anti-aircraft guns, more ships suffered major damage. The *Arizona*, tethered inboard alongside the support ship USS *Vestal* blew up under heavy bombing, losing 80% of her crew. James Leamon Forbis, a coxswain on the *Arizona*, related how 'the stern part of the ship was sticking up dry. The ship was down by the bow and sitting on the bottom. Everything was in sad shape. It was torn up. There was bombing, burning, and people were in the water'. The *Tennessee* and *Maryland* too were badly damaged, and Kimmel's flagship the *Pennsylvania* was also hit, together with cruisers, destroyers, and other ships in the harbour.

The Aftermath

By 10.15 a.m. the attack was over. In all, 18 ships of the Pacific Fleet had been sunk, capsized, or badly damaged, including 8 battleships, 3 destroyers, and 4 auxiliary vessels. The damage to US air capability was also considerable. The US Navy had lost 80 aircraft, and as well as 77 Army planes destroyed, another 128 were badly damaged. The attack had taken its toll on human life too. In total 2,403 people were killed at Pearl Harbor, with a further 1,178 injured. The Japanese lost 29 planes, one submarine, and all five of their midget submarines as they tried to penetrate the harbour, only one man surviving. These losses were minimal in the context of an attack upon a heavily defended enemy base over 3,000 miles from home.

And yet the damage could have been worse, much worse. Fuel and ammunition reserves had been spared, as had the repair shops, dry docks, and submarine pens essential to the maintenance of the Pacific Fleet. Nagumo spurned the opportunity to mount a second, and surely terminal attack – the now largely undefended Pear Harbor would have been easy pickings. But Nagumo, fearful of a counter-attack on his fleet being mounted from the mainland or from US carriers, ordered his task force to set course for home.

The Japanese attack on Pearl Harbor was a startlingly tactical success. For relatively few losses they had inflicted major damage on the US Pacific Fleet. In so doing Japan gained a short-term advantage over its rivals in the Pacific. But in military terms this advantage would have been greater had Nagumo pressed home his advantage with a second attack. The prized targets, the US aircraft carriers, were still intact, as were the heavy cruisers and the US submarine fleet. Moreover, the damage inflicted on Pearl Harbor was quickly repaired.

In political terms Pearl Harbor would prove an unmitigated strategic disaster for Japan. By hastening the USA's entry into the war, the attack proved to be a turning point in the war – indeed a turning point in the century. Although it was Japan's intention to present a declaration of war in Washington a few minutes before the attack, their diplomats failed to do so for complex reasons of timing. This led to a perception of the Japanese as a brutal and amoral enemy who would stop at nothing, an enemy against whom resort to weapons as yet unimagined would be the only option.

IAN STEWART

Further Reading

Gaily, H A *The War in the Pacific* (Presidio, 1997)

Howarth, S *Morning Glory* (1983)

Prange, G W *At Dawn We Slept* (London, 1982)

Slackman, M *Target: Pearl Harbor* (Honolulu, 1990)

Operation Pedestal
The Malta Convoy
3 – 15 AUGUST 1942

British Royal Navy's Force 'H' under Vice Admiral
Sir Neville Syfret

VERSUS

German and Italian forces under Field Marshal
Albert Kesselring, Commander-in-Chief South

CHRONOLOGY

3 August 1942 –	The Pedestal convoy leaves the Clyde
10 August 1942 –	The convoy enters the Mediterranean
11 August 1942 –	The convoy takes its first losses
12 August 1942 –	The main body of Force 'H' leaves the convoy
13 August 1942 –	The main convoy reaches Valletta harbour
15 August 1942 –	The last stragglers reach Valletta

"The loss of Malta would be a disaster of the first magnitude to the British Empire." WINSTON CHURCHILL

WARFARE AT SEA is forever associated with the clash of warships – battleships, submarines, aircraft carriers, manoeuvring and striking at each other often over great distances. But one of the most important roles of sea power, in war as in peace, is to transport cargo, supplies, and people from one land mass to another. The convoy system of protecting merchant ships, an ancient practice revived by the British in World War I in response to marauding German submarines (*Unterseebooten* or U-boats), played a critical if unglamorous part in determining victory and defeat in World War II. The convoy battles were among the hardest fought of the war, made all the more terrible by the fact that the prime targets were not enemy warships, but merchant vessels with civilian crews with little or no means of protecting themselves. The often vital importance of a convoy was reflected in the lengths to which both sides would go and the losses that they were prepared to take in fighting ships and aircraft, either to get the convoy through or to sink it. This critical convoy despatched from the United Kingdom to Malta at the height of the war in the Mediterranean and Middle East, produced a battle that was one of the hardest fought of all.

The Strategic Situation

By the middle of 1942 the situation on the island of Malta, one of the British bases in the Mediterranean, had become critical, with stocks of food for the population and fuel and munitions for the Royal Air Force (RAF) and the Royal Navy's submarines reaching dangerously low levels. Axis air domination of the central Mediterranean had been attained by the middle of 1941, following the capture of Crete. This, combined with the ease with which German and Italian submarines and coastal craft could operate from bases in Italy and North Africa, more than compensated for the relative ineffectiveness of the Italian surface fleet. Consequently it was becoming increasingly difficult for the British to fight resupply convoys through to Malta, and attempts to do so met with limited success and endured heavy casualties.

If Malta had fallen, the Allied war effort in the region would have been severely degraded. Not only would maritime control have been surrendered, but the ability to interrupt Axis supply shipping for Field Marshal Erwin Rommel's *Afrika Korps* would also have been lost. Thus the existence of the bases on Malta was critical to the British Eighth Army's attempts to halt and reverse the German advance towards the Suez Canal and the Middle East oilfields. Prime Minister Winston Churchill, in particular, feared that the loss of Malta would mean the eventual loss of Egypt.

The Axis powers were also very concerned about Malta. The use of the island as a British base was starting to cause substantial casualties to resupply routes to North Africa. By early 1942, these losses were beginning to delay Rommel's advance through Tunisia and into Libya. There was, therefore, a severe risk to the overall German grand strategy of taking the Suez Canal, turning northwards through the Levant, and eventually linking with the German armies advancing through the Soviet Union.

The British Plan

Following a disastrous attempt to resupply Malta in June 1942 from Gibraltar and Alexandria (Operations 'Harpoon' and 'Vigorous'), the British decided against trying to fight a convoy through to the island in July until the lessons of the June experience had been studied and full preparations had been made. Consequently the Admiralty assured Middle East Command that a single convoy of fast merchant ships sailing from Gibraltar could reach Malta with 'a reasonable number' of ships surviving the inevitable onslaught from Axis air and sea attacks. The main difference between this convoy, to be named 'Operation Pedestal', and its predecessors was to be the size of the escort. The convoy was to consist of 14 merchantmen. To protect them no fewer than four fleet aircraft carriers – over half the Royal Navy's total strength – were to be deployed. Of these, the old carrier HMS *Furious* was to act as an aircraft transport to supply reinforcement Spitfires to the RAF on Malta. The other three, HMS *Victorious*, HMS *Indomitable*, and HMS *Eagle*, were to provide air defence for the convoy as far as the Tunisian coast off Bizerte. The remainder of the escort was to include two battleships – HMS *Nelson* and HMS *Rodney* – seven cruisers, and 24 destroyers (a number equipped as fast minesweepers); a ratio of two and a half escorts for each merchant ship.

The operation was to be under the command of Vice Admiral Sir Neville Syfret, commander of the Royal Navy's famous Force 'H', normally based at Gibraltar. The convoy was to form in the UK and pass through the Strait of Gibraltar at night without stopping. Simultaneously, the British Mediterranean Fleet based in Alexandria was to sail in order to create a diversion. This, it was hoped, would give the impression that convoys were to be forced through to Malta from both directions, as had happened in the June operations.

The main threats were identified as Italian and German submarines, aircraft flying from Sardinia and Sicily, and small torpedo boats ('E-boats') based along the Tunisian coast, as well as minefields in coastal waters off Tunisia. Consequently, the route of the convoy was to be based on whichever of these threats was analysed as being the most serious for each sector. As far as the narrows between Tunisia and Sardinia, the convoy was to remain on a middle track, maintaining equidistance from the North African coast and the Balearic Islands to the north. Once the convoy came within the range of Axis aircraft based in Sicily, then air attack was identified as the main threat and the convoy, minus its heavy units (carriers, battleships, and some escorts), which were now considered too vulnerable, was to hug the Tunisian coast despite the probability of attacks from torpedo boats and the inevitability of enemy minefields.

The final dash to Malta, the convoy having rounded Cap Bon, was to take place at maximum speed with British submarines mounting a barrier through which the merchant ships could pass and with the RAF from Malta providing air cover. It was hoped that half the supply ships beginning the operation would reach their destination. Even then success would not be guaranteed, as the island was under almost permanent air attack and ships were regularly bombed while in Valletta and other ports.

The Axis Plan

Through the early part of 1942, the Axis higher commands – particularly the new German Commander-in-Chief South, Field Marshal 'Smiling Albert' Kesselring of the Luftwaffe – were uncertain of how to approach the problem of Malta. There was little doubt that Hitler was taking the Mediterranean campaign more seriously than he had in 1941, especially with Rommel's seemingly unstoppable successes. The Russian winter of 1941–42, in which the Luftwaffe had little opportunity to fly, had enabled a significant redeployment of German aircraft from that theatre to Italy and North Africa. If Malta was to be taken, then the summer of 1942 seemed the optimum time, especially as the island was believed to be close to starvation and had been battered by continuous air bombardment. Consequently, 'Operation Hercules', a chiefly airborne German assault on Malta, was conceived and planned.

But by the end of June, Rommel's progress was so impressive that it was believed that the threat Malta could pose to his resupply routes was outweighed by the probability that the remaining British resistance in North Africa would be overcome quickly as Rommel advanced into Egypt. So rather than commit valuable resources and time to taking Malta (bearing in mind the cost of the similar operation to take Crete), the German high command told Rommel to proceed with his desert campaign. The Luftwaffe and the German Navy, as well as their Italian allies, were to ensure that no further supplies reached Malta.

At the time 'Operation Pedestal' began, some 1,000 Axis combat aircraft had been assembled in Sardinia and Sicily. Six Italian and three German submarines were stationed between the Balearic Islands and the Algerian Coast. A further 12 Italian submarines were deployed in the narrows between Sicily and Tunisia. A new minefield had been laid off Cap Bon, and south of the minefield 25 E-boats and their Italian equivalents were prepared to attack. In the coastal waters off Sicily a major Italian surface fleet consisting of six cruisers and 12 destroyers was ready to intercept any convoy. It could be safely assumed that such a force would be more than adequate to prevent 'Operation Pedestal' from reaching Malta.

The First Phase

Vice Admiral Syfret joined Force 'H' in Scapa Flow on 27 July 1942, and hoisted his flag in HMS *Nelson*. After final preparations the fleet sailed to meet the Pedestal convoy in the approaches to the River Clyde on 3 August. The passage to the Mediterranean took place without incident except for a minor collision. On 10 August the convoy passed Gibraltar in thick fog. However, the eastern Mediterranean deception plan did not cause any serious confusion to the enemy, as Axis reconnaissance aircraft had located and were shadowing Pedestal shortly after it had entered the Mediterranean. Within a few hours the Italian submarine *Uarsciek* had reported the convoy's position and composition from a location some 60 miles south of Ibiza.

On 11 August, Pedestal's first objective was achieved without difficulty when the carrier HMS *Furious* was able to despatch her complement of 38 Spitfires towards Malta, some 550 miles away. With her escort she then returned to Gibraltar leaving the three remaining fleet aircraft carriers to accompany the convoy. Unfortunately, the first serious casualty occurred the same day as the convoy entered the area perceived as being the most dangerous as regards the submarine threat. The German submarine U-73 struck the elderly carrier HMS *Eagle* with four torpedoes, 70 miles north of Algiers. *Eagle* had operated in the Mediterranean virtually since the beginning of the war, but her age made her particularly vulnerable as she had been converted into an aircraft carrier from an early (Chilean) *Dreadnought* class battleship. She sank quickly with the loss of 260 of her complement of 1,160 men. However, the main loss to the force was her Hurricane fighters, almost all of which went down with the ship. The number of carriers able to give the convoy air cover was now reduced to two.

In the early evening of 11 August, Pedestal experienced its first air attacks from Axis bases in Sardinia. Altogether 36 Luftwaffe Junkers Ju-88 and Heinkel He-111 medium bombers were involved, but none of the attacks was delivered with much conviction and no damage was sustained. Four aircraft were shot down. While these aircraft were away, their bases were struck by RAF Bristol Beaufighters from Malta.

By the next day the convoy had sailed much closer to the Axis bases in Sardinia, and the attacks were more determined and more sustained. That afternoon some 80 torpedo and dive-bombers attacked. The defending fighters were to minimize the effect, although the aircraft carrier *Victorious*

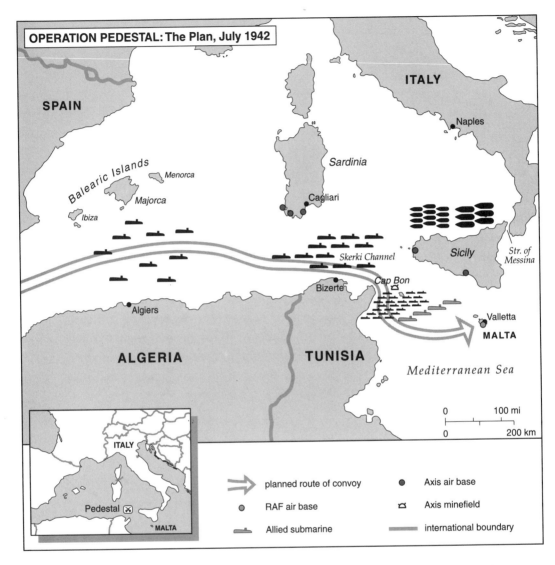

OPERATION PEDESTAL: The Plan, July 1942

SPAIN

ITALY

Naples

Balearic Islands

Menorca

Majorca

Sardinia

Ibiza

Cagliari

Sicily

Str. of Messina

Skerki Channel

Bizerte

Cap Bon

Algiers

Valletta

MALTA

ALGERIA

TUNISIA

Mediterranean Sea

| 0 | 100 mi |
| 0 | 200 km |

ITALY

Pedestal ⊠

MALTA

planned route of convoy   ● Axis air base

● RAF air base   ⌂ Axis minefield

Allied submarine   international boundary

was hit but not seriously damaged. The first merchant ship was lost, however, when the Blue Funnel liner *Deucalion* was hit. She turned towards the Tunisian coast hoping to avoid further attack, but later she was found by Italian dive bombers and sunk.

By the evening of 12 August it was believed that the convoy had left the area of the main enemy submarine concentration. But in the evening air attacks began again, in very serious numbers. The carrier *Indomitable* was a casualty of this attack, having her flight deck so badly damaged that she was no longer effective and had to return to Gibraltar, leaving only *Victorious* left to provide air defence. The escort also lost one of its destroyers, HMS *Foresight*. Pedestal

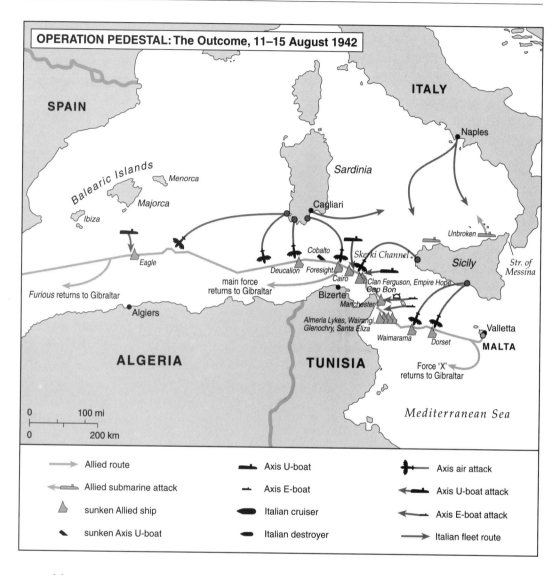

OPERATION PEDESTAL: The Outcome, 11–15 August 1942

SPAIN

ITALY

Naples

Balearic Islands

Menorca

Sardinia

Majorca

Cagliari

Ibiza

Unbroken

Eagle

Cobalto

Skerki Channel

Sicily

Str. of Messina

Deucalion *Foresight*

main force
returns to Gibraltar

Cairo

Clan Ferguson, Empire Hope
Cap Bon

Furious returns to Gibraltar

Manchester

Bizerte

Almeria Lykes, Wairangi,
Glenochry, Santa Eliza

Algiers

Waimarama

Dorset

Valletta

MALTA

ALGERIA

TUNISIA

Force 'X'
returns to Gibraltar

Mediterranean Sea

| 0 | 100 mi |
| 0 | 200 km |

	Allied route		Axis U-boat		Axis air attack
	Allied submarine attack		Axis E-boat		Axis U-boat attack
	sunken Allied ship		Italian cruiser		Axis E-boat attack
	sunken Axis U-boat		Italian destroyer		Italian fleet route

was able to record a success though, when the destroyer HMS *Ithuriel* forced
the Italian submarine *Cobalto* to the surface and rammed her.

In the early evening of 12 August, Pedestal reached the point off the
Tunisian port of Bizerte where Admiral Syfret and the major surface units of
the escort were to turn round and rejoin the rest of Force 'H' at Gibraltar. No
further major warships were lost after this point, but the convoy was left to
continue its passage with an escort reduced to four cruisers and 12 destroyers
(known as Force 'X') under Rear Admiral H M Burrough. It was believed this
force would be adequate to deter the Italian Navy.

The Critical Stage

Until this time, 'Operation Pedestal' had gone roughly to plan and the commanders were optimistic as to the overall outcome. But as the convoy reached the most critical point, closing the Tunisian coast, the Italian submarine *Axum* torpedoed both the cruiser HMS *Nigeria*, Burrough's flagship, and the smaller anti-aircraft cruiser HMS *Cairo*. Through superb damage-control action, *Nigeria* survived to reach Gibraltar but Burrough had to transfer his flag to the destroyer HMS *Ashanti*. HMS *Cairo* was so badly damaged that her crew was evacuated and she had to be sunk by British ships. As Pedestal altered its formation to pass through the Skerki Channel, it also suffered another large-scale air attack, which resulted in the sinking of two merchant ships, the *Clan Ferguson* and the *Empire Hope*. Shortly after this blow the escort almost lost another of its major units when the cruiser HMS *Kenya* was torpedoed. But fortunately damage was light, and the ship was able to remain as part of the convoy.

On hearing of this, Admiral Syfret, on his way back to Gibraltar, ordered one of his light cruisers, HMS *Charybdis*, and two destroyers back to rejoin Pedestal to make up for some of the losses. These reinforcements had not arrived by the time the convoy rounded Cap Bon and turned south keeping close to the Tunisian coast. It was appreciated that the area was heavily mined, but it was hoped that the specially adapted minesweeping destroyers would be able to clear a passage effectively and quickly, an operation which was generally successful. The serious new threat that did materialize, however, was that mounted by the torpedo boats based along the coast. They were highly effective, especially at night when their low profile made them especially difficult to see. By the end of the night of 12–13 August, the convoy had lost four further merchant ships sunk and another seriously damaged. The escort was also to lose another major warship when two Italian torpedo boats, *M16* and *M22*, torpedoed the cruiser HMS *Manchester*, leaving her so badly damaged that she had to be scuttled.

Further north, surface units of the Italian fleet had put to sea from bases in Sardinia, Sicily, and Naples hoping to emulate the success of the Italian surface ships in 'Operation Vigorous' by stopping the convoy. However, inter-service rivalry forced the fleet to turn around, as the German higher commanders decided to leave the air forces to destroy what was left of Pedestal. As the Italian ships headed back to their bases, one of the two Malta-based submarines deployed to the areas north of Sicily, HMS *Unbroken*, succeeded in torpedoing the Italian cruisers *Bolzano* and *Attendolo* as they approached the Strait of Messina. Both ships were severely damaged. Consequently no major Italian surface warships were deployed south of Sicily.

Shortly after dawn on 13 August, air attacks resumed accounting for one more merchant ship lost and three damaged. Among the damaged ships was the tanker *Ohio*, one of Pedestal's more valued units. Destroyers were told to remain behind in order to escort the damaged ships while the remainder of the convoy, which was now reduced to three merchantmen, made the final dash to Malta. By this time Malta-based forces had assumed responsibility for the remaining ships, thus enabling Force 'X' to return to Gibraltar. RAF Spitfires, Beaufighters, and Liberator bombers, together with naval minesweepers and light patrol craft, shepherded the remnants of Pedestal towards Malta. Despite further air attacks the three ships – the *Melbourne Star*, *Port Chalmers*, and *Rochester Castle* – entered Valletta harbour to a tumultuous welcome on the afternoon of 13 August.

The End of the Convoy

The remaining task was to try and get as many of the damaged ships as possible safely into Malta. On the evening of 13 August an air attack sank one of them, but despite being further damaged, the tanker *Ohio* reached the island relatively intact on 15 August. The effort that went into saving this ship was one of the most notable episodes of the whole operation. One other damaged merchantman, the *Brisbane Star*, also successfully reached the island.

'Operation Pedestal' ended with just five of the original 14 supply ships actually reaching Malta. As a result, 32,000 tons of general cargo and 15,000 tons of fuel oil were finally delivered to the garrison. Even this number was more than had succeeded in previous operations. The supplies delivered were sufficient for the island to continue to defend itself for a few more weeks, although they did not significantly improve the lives of the Maltese population or the British garrison. The price paid was high and probably unsustainable on such a scale. The Royal Navy had lost a fleet aircraft carrier, two light cruisers, and a destroyer. Another fleet carrier, two more cruisers, and several destroyers had been damaged. Nine fast merchant ships had also been destroyed. But Pedestal gave Malta that little breathing space that is often crucial in military campaigns. The siege of Malta was still far from over, but despite further reverses in the theatre, the situation in the Mediterranean was to improve dramatically in the coming months. The successful arrival of a convoy of four merchant ships from Alexandria on 20 November marked the effective relief of the island.

DAVID PICKUP

Further Reading

Mackintyre, D *The Battle for the Mediterranean* (London, 1964)

Roskill, S W *The War At Sea, Volume II* (London, 1956)

Roskill, S W *The Navy At War 1939–1945* (London, 1960)

Shankland, P, and Hunter, A *Malta Convoy* (London, 1961)

THE AIRBORNE ASSAULTS

"It would be wrong to consider a parachutist only as a soldier who has learned an extremely important kind of modern warfare. Parachute training is a school of character and a test of leaders' capacities." MAJOR GENERAL STANISLAV SOSABOWSKI, COMMANDER OF POLISH AIRBORNE FORCES IN WORLD WAR II

ONE OF THE most remarkable features of battle in World War II was that it saw the both the beginning and the end of an entirely new form of warfare: the mass airborne assault by parachute and glider, involving thousands of specially trained and dedicated soldiers. First envisaged by the Americans in World War I, and rehearsed in Germany and the Soviet Union in the interwar years, airborne assaults were carried out by almost all the major countries involved in World War II, and in every theatre of war. But by 1945 the sheer scale of effort required to mount such operations, together with the increased power of air and land defences against airborne troops, meant that the idea was already in decline. Since then, only a handful of airborne assaults involving more than a few hundred men have ever taken place, and airborne troops are more likely to land from helicopters than by parachute. Airborne troops depended on surprise for success, but could not carry or bring heavy weapons. Instead they relied on very high levels of training and courage, which were all too often tested to their limits.

The Battle for Crete
The Pyrrhic Victory
20 MAY – 1 JUNE 1941

Commonwealth and Greek forces under
Major General Bernard Freyberg VC

VERSUS

German XI Air Corps under General Kurt Student
and VIII Air Corps under General Wolfram Freiherr
von Richthofen

CHRONOLOGY

25 April 1941 – Hitler orders invasion of Crete
20 May 1941 – German airborne forces land on Crete
21 May 1941 – German airborne reinforcements land
at Maleme; seaborne reinforcements
intercepted by Royal Navy
23 May 1941 – Germans push east from Maleme, Royal
Navy retires south of Crete
26 May 1941 – Allied defence line west of Chania
collapses
27 May 1941 – Allied evacuation from Crete
authorized
1 June 1941 – Evacuation ends, remaining Allied
forces surrender

*"Of course, you know that we shall never do another airborne
operation. Crete proved that the days of parachute troops are over."*
ADOLF HITLER

THROUGHOUT WORLD WAR II, considerable debate existed on all sides as
to the best way to use the evolving airborne forces. Were they to
emphasize gliders, or parachutists? Were they better off being used in

small numbers for raids and special operations, or in divisional strength? Above all, could forces be landed and supported from the sky alone that were strong enough to defeat a major enemy and win a battle without support from other troops, or was rapid reinforcement of airborne forces essential? In Spring 1941 the island of Crete provided a grim testing ground. The resulting battle was a victory for the German airborne forces, and the only major battle won by airborne forces alone in the whole course of World War II. But when counting the cost, whether it was a victory for the idea of airborne assault was far less clear.

The Strategic Situation

In April 1941 Adolf Hitler unleashed a campaign of unprecedented ferocity in the Balkans. Determined that nothing should threaten the southern flank of 'Operation Barbarossa' (the planned invasion of the Soviet Union), German air and land forces delivered a series of devastating blows against Yugoslavia, defeating the latter in less than two weeks. Simultaneously Greece was attacked and overrun, in the process ending its army's valiant struggle against the Italians in Albania. To add insult to injury, the Germans also drove a British-led expeditionary force, sent from Egypt to help the Greeks, into a humiliating and precipitate withdrawal. By 3 May southeastern Europe lay firmly under the control of the Axis powers.

There was, however, one significant exception – the island of Crete. Although separated from the Greek mainland by a not inconsiderable stretch of water, Crete remained both a thorn in the Germans' side and a tempting prize. From airbases there a rejuvenated Royal Air Force (RAF) could not only attack Axis shipping to North Africa, but might also launch raids on Germany's main source of fuel, the Romanian oil fields. Similarly, from the developing naval base of Suda Bay the powerful British Mediterranean Fleet could strike north into the Aegean, threatening their enemy's grip on the region and exerting political influence on neutral Turkey. By contrast, if Crete could be captured these dangers would largely evaporate, while a strong position from which to defend Greece or to support further operations in the Mediterranean would fall into Axis hands. By attacking Crete, Hitler might also deceive the British and Soviets into believing that German intentions lay elsewhere than the Soviet Union. The result was the issuing on 25 April 1941 of 'Führer Directive 28', ordering a direct assault on Crete under the code name of 'Operation Mercury'.

The German Plans

'Mercury' was to be a hurriedly improvised but audacious operation. Lacking command of the sea and the maritime assets necessary to launch a full-scale amphibious attack, but conscious of their overwhelming superiority in the air, the Germans decided to carry out their initial landings with airborne forces commanded by Luftwaffe General Kurt Student. Spearheading the assault would be well-trained paratroopers and glider-borne infantry from XI Air Corps and, in particular, 7th Air Division (despite its name, a parachute division that had played an important role in the 1940 campaign in the West). Attacking in two waves on the first day, the parachutists and gliders were to seize airfields at Maleme, Rethymnon, and Heraklion, as well as the principal Cretan town of Chania. Once this had been done, reinforcements from 5th Mountain Division would be flown in to the captured airfields or landed from a mixed merchant fleet of powered sailing ships despatched from Greek ports. Together with the airborne units, they would link up the bridgeheads along the north coast, before driving south in pursuit of any enemy forces attempting to escape across the mountainous spine of the island. Altogether, some 15,750 airborne and 7,000 seaborne troops, as well as over 500 Junkers Ju 52 transport aircraft and 80 gliders would be used. Supporting them would be 280 bombers, 150 dive-bombers, 180 fighters, and 40 reconnaissance aircraft from General von Richthofen's VIII Air Corps. It was hoped that this armada would guarantee the safe arrival of the airborne forces and deter the Royal Navy from interfering with the weakly escorted merchant convoys. The operation was to be launched on 20 May.

The British Plans

Against their opponents' elite formations the forces on Crete could offer superior numbers and bravery, but little else. Mainly because the island had acted as a receptacle for troops withdrawn from Greece, there were in fact some 30,000 British and Commonwealth and 11,000 Greek military personnel on Crete by mid-May. Some of these, especially the New Zealand 4th Brigade and 5th Brigade, the Australian 19th Brigade and the British 14th Brigade, were capable and courageous soldiers. However, most had left their equipment behind on evacuation from the mainland, and many even lacked such basic needs as entrenching tools. Although willing to fight, the Greeks had hardly any firearms, while thousands of the Commonwealth troops were auxiliary personnel of minimal combat value. General Sir Archibald Wavell, British Commander-in-Chief in the Middle East, did what he could to help but, overstretched by the fighting in North Africa, could send only a couple of dozen hastily repaired light and medium tanks and around 100 guns taken from the Italians, mostly without sights. Having suffered disastrous losses in Greece, the RAF was unable to provide more than token air cover, and even this disappeared on 19 May when the last five fighters based on Crete were withdrawn to Egypt. Neither, in the face of German air supremacy, was the Royal Navy in any position to carry out major daylight operations north of the island. To all intents and purposes, the troops on Crete were on their own.

The garrison commander on Crete, the New Zealander Major General Bernard Freyberg VC, did have one major advantage: he had considerable knowledge of German intentions. Owing to success in breaking top secret German codes, several weeks before 'Mercury' was launched British intelligence was able to identify the basic elements of the German plan. Together with subsequent details, this information was passed on to Freyberg. However, although this helped him to deploy his forces and confirmed what analysis of the ground already suggested would be the likely decisive points, there were problems with using this information. It was less than complete, and Freyberg remained concerned that an amphibious assault might be an important element of the German plan. As a result, his forces were compelled to split their attention between defence of the airfields and possible beach landing sites. Furthermore, there is evidence to suggest that fear of compromising the fact that the British were breaking German codes meant that Freyberg was unable to adjust his plans as new information was received. This may have been one reason why the three landing strips were not destroyed when the RAF evacuated its surviving aircraft. Last, the central problem remained that Freyberg's forces were weak, overextended, and immobile. Sadly, no amount of accurate intelligence could compensate for these facts.

The Opening Stages

At 7.15 a.m. (German time) on 20 May, after a week of intensive air attacks, the assault on Crete began. With heavy bombing and ground strafing still going on, gliderborne troops from lst Battalion of XI Air Corps' Assault Regiment landed near Maleme airfield, towards the western end of the island. Others descended near Chania, while in their immediate wake came several thousand paratroopers of 'Group West', which was to overrun Maleme, and 'Group Centre', which was to land in the Aiya Valley and seize Chania and Suda Bay to the east. They were to be followed the same afternoon by the rest of 'Group Centre', which was to land at Rethymnon, and by 'Group East', a powerful parachute force which was to capture the airfield at Heraklion.

Anticipating relatively weak resistance, the Germans went into action confident that they would achieve their objectives by nightfall, thus unlocking the island's defences and guaranteeing a rapid victory.

Instead, the German assault met disaster. Warned in good time of the attack, and despite the effects of the air bombardment, all along the north coast Commonwealth and Greek forces responded to the Germans' arrival with brutal resistance. Southeast of Maleme, 3rd Battalion of the Assault Regiment lost 400 men in less than an hour, when it dropped among elements of New Zealand 5th Brigade. The 3rd Parachute Rifle Regiment from 7th Air Division also suffered heavy casualties as it landed in and around the Aiya Valley. In several places Cretan civilians armed with agricultural implements lent their weight to the defence, literally cutting a German company to pieces at Kastelli and savaging isolated German detachments in the hills around Maleme. Nor were things better for the troops arriving in the afternoon. At Rethymnon two battalions of 2nd Parachute Rifle Regiment fell among Australian and Greek forces, losing hundreds of men, while at Heraklion the reinforced 1st Parachute Rifle Regiment saw more than a third of its number become casualties to a Commonwealth and Greek defence estimated beforehand by the Germans at 400 men, but which actually amounted to over 8,000 effectives.

By the evening of 20 May it was clear to Student, at his headquarters in Athens, that the initial airborne attacks had failed. None of the airfields had been seized, no contact could be made with the traumatized remnants of the assault force at Rethymnon, and heavy losses had been incurred by his troops. Nevertheless, there was one glimmer of hope, and Student was determined to seize it. West of Maleme two battalions of the Assault Regiment, together with other survivors, had consolidated a position along the dry bed of the Tavronitis River and at the foot of Hill 107, south of the airfield. If they could be supported, the landing strip might still be captured and further exploitation made possible. Directing that attempts be carried out to land ammunition at Maleme regardless of whether the airfield was secure, and that all available airborne and seaborne reinforcements be directed to the western part of Crete, Student – as he admitted – was staking everything on a single card. But, as he also knew, he had little choice if complete failure was to be avoided.

The Climax of the Battle

Unlike Student, Major General Freyberg was able to reflect on the first day's fighting with a degree of satisfaction. Nevertheless, from the moment he had assumed command on Crete he had been aware of the weakness of his

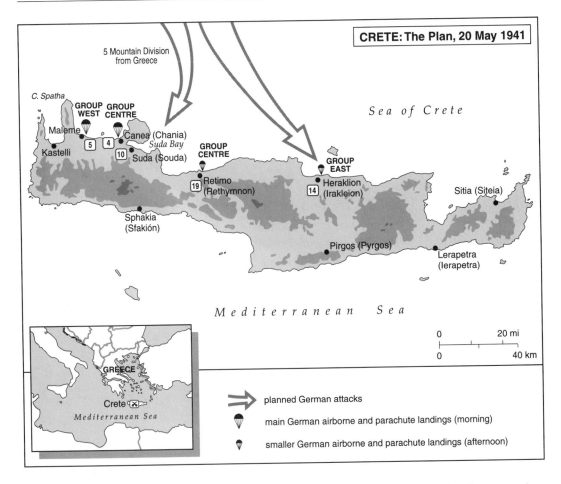

CRETE: The Plan, 20 May 1941

5 Mountain Division from Greece

C. Spatha

GROUP WEST GROUP CENTRE

Maleme

Canea (Chania)
Suda Bay

Kastelli

GROUP CENTRE

Suda (Souda)

Sea of Crete

GROUP EAST

Retimo (Rethymnon)

Heraklion (Irakleion)

Sitia (Siteia)

Sphakia (Sfakión)

Pirgos (Pyrgos)

Lerapetra (Ierapetra)

Mediterranean Sea

0   20 mi
0   40 km

GREECE

Crete

Mediterranean Sea

planned German attacks

main German airborne and parachute landings (morning)

smaller German airborne and parachute landings (afternoon)

position, and his problems were to be magnified by failures of judgement that would prove decisive in turning the tide of battle. First, owing to fears of an imminent amphibious attack, Commonwealth commanders had generally proved reluctant to move troops away from their coastal defences when the German paratroopers landed. As a result, the survivors of the airborne forces were usually able to prevent attempts by locally available reserves to mop them up, thus tying down units that might otherwise have been used for concentrated counter-attacks. Even worse, during the night of 20–21 May the commander of the New Zealand battalion defending the perimeter of Maleme airfield decided to withdraw to the east, fearing that otherwise his forces would be destroyed. He was almost certainly wrong, but disastrously, his brigade commander failed to reverse his decision. As a result Hill 107, which dominated the landing strip from the south, was left undefended.

The costs of this withdrawal were to be fully felt the next day. Hardly able to believe their luck, at dawn on 21 May the Germans in the Tavronitis Valley

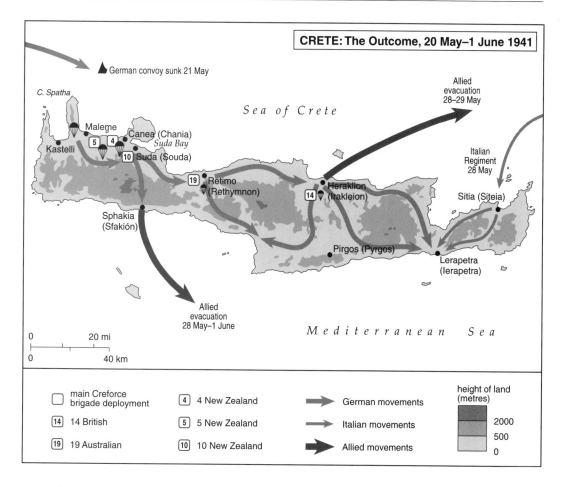

CRETE: The Outcome, 20 May–1 June 1941

German convoy sunk 21 May

C. Spatha

Sea of Crete

Allied
evacuation
28–29 May

Maleme

Kastelli

Canea (Chania)
Suda Bay

5 4

10 Suda (Souda)

Italian
Regiment
28 May

19 Retimo
(Rethymnon)

Heraklion
(Irakleion)

14

Sitia (Siteia)

Sphakia
(Sfakión)

Pirgos (Pyrgos)

Lerapetra
(Ierapetra)

Allied
evacuation
28 May–1 June

Mediterranean   Sea

0   20 mi

0   40 km

☐ main Creforce
brigade deployment

4 4 New Zealand

German movements

height of land
(metres)

2000

14 14 British

5 5 New Zealand

Italian movements

500

19 19 Australian

10 10 New Zealand

Allied movements

0

moved forward, occupying Hill 107 and establishing a defence line east of
Maleme. Their numbers at this point were still small – perhaps 1,000 men –
but in the face of continuous attacks from the Luftwaffe, the New Zealanders
were unable to push them back, although they did keep the landing strip
under indirect artillery and machine-gun fire.

By late afternoon German reinforcements were arriving, some by parachute
and others in Ju-52 transports. Coming down under heavy fire at the airfield,
or deliberately crash landing on the beaches to the north, aircraft losses were
heavy. Nevertheless, by nightfall a battalion of 5th Mountain Division and
several hundred more paratroopers were present to bolster the Germans'
position. To Student, it began to appear that the crisis had passed.

The battle for Crete, however, was still hanging in the balance. For the
Germans the arrival of seaborne reinforcements (4,600 men of 5th Mountain
Division, together with artillery) appeared vital if momentum was to be
sustained. Yet in the late evening of 21 May, the first convoy to approach

Crete suffered disaster when it was intercepted by British naval forces north of the island. Admiral Sir Andrew Cunningham, Commander of the Mediterranean Fleet, had been extremely unenthusiastic about using his ships in an area dominated by the Luftwaffe. However, in view of the importance of his task, he had taken the risk and the initial results were impressive. Unfortunately, although one enemy convoy was destroyed and another forced to turn back to Greece, the inevitable result was to bring down the full weight of German and Italian air power onto his vessels. By 23 May, when Cunningham's surviving forces retired to the south, they had lost two cruisers and four destroyers sunk and two battleships and several other warships damaged. These were by any standards grievous losses.

While the air-sea battle was raging around Crete, and notwithstanding the fate of their merchant convoys, events on the ground began to move steadily in the Germans' favour. Although the paratroopers at Rethymnon and Heraklion had enough to do to stay alive, the loss of Maleme and the failure to crater its runway before the invasion now began to weigh heavily against Commonwealth and Greek forces. On 22 May an attempt to recapture Maleme collapsed, when Freyberg proved unwilling to release the necessary troops from coastal defence around Chania, and when those who were committed to the operation failed to set off on time and were stopped in daylight by German close air support and ground fire. On the same day three more battalions of 5th Mountain Division were flown in to Maleme, and, although in the process the Germans lost many more aircraft, the overall effect was to render their position invulnerable. Split into three units, on the morning of 23 May the mountain troops and remnants of Group West set off to push the New Zealanders out of artillery range of the airfield. The battle for Crete was about to be decided.

The Final Stages

The 72 hours from the initial landings on 20 May had seen the situation on Crete change completely. For all their gallantry the defenders had lost the initiative, and they were never to regain it. Conscious of the disastrous political ramifications should the entire New Zealand contingent be captured, Freyberg decided to order a withdrawal from the Maleme sector. Followed closely by the Germans, on 23 May New Zealand 5th Brigade retreated towards Galatas, at the northern end of the final defence line before Chania and Suda Bay. Almost simultaneously, contact was established between elements of 5th Mountain Division and the survivors of 3rd Parachute Rifle Regiment in the Aiya Valley. Supported by frequent air strikes from VIII Air Corps, together they began to prepare an attack to seize the Cretan capital and to break through to their beleaguered comrades in the east.

At dawn on 25 May, after a heavy air and mortar bombardment, the Germans commenced their assault. In a desperate, often hand-to-hand struggle in blistering heat, the battle swayed to and fro. As on most occasions during the island fighting few prisoners were taken by either side, and casualties rapidly mounted. But against the relatively fresh and newly supplied mountain troops, and in the face of almost complete Luftwaffe air supremacy, the outcome was in little doubt. On 26 May the defenders' line broke, and next day the Germans entered Chania.

The collapse of the last defensive position in western Crete made it clear that the battle was lost. Having informed Wavell that his soldiers had reached the limits of their endurance, on the afternoon of 27 May Freyberg received authorization to begin a withdrawal from the island. This was by no means easy, and a series of bloody rearguard actions ensued as the Germans sought to outflank and encircle the bulk of the garrison before it could retreat to the east. However, by the time Suda fell most of Freyberg's troops were already painfully hauling themselves across the winding mountain road that linked the northern sector with the village of Sfakión on the south coast. It was from here that the evacuation was mainly to take place.

The last few days of the battle for Crete saw fortune turn once again marginally in favour of the defenders. Determined to prevent a rallying of forces towards the other end of the island, the Germans focused their attention on an eastward drive that reached the remnants of 2nd Parachute Rifle and 1st Parachute Rifle Regiments at Rethymnon and Heraklion respectively on 29 May. In doing so they failed to notice that the direction of their enemy's withdrawal was actually to the south, so that although several thousand Australian prisoners were taken east of Rethymnon, the main Commonwealth forces were able to reach Sfakión unscathed, if exhausted. Because of the relatively short distance from North Africa to the southern shoreline of Crete, Royal Navy ships were able to make night crossings to rescue 4,000 troops from Heraklion on 29 May and another 12,000 from Sfakión between 28 May and 1 June. Tragically, hundreds of these were killed when the Heraklion convoy was struck by the Luftwaffe, and several ships were lost before the final evacuation took place, but this was still a significant achievement. Freyberg himself escaped by flying boat on 30 May.

The Aftermath

On Sunday, 1 June 1941, the fighting on Crete came to an end. The killing, however, did not stop, for the Germans had been incensed by the actions of the Cretan population during the battle and embarked on a campaign of retribution that was to drag on for months and cost hundreds of lives. Many of the defending soldiers also took refuge in the hills, and, although most were eventually hunted down, several hundred would eventually escape to continue the struggle. But for the rest of the Allied forces – 11,835 Commonwealth troops and all but 1,000 Greeks – a prison camp was all that could be expected. Added to the 4,200 soldiers and 2,000 sailors killed and wounded on the British side and the severe damage done to the Mediterranean Fleet and British prestige, this was indisputable evidence of a humiliating defeat.

By contrast, the Germans could claim a genuinely impressive and hard won victory. Whether or not in the long term it did more than make them commit yet another garrison to a secondary theatre is a matter for debate, but what is clear is that for the first time in warfare a force transported entirely by air had stormed and captured an island protected not only by large numbers of valiant defenders, but also by a powerful surface fleet. Nevertheless, the costs had been high: 7th Air Division alone had suffered over 4,500 casualties, and altogether 6,698 Germans were killed, wounded, or went missing during the battle. Also, 284 aircraft, among them 117 precious transports, were lost. But most significant of all was the psychological effect on the Führer himself. Although the German parachute arm would continue to expand and fight bravely until 1945, never again did the Germans carry out a large-scale airborne operation.

SIMON TREW

Further Reading

Beevor, A *Crete, the Battle and the Resistance* (London, 1991)

Hinsley, F H *British Intelligence in the Second World War, Volume I* (London, 1979)

MacDonald, C *The Lost Battle: Crete 1941* (London, 1993)

Vogel, D *Germany and the Second World War* (Oxford, 1995)

Operation Market-Garden

The Bridge at Arnhem

17 – 26 SEPTEMBER 1944

Allied 21st Army Group under Field Marshal
Sir Bernard L Montgomery
and First Allied Airborne Army under Lieutenant
General Lewis Brereton

VERSUS

Army Group B under Field Marshal Walther Model
and Armed Forces Command Netherlands under
General Friedrich Christiansen

CHRONOLOGY

17 September 1944 –	'Operation Market-Garden' begins
19 September 1944 –	XXX Corps reaches Nijmegen
20 September 1944 –	British form Oosterbeek pocket
21 September 1944 –	XXX Corps cross Nijmegen bridge; Germans recapture Arnhem bridge
26 September 1944 –	'Operation Berlin', the Allied withdrawal from Arnhem

*"In the annals of the British Army there are many glorious deeds…
But there can be few episodes more glorious than the epic of
ARNHEM, and those that follow after will find it hard to live up to
the standards that you have set… In years to come it will be a great
thing for a man to be able to say: 'I fought at ARNHEM'."*
MONTGOMERY TO URQUHART, 28 SEPTEMBER 1944

THE WORDS 'AIRBORNE ASSAULT' encapsulate all that is most exciting, daring, and dangerous in the profession of arms. Inserting lightly armed troops by air and using their speed and surprise to dislocate the enemy can bring about the most remarkable results, but it has always been a high-risk fighting method. World War II saw all manner of airborne assaults and the years 1940–45 were the brief but turbulent heyday of the large-scale airborne operation and the use of the parachute and the glider. 'Operation Market-Garden' was the largest airborne operation in history and, although conducted at a time when both Germany and the Soviet Union had lost faith in such assaults, aimed to end the war in Europe by Christmas 1944.

The Rival Plans

The Battle of Normandy was a disaster for Adolf Hitler. In trying to halt the Allied advance into France the Germans suffered very heavy casualties, and, by 3 September 1944, both Paris and Brussels had been liberated. General Dwight D Eisenhower, Supreme Commander of the Allied Expeditionary Forces, employed a broad fronted strategy during the campaign, and the speed of the Allied advance during the late summer led many Allied soldiers to think that the war in Europe was as good as won. However, Eisenhower's success during this period belied a number of growing problems that had to be sorted out with some urgency. These problems, ironically, were to a very large extent caused by the success of the Allied advance across France and Belgium – as Field Marshal Bernard Montgomery's 21st Army Group, led by British Second Army, was finding out.

Lieutenant General Sir Brian Horrocks's XXX Corps, the spearhead of Second Army, was advancing at a rate of 50 miles a day in late August, a rate of advance that just could not be sustained with supplies having to be brought up from the Normandy beaches some 300 miles to the rear. Halting for resupply, however, would have given the Germans exactly the sort of breathing space that they required to reorganize themselves, a situation that Montgomery thought could be avoided if Eisenhower allowed a narrow fronted thrust by 21st Army Group to crack open the German front before a rapid advance to Berlin. Montgomery continually badgered Eisenhower for a reorientation in strategy from mid-August onwards, but to no avail, and on 4 September Second Army's advance ground to a halt around Antwerp for want of supplies.

Nevertheless, six days after this loss of Allied momentum, Eisenhower finally agreed to some of Montgomery's wishes and to a scheme which aimed to use Lieutenant General Lewis Brereton's First Allied Airborne Army, sitting in reserve in Britain, to get Second Army moving again. 'Operation Market-

Garden' sought to insert three airborne divisions behind enemy lines to seize a number of vital bridges in the Netherlands over which Second Army would advance: the American 101st Airborne Division ('Screaming Eagles') around Eindhoven; the American 82nd Airborne Division ('All American') around Nijmegen; and the British 1st Airborne Division with the attached 1st Polish Independent Parachute Brigade around Arnhem. The aim was to pave the way for the capture of the Rhur, Germany's industrial heartland, and to end the war in Europe in just a few months. Planning started immediately on 10 September; the operation was to take place just seven days later.

The Germans that were facing this Allied onslaught were Field Marshal Walther Model's German Army Group B. It was Model's job to turn chaotic withdrawal into capable defence – and do it quickly. Under his command Model used the meagre forces of Colonel General Kurt Student's First Parachute Army and General Gustav von Zangen's Fifteenth Army to defend up to Nijmegen, while Kampfgruppe 'von Tettau' and Lieutenant General Willi Bittrich's II SS Panzer Corps, specialists in defence against airborne landings, were located around Arnhem. The two battered armoured divisions that made up Bittrich's II SS Panzer Corps, 9th SS Panzer Division and 10th SS Panzer Division, amounted to no more than 3,000 men each and had only about 12 functioning tanks between them. As a consequence, they were reconfigured as SS-Kampfgruppe 'Hohenstauffen' and SS-Kampfgruppe 'Frundsberg' respectively (a 'Kampfgruppe' or 'battlegroup' being an improvised formation smaller than a division).

The Allies were aware of German weaknesses, although the euphoria of their speedy advance and the amount of information flowing into various headquarters did tend to muddy the intelligence waters somewhat. Nevertheless, information from 'Ultra' codebreaking was reliable and 21st Army Group did have a good idea of enemy strengths and dispositions. Although not privy to Ultra intelligence, First Allied Airborne Army did know of the existence of II SS Panzer Corps at Arnhem and that it was very weak. However, although 'Operation Market-Garden' commanders did not necessarily lack information about the enemy, many did underestimate what the enemy was still capable of achieving. Model had created order out of disorder very quickly and, faced with defenders of the calibre of Student and Bittrich, Allied optimism was not well founded.

Major General Robert 'Roy' Urquhart, the commander of British 1st Airborne Division, was well aware that his troops would need speed and surprise if they were to attain their objectives, and had more reasons than most to be worried about the enemy's potential. His division, which had never fought together before, was being inserted some 64 miles behind enemy lines in daylight and up to 8 miles from their objectives, in airborne lifts that spanned over three days. Urquhart was concerned about the resistance that his men would meet in Arnhem.

The Airborne Assault

Sunday 17 September was warm, dry, and bright – ideal conditions for an airborne assault. German anti-aircraft defences were suppressed by Allied aircraft that morning and the airborne divisions began to land in the Netherlands soon after. By just after 2.00 p.m., some 20,000 combat troops, 511 vehicles, 330 artillery pieces, and 590 tons of equipment had been safely landed. Meanwhile, the lead element of XXX Corps, the Guards Armoured Division, opened the ground-based part of the operation and began to move forwards up the Eindhoven road from Neerpelt.

West of Arnhem, the landing of Brigadier 'Pip' Hicks's 1st Airlanding Brigade in 320 gliders and the drop of the 2,278 men of Brigadier Gerald Lathbury's 1st Parachute Brigade were extremely successful and met with very little German opposition. As the airlanding troops set off to defend their landing zones for the second lift, the parachutists prepared to march to their objectives. The 1st Battalion of the Parachute Regiment was to advance along 'Leopard' route to take the high ground to the north of Arnhem; 2nd Battalion followed by 1st Parachute Brigade Headquarters was to head along 'Lion' route and take the railway bridge and Arnhem road bridge, while 3rd Battalion was to push down 'Tiger' route and assist at Arnhem road bridge.

The first stubborn opposition that the 1st Parachute Brigade ran into was to have great consequences for the Battle of Arnhem. Training in the woods of Wolfheze just by the Landing Zones were 435 men of an SS battalion commanded by Major Sepp Krafft. Quickly appraising the situation and realizing that time was of the essence, Krafft moved his men into a defensive block. This immediately stopped the jeeps of an important *coup-de-main* force, Major 'Freddie' Gough's Reconnaissance Squadron, which had been sent along 'Leopard' route to seize the Arnhem road bridge. When 1st Battalion followed them a little later and found the route blocked, they desperately tried to outflank Krafft to the north, but finally gave up and headed southeast towards Oosterbeek.

Meanwhile, 2nd Battalion and 3rd Battalion were marching towards Arnhem. As they advanced there was little to slow them, but they were not moving fast enough for the liking of either Urquhart or Lathbury, a problem compounded by radio failure, which led to both men leaving their headquarters to personally urge the battalions on. The two commanders eventually met in Oosterbeek behind a 3rd Battalion that was stalling as they ran into more improvised opposition from SS-Kampfgruppe 'Spindler', and Urquhart found himself unable to return to headquarters.

From 1st Parachute Brigade, only Lieutenant Colonel John Frost's 2nd Battalion made substantial progress, and even then their railway bridge objective was blown up as they approached it. The relative speed of the battalion, however, meant that by the time most of them reached the Arnhem road bridge that evening, they found it virtually deserted. Although attempts to cross the bridge were thwarted by a German pillbox on the far side, by the end of the day Frost held a comfortable defensive position at the northern end consisting of 750 men, including 'C' Company of 3rd Battalion, who had managed to wriggle through the German defences, and some Reconnaissance Squadron men with Major Gough.

The Attempt to Break Through

Also by the end of 17 September, the Guards Armoured Division had managed to crack the outer crust of the German defences around the Dutch border and had reached Valkenswaard for the loss of nine tanks. However, the critical bridge at Son had been blown despite attempts by 101st Airborne to capture it intact, and the Germans' ability to stall XXX Corps' attack was evident in the first hours of the battle. The next day saw the reinforcement of all three airborne divisions. At 3.00 p.m. on 18 September west of Arnhem, 4th Parachute Brigade, divisional troops, and the remainder of 1st Airlanding Brigade touched down on Dutch soil. But the resupply drop that took place soon after their arrival was of very limited use as the drop zone was still in German hands.

At this point Brigadier Hicks, who had taken over command of the division in Urquhart's absence, sent 2nd South Staffordshire Regiment (one of the airlanding battalions) and 11th Battalion of the Parachute Regiment to reinforce 1st Battalion and 3rd Battalion, who were attempting to break through to the bridge from the west in the vicinity of St Elizabeth's hospital. In this confused street fighting Lathbury was wounded and Urquhart was forced to take refuge in an attic. At this critical stage in the battle, the division could ill-afford their commander not to be commanding.

Monday morning also saw an attack by yet another German formation, Kampfgruppe 'von Tettau' from the west, and with this 1st Airborne Division felt itself gradually being surrounded. At the bridge, however, Frost still felt confident despite probing assaults from the north by SS-Kampfgruppe 'Knaust', part of the 'Hohenstauffen' formation. This confidence was further

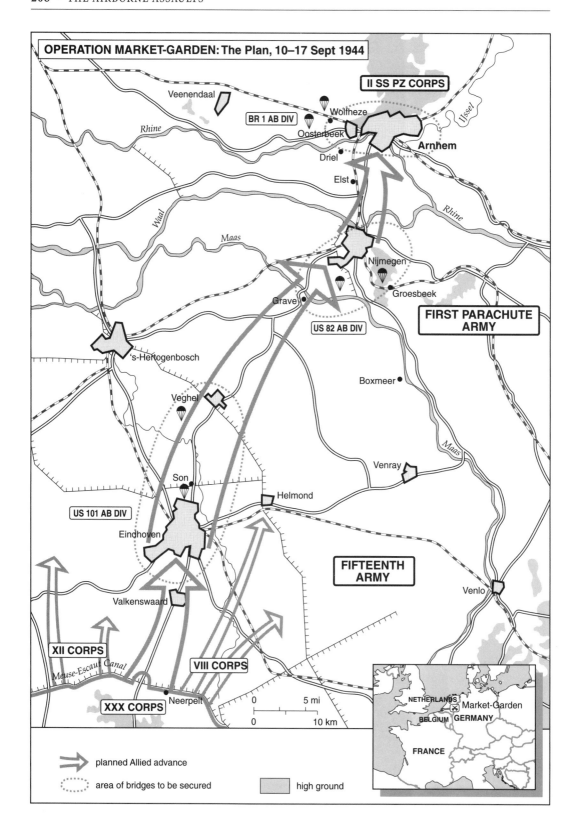

OPERATION MARKET-GARDEN: The Plan, 10–17 Sept 1944

Veenendaal

II SS PZ CORPS

BR 1 AB DIV

Wolfheze

Rhine

Oosterbeek

Arnhem

IJssel

Driel

Elst

Rhine

Waal

Maas

Nijmegen

Groesbeek

Grave

FIRST PARACHUTE ARMY

US 82 AB DIV

's-Hertogenbosch

Boxmeer

Veghel

Maas

Venray

Son

Helmond

US 101 AB DIV

Eindhoven

FIFTEENTH ARMY

Venlo

Valkenswaard

XII CORPS

Meuse-Escaut Canal

VIII CORPS

XXX CORPS

Neerpelt

0   5 mi

0   10 km

NETHERLANDS   Market-Garden

BELGIUM   GERMANY

FRANCE

→ planned Allied advance

⬭ area of bridges to be secured

▨ high ground

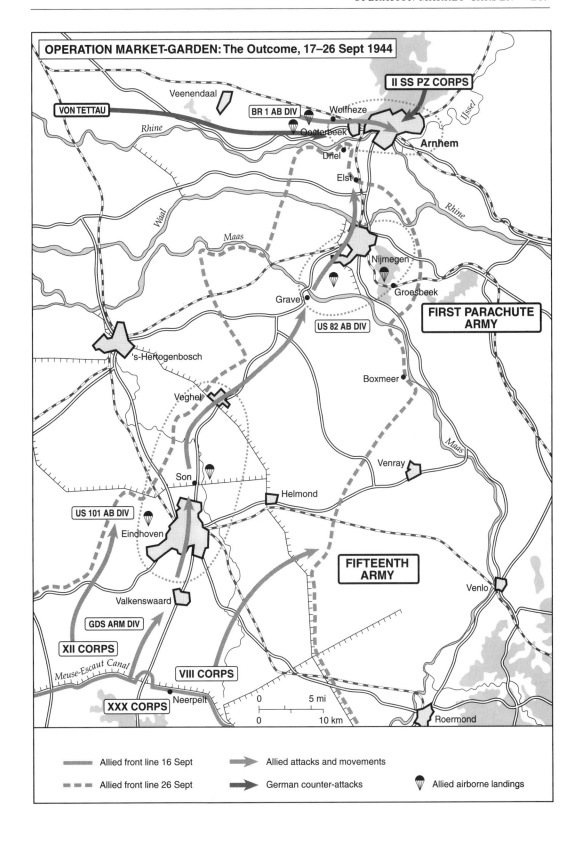

OPERATION MARKET-GARDEN: The Outcome, 17–26 Sept 1944

II SS PZ CORPS

Veenendaal

VON TETTAU

Rhine

BR 1 AB DIV

Wolfheze

Oosterbeek

Arnhem

IJssel

Driel

Elst

Rhine

Waal

Maas

Nijmegen

Grave

Groesbeek

US 82 AB DIV

FIRST PARACHUTE ARMY

's-Hertogenbosch

Boxmeer

Veghel

Maas

Venray

Son

Helmond

US 101 AB DIV

Eindhoven

FIFTEENTH ARMY

Venlo

Valkenswaard

GDS ARM DIV

XII CORPS

Meuse-Escaut Canal

VIII CORPS

XXX CORPS

Neerpelt

Roermond

0	5 mi
0	10 km

Allied front line 16 Sept   Allied attacks and movements

Allied front line 26 Sept   German counter-attacks   Allied airborne landings enhanced when at about 9.30 a.m. some 22 vehicles of 9th SS Reconnaissance Battalion returned from Nijmegen and tried to cross the bridge. Only the first few vehicles made it to the north side, but those that followed did not. In a battle that raged for several hours, the airborne troops stopped the Germans on the ramp of the bridge.

The battle in Arnhem certainly had not been progressing according to the Allied plans as expected. But by the evening of 18 September XXX Corps had linked up with 101st Airborne Division and had reached the blown Son bridge, where work on a Bailey bridge began immediately. As this was happening, 82nd Airborne, which had secured its other target bridges, endeavoured to take the Nijmegen road bridge – but the German defences held firm.

Tuesday 19 September brought with it little good news for British 1st Airborne: bad weather thwarted attempts to fly in the Polish Brigade; the attack of 4th Parachute Brigade supported by another airlanding battalion, 7th King's Own Scottish Borderers, was halted in the woods north of Oosterbeek. Various attacks around the St Elizabeth's hospital by a mixture of units, although releasing Urquhart from his attic to resume command, failed to break through to Frost at Arnhem bridge. These failures resulted in Urquhart pulling the remnants of his division back towards his headquarters at the Hartenstein Hotel in Oosterbeek.

Frost's men at the bridge were also under increasing pressure. German air raids, shelling and mortaring from the north and the east, cost the airborne troops heavy casualties, but even though ammunition, food, and water were all running low, little ground was conceded. It was now clear to Frost that he was unlikely to be reinforced by the rest of the division and that his lot was to hold on as long as possible with precious few resources and await the arrival of XXX Corps.

The Guards Armoured were making progress towards Arnhem – they crossed the newly constructed Son Bailey bridge and reached Grave that morning, but the advance of XXX Corps lacked momentum. American airborne troops attacked Nijmegen Bridge again that afternoon in order to give the tanks a clear run through – but again the German defenders were too strong. So keen was Major General 'Jumping Jim' Gavin, commander of the 82nd Airborne, to clear the way in front of XXX Corps, that he ordered an assault crossing of the River Waal in order to take the bridge from both ends. However, his men needed boats and these had to be brought up through the vehicle clogged highway. Time, clearly, was as much an enemy to the Allies during Market-Garden as the German themselves – and Model knew this.

Forming the Oosterbeek Perimeter

With German pressure on 1st Airborne Division increasing and, with no sign of the imminent arrival by XXX Corps, Urquhart decided on 20 September to defend a thumb-shaped perimeter at Oosterbeek, with its base on the river. The fact that troops were still fighting at Arnhem bridge certainly took some pressure off Urquhart's position, but Frost's men were suffering as the Germans systematically destroyed their buildings. The fragmented nature of the battle here also meant that coordination of the defence became increasingly difficult, and was hardly helped when Frost himself became a casualty and was put out of action. Gough took command of the remaining men and although able to negotiate a truce in order to evacuate some of the wounded into German care, he knew that the defenders could not fight for much longer.

As the leading tanks of XXX Corps crossed the Waal that evening after the successful assault crossing of the river by men of 82nd Airborne, they were close enough to see the smoke rising from Arnhem. But although only 8 miles from the town, the exhausted Guards Armoured, without infantry support or air cover and lacking artillery ammunition, stopped for the night.

The Fall of Arnhem Bridge

At Arnhem bridge the fighting continued during the morning of 21 September, but gradually petered out as the airborne troops were overrun. With the bridge open to German traffic, SS-Kampfgruppe 'Knaust' raced across and set up defensive positions south of Arnhem at Elst in order to halt XXX Corps. Meanwhile, in the Oosterbeek perimeter, Urquhart's men were finding it difficult to maintain their positions. That morning an attack by Kampfgruppe 'von Tettau' drove the third airlanding battalion and last divisional reserve, 1st Border Regiment, off the Westerbouwing Heights, the crucial high ground that overlooked the base of the divisional perimeter, the Heveadorp Ferry (out of action by this time) and the village of Driel on the far bank of the lower Rhine. From these heights German fire could dominate any attempted river crossing.

That 1st Airborne Division was not overwhelmed on this day was largely due to an advance by XXX Corps as far as Elst, and the subsequent skill with which their artillery laid down fire around the perimeter to suppress German attacks. As the battle for Elst raged that afternoon, most of 1st Polish Parachute Brigade, delayed since Tuesday, dropped at Driel under heavy German fire. That night the Poles planned a crossing of the lower Rhine to reinforce the perimeter, but, as with the American airborne troops at the Waal the day before, they first had to await the arrival of assault boats.

A brigade of 43rd (Wessex) Division attacked towards Driel the following morning, Friday 22 September, and completed the link up between XXX Corps and the airborne forces. But this was no time for self-congratulation, as Urquhart's division was in a precarious state and desperately required reinforcement. That evening 35 Poles managed to cross to Heveadorp in four rubber boats and joined the defensive of the perimeter, but so few made little difference to the division's prospects. As they crossed, the German commanders planned the final destruction of Urquhart's men for the next day. These German attempts to destroy the perimeter on Saturday 23 September were thwarted not only by the guns of XXX Corps, but also by close air support that the fine weather at last made possible. By this stage the fighting in Oosterbeek had developed into infantry probes, sniping and mortar attacks with the exhausted troops on both sides finding it difficult to stay awake. Nevertheless, the superior fire power of the Germans was beginning to tell, and, as at Arnhem bridge, the threat of being overrun was ever present. After nightfall a further 200 Poles crossed the river and plunged into the perimeter, but by the following day it had become clear to Urquhart that an evacuation of his division would have to take place soon.

A medical truce on Sunday 24 September allowed 1,200 wounded, many of whom were threatened with being burned alive in the cellars of the buildings that they were sheltering in, to be handed over to German medical staff. Thus, at the end of a day that saw the Germans unleash 15 of their heaviest tanks, the PzKw VIB King Tiger, against the eastern side of the perimeter, Urquhart was left with just 1,800 troops. There was plenty of activity at Heveadorp during the night of 24–25 September, as 315 men of the 4th Dorsetshire Regiment, part of 43rd Division, crossed the Lower Rhine and briefly held part of Westerbouwing. But German armour and infantry were slowly infiltrating the airborne positions and the withdrawal across the lower Rhine, 'Operation Berlin', had to take place that night.

The End at Arnhem

At 9.00 p.m. the evacuation began with a XXX Corps artillery bombardment that lasted 11 hours. British and Canadian engineers with 37 boats then started to cross the river. Leaving the wounded behind with volunteers, 1st Airborne withdrew to the river bank through the base of the perimeter which was a mere 750 yards wide. Although the Germans continued mortaring, the darkness and the heavy rain masked the evacuation and there was no attempt to attack and rout Urquhart's men. The little boats made many journeys across the lower Rhine that night, and only stopped when dawn made it too dangerous to continue. With the end of 'Operation Berlin' came also the end of 'Operation Market-Garden'.

In the Battle of Arnhem, 1,485 Allied troops were killed or died from their wounds, 3,910 came back in the evacuation over the river, and 6,525 became prisoners of war or attempted to evade capture. Approximately 2,250 of the prisoners were wounded. British 1st Airborne Division's casualty figures were twice as heavy as the combined totals for the two American airborne divisions. Second Army casualties were approximately 5,354, including 1,480 for XXX Corps. The German casualties are very difficult to assess: Model admitted to about 3,300, although other estimates put the figure as high as 8,000.

Clearly the cost of 'Operation Market-Garden', especially as it failed to achieve its objectives, was very high. The reasons for this failure are myriad and clearly show many of the difficulties involved in mounting successful airborne assaults. However, although it is easy in hindsight to say that 'Market-Garden' should never have taken place, we must remember the circumstances in which the operation was conceived, planned, and conducted. With the Germans on the retreat, September 1944 was the time for a daring operation to shorten the war and bold decisions had to be taken quickly if the opportunity was not to be lost. 'Market-Garden' was a sensibly conceived plan at the right time, but it was ultimately a plan flawed in too many ways to be a success. Nevertheless, to the British 1st Airborne Division who held on for the arrival of XXX Corps for so long, the Battle of Arnhem will always be seen as a victory.

LLOYD CLARK

Further Reading

Frost, J A *Drop Too Many* (London, 1980)

Kershaw, R *It Never Snows in September* (Marlborough, 1990)

Middlebrook, M *Arnhem 1944 – The Airborne Battle* (London, 1994)

Powell, G *The Devil's Birthday* (London, 1984)

Urquhart, R E *Arnhem* (London, 1958)

Operation Thursday
Wingate and the Chindits
5 MARCH – 27 AUGUST 1944

Japanese Fifteenth Army under Lieutenant General Mutaguchi
VERSUS
British Chindit Brigades under Major General Orde Wingate

CHRONOLOGY

5 February 1944 –	Chindit ground movement begins
5 March 1944 –	Chindit fly-in to 'Broadway' and 'Piccadilly' begins
15 March 1944 –	Japanese offensive against Imphal and Kohima begins
24 March 1944 –	Wingate killed in air crash near Bishenpur
27 March 1944 –	Japanese attacks on Chindit strongholds begin
10 May 1944 –	Chindit evacuations begin
17 May 1944 –	Myitkyina airfield captured
27 August 1944 –	Last Chindits are evacuated to India

"Our first task is fulfilled … all our columns are inside the enemy's guts. Let us press forward with our sword in the enemy's ribs to expel him from our territory." ORDE WINGATE

IN 1946 THE British Field Marshal Viscount Wavell wrote, 'All plans in the dubious hazard of war must have risks; the great commander is he who has both the courage to accept them and the skills to minimise them'. In both world wars individual commanders invariably emerged prepared to advance unorthodox ideas and take great, often spectacular risks. Major General Orde Wingate was indeed one such commander. While his operational skills and judgement continued to be questioned, his leadership arguably reflected these and many other qualities. The risk involved in 'Operation Thursday', one of the biggest airborne operations ever mounted, was to deploy a reinforced division of thousands of men chiefly by gliders and keep them supplied deep in the jungle, behind enemy lines in Japanese-occupied northern Burma.

The Strategic Context

Since Japan's entry into World War II in December 1941, the Burma theatre of war had received the lowest priority in the Allied war effort. Allied morale in this theatre had correspondingly reached its lowest ebb – prior to December 1943, British Commonwealth and US forces had experienced a virtually unbroken run of defeats at the hands of Imperial Japanese forces. The fall of Hong Kong and Singapore, and the humiliating retreat of British forces from Malaya and Burma in 1942, encouraged an image of Japanese troops as supermen. It was a perception reinforced yet again by the reversals of the first Arakan campaign of September 1942 to May 1943.

In the aftermath of these setbacks, however, came the first signs of a revival of Allied political and military resolve. At three top-level Anglo-American planning conferences held in 1943, Casablanca in January followed by the 'Trident' conference in Washington, DC, in May and 'Quadrant' in Quebec, Canada, in August, a new policy and command structure for the Southeast Asia theatre emerged. To give effect to the formation of the new Southeast Asia Command (SEAC), Admiral Lord Louis Mountbatten was appointed Supreme Commander on 25 August 1943, with the US Lieutenant General Joseph W Stilwell as his deputy. Known as 'Vinegar Joe', Stilwell was often rabidly anti-British in his attitudes. Equally significant was the appointment of General William ('Bill') Slim to command the British Fourteenth Army in Burma, a mixture of British, Commonwealth, and Imperial troops. Slim was a dynamic leader whose dedicated task was to restore the morale, fitness, and overall efficiency of the so-called 'Forgotten Army'.

Strategic imperatives were now, if anything, even more pressing. Not only were the British particularly anxious to halt the now imminent Japanese threat to India, the 'jewel' in their imperial crown, but the Americans desperately wanted to recover Burma as part of their overall strategy to both develop and rebuild China as an active theatre of military operations, and to re-establish overland communications with Chiang Kai-shek's regime at Chongqing.

In the midst of these changes in late 1943 stood a dynamic leader, Brigadier Orde Wingate. He had already gained wide experience of irregular warfare, in Palestine in the 1930s, and Ethiopia and Burma during the war, and he was now anxious to promote and extend his revolutionary tactics of deep penetration behind enemy lines. These tactics, Wingate insisted, would both forestall and undermine what he – rightly – predicted was an imminent Japanese offensive against the Allied garrisons at Kohima and Imphal in Spring 1944.

The Allied Plan

Wingate's battle plans under the code name 'Operation Thursday' represented a more complex version of his original conception of the use of Long Range Patrol (LRP) forces as a means of penetrating deep into enemy-held territory. His small, lightly equipped 'columns' of infantry were initially designed to raid lines of communication and direct aircraft onto suitable targets. A small-scale version of this concept had already been tried earlier in 1943 with mixed results. In 'Operation Longcloth', two groups of Wingate's Chindits (a corruption of *chinthé*, the Burmese for lion) had crossed the River Chindwin into the jungle to harass Japanese communications, but were eventually withdrawn on 24 March 1943 after encountering stiff Japanese resistance and suffering heavy losses due to disease as much as combat.

Wingate's tactics had caught the imagination not only of the British public but also of Prime Minister Winston Churchill and President Franklin Roosevelt, both of whom he met at the 1943 Quebec conference. Churchill, always favouring unorthodox commanders, was captivated by both Wingate's messianic zeal and his claim to be able to destroy the myth of Japanese invincibility. 'Wingate should command the army against Burma', he declared, 'He is a man of genius and audacity and has rightly been discerned by all eyes as a figure quite above the ordinary level'. Such higher support was sufficient to overcome the major political obstacles Wingate faced at local level, with considerable distrust and scepticism directed towards him by the more orthodox senior officers in both India and Burma.

The purpose of 'Operation Thursday' was to act as an integral of the Allied second Arakan campaign of December 1943–April 1944 and further advance Wingate's tactical concept of the 'stronghold'. This involved establishing powerful fortified encampments protected by mines, machine guns, and wire from which marauding columns would attack weakly held Japanese supply and communication centres, principally at Myitkyina, Mogaung, and Indaw. On 14 February 1944, Wingate was accordingly given three key tasks or aims by Slim. These were, in order of importance: first, to help the advance of Stilwell's Chinese-American forces on Myitkyina airfield by drawing off forces opposing it and preventing reinforcements from reaching them; secondly, to create a favourable situation for the Nationalist Chinese Yunnan Armies to advance westwards from China; and finally, Wingate was tasked to inflict overall maximum damage, confusion, and loss on the Japanese in northern Burma.

To facilitate these objectives Wingate was to specifically operate in the oblong-shaped area bounded by Mogaung, Bhamo, Pinlebu, and Lonkin. The four designated assembly places originally selected, open clearings in the jungle that were in Slims' words 'fancy names written on a map', were called 'Aberdeen', 'Piccadilly', 'Broadway', and 'Chowringhee'. All these sites were based away from roads, near water supplies, and consisted of largely flat ground for landing purposes. Wingate's initial plans comprised three complementary and interlocking deployments. Chindit 16th Brigade under Colonel Bernard Fergusson would march south from Ledo towards Indaw. Then 77th Brigade under Colonel Michael Calvert, a close disciple of Wingate and his tactics, would be flown by glider to 'Broadway' and 'Piccadilly' in the Kaukkwe Valley, where it was known that their gliders could land. Finally, 111th Brigade under Brigadier D W A Lentaigne would follow 77th Brigade, also in gliders and in aircraft.

The problems were immense. In Wingate's view the number of gliders and, in particular, troops designated for 'Operation Thursday' were insufficient; in fractious meetings with Slim he demanded four extra infantry battalions to garrison his strongholds. In the end he was awarded only one, the other three weak battalions to come from 3rd West African Brigade. So the remaining three Chindit brigades, 14th Brigade, 23rd Brigade, and 3rd West African Brigade, were held back for the second wave of fly-ins. In addition to this there were the ever-present risks of largely unknown terrain, dispersed enemy patrols, and the inevitable debilitating climate which harboured a whole host of potentially fatal jungle diseases, such as beri-beri, amoebic dysentery, and malaria.

The Japanese Plan

It was evidence of this Allied revival and renewal in late 1943, coupled with acute awareness of the potential of LRP forces following Wingate's first Chindit expedition, which catalysed the Japanese high command into plans for a pre-emptive offensive. The adage that 'offence is the best method of defence' played a key role in Japanese as well as British strategic planning. The commander of the Japanese Fifteenth Army, General Mutaguchi, therefore focused his thoughts upon Imphal and Kohima, both of which offered a gateway to India. In October 1943, Mutaguchi's staff began detailed planning and, on 7 January 1944, Imperial Headquarters in Tokyo issued the necessary orders. Three Japanese divisions – 15th Infantry Division, 31st Infantry Division, and 33rd Infantry Division – would cross the Chindwin River on 15 March 1945, two of them heading for Imphal and the third for Kohima. Despite being outnumbered and outgunned by the British IV Indian Corps defending Kohima and Imphal, and potentially outflanked by Stilwell's Chinese-American forces (together with his irregular 'Galahad' force, later known as 'Merrill's Marauders') the Japanese hoped to break through British defences by using surprise tactics of encirclement and night attack, so cutting communications.

The Opening Moves

In the event, it was Wingate's daring interposition behind Japanese lines which, by great fortune, itself pre-empted the Japanese Imphal–Kohima offensive by over a week. On Sunday 5 March 1944, after weeks of gruelling training and meticulous planning, the first wave of 83 RAF and USAAF transport aircraft, the C-47 Douglas Dakota ('Skytrain'), and 80 gliders carrying 77th Brigade were ready for take-off. It was one of the most original and dangerous exploits of the war. This glider force of 12,000 men was being deployed not into the flat fields of Normandy or Holland, but tugged over mountain ranges 7,000 ft high, aiming in pitch darkness at small jungle clearings with little scope for overshoot or second runs, and with the ever-present danger of Japanese ambush. The three brigades that made the initial Chindit deployment were to play a key role in the second Arakan offensive.

The problems of air reconnaissance were evident from the start of the operation. Literally at Zero Hour on 5 March, Wingate's plans faced crisis when US pilots of the Allied Air Commando (the improvised airforce formed to support the Chindits) flew in with two-hour-old photographs showing the 'Piccadilly' landing ground mysteriously obstructed by tree trunks. After tense negotiations between Slim, Wingate, and Calvert and other senior officers, during which a distraught Wingate voiced fears of betrayal and possible ambush, the courageous decision was taken to proceed. A reduced number of 61 gliders eventually took off, of which only 35 reached 'Broadway'. Calvert's initial despair led him to prematurely use the codeword for disaster for his brigade, 'Soya Link' (a reference to the most hated item in British rations). But this was soon reversed when a clearer picture emerged and it was clear that despite a few catastrophic crashes, there had been no Japanese ambush. Nevertheless, 30 men were killed and 20 wounded out of 400 on this first day, while of those planes and gliders that failed to reach 'Broadway', 66 men perished. After this, roughly 100 Dakotas arrived nightly at 'Broadway' and 'Piccadilly', ultimately bringing in around 12,000 men and 2,000 mules with sufficient supplies of weapons, ammunition, and food.

The initial landings had therefore been a success: the only Japanese response was a futile air attack on Chowringhee on 10 March, occurring a couple of hours after Lentaigne's 111th Brigade had marched off, leaving only derelict gliders behind. By 13 March Wingate felt confident enough to proclaim, 'Our first task is fulfilled... this is a moment to live in history'. The Chindit success can be measured by the extent of Japanese confusion, with 'lost' gliders landing all over the Indaw area ironically adding to their disarray. Moreover, the sudden appearance of a flight of Supermarine Spitfires of 221 Group RAF, significantly superior to the main Japanese 'Zero' fighter, also cost the Japanese over half of their local air strength in their first abortive attacks on the stronghold positions.

With 'Broadway' stronghold fortified and securely garrisoned by 77th Brigade (three British battalions and one of Gurkhas) and morale massively boosted by a flying visit from Wingate, the stage was set for the next stage of the plan: the establishment of the 'White City' stronghold. Calvert accordingly marched a strong force of about half his brigade to block the main Japanese road and railway depot at Mawlu. A vicious but victorious hand-to-hand battle at Pagoda Hill, near Henu village, cost the Chindits 69 casualties and led to the award of a posthumous Victoria Cross to Lieutenant George Cairns, who continued fighting even after losing his arm – severed by a Japanese sword! Nearby, Calvert chose the site for 'White City' (named after the scores of white supply parachutes adorning the trees), an ideal position with good water supply and visibility for its defenders. As at 'Broadway', mines, fire zones, barbed wire, and trenches were established in preparation for the expected Japanese attacks. The first serious attack, by five companies of the Japanese 18th Infantry Division, was repelled deploying a coordinated fire plan, intense mortar fire, and continual air strikes by US P-51 Mustang aircraft.

Meanwhile the third key Chindit formation, Fergusson's 16th Brigade, although exhausted by its long march of over 50 days from Ledo, was in position to establish the 'Aberdeen' stronghold at the junction of Kalat Chaung and the Meza River. Despite Fergusson's reservations, Wingate insisted he move on to attack Indaw, where he would be reinforced by 14th Brigade. This deployment led to further personal clashes between Slim and Wingate, who again demanded more reinforcements.

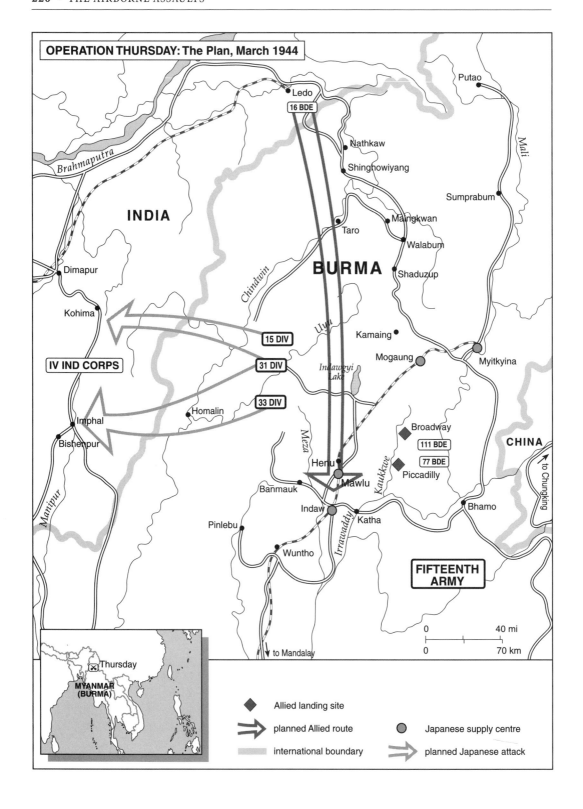

OPERATION THURSDAY: The Plan, March 1944

Legend:
- ◆ Allied landing site
- ➡ planned Allied route
- ▬ international boundary
- ◯ Japanese supply centre
- ➡ planned Japanese attack

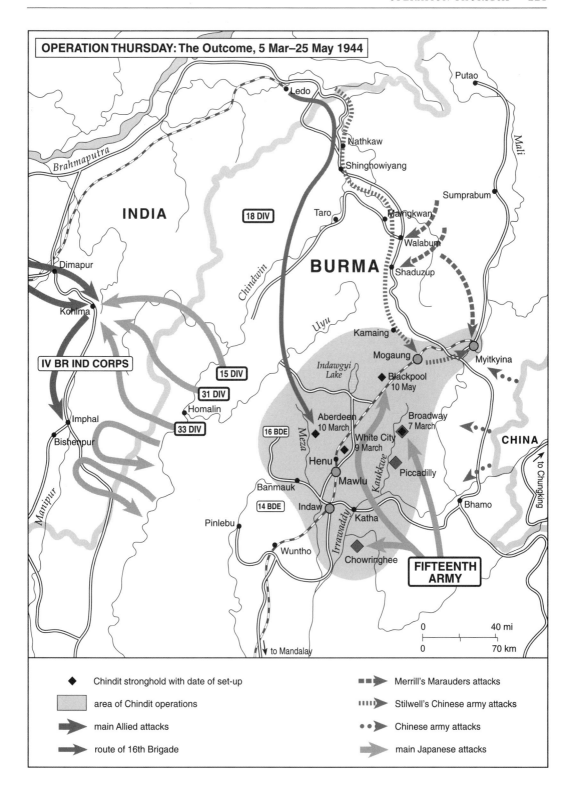

OPERATION THURSDAY: The Outcome, 5 Mar–25 May 1944

Putao

Ledo

Nathkaw

Shinghowiyang

Sumprabum

Brahmaputra

INDIA

18 DIV

Taro

Maingkwan

Walabum

Mali

BURMA

Shaduzup

Chindwin

Dimapur

Kamaing

Uyu

Kohima

Mogaung

Myitkyina

IV BR IND CORPS

Indawgyi Lake

◆ Blackpool
10 May

15 DIV

31 DIV

Homalin

Aberdeen
10 March

Broadway
7 March

CHINA

Imphal

33 DIV

16 BDE

Meza

White City
9 March

Bishenpur

Henu

◆ Piccadilly

to Chungking

Kaukkwe

Banmauk

Mawlu

Manipur

14 BDE

Indaw

Katha

Bhamo

Pinlebu

Irrawaddy

Wuntho

Chowringhee

FIFTEENTH
ARMY

0   40 mi

0   70 km

↓ to Mandalay

◆   Chindit stronghold with date of set-up

▪▪▶ Merrill's Marauders attacks

     area of Chindit operations

▮▮▮▶ Stilwell's Chinese army attacks

➤   main Allied attacks

●●▶ Chinese army attacks

➤   route of 16th Brigade

➤   main Japanese attacks

The Change of Plan

The main Japanese attack on Kohima and Imphal began on 15 March, with Wingate's three brigades deep in their rear. Road, rail, and river transport to the northern Japanese divisions around Kohima and Imphal were completely halted by continual Chindit forays. It was not until 27 March that 'Broadway' was attacked by the Japanese, confirming the extent of surprise that the Chindits had achieved. When several battalions from 56th Infantry Division in Yunnan finally arrived at 'Broadway' they were bloodily repulsed by the British and Gurkhas. But the Chindits also experienced their first major setback with the tragic loss of their leader. Wingate was killed on 27 March in an air crash near Bishenpur. His successor was Lentaigne of 111th Brigade, not known for his personal empathy for Wingate or for his total support of the unorthodox Chindit tactics.

The end of March represented the critical turning point for the Chindits. Until then, Japanese attacks on both 'Broadway' and 'White City' had been successfully repulsed. From early April, however, it was clear that the impact of 'Operation Thursday', particularly following the death of its inspired leader, would be more limited. Fergusson's attacks on Indaw stalled, arguably because Wingate had, in ordering the attack just before his death, abandoned his basic principle that LRP columns should not attack prepared enemy fortified positions. On 9 April, in the wake of this problem and the growing awareness that the small numbers of Chindits could not decisively influence the savage struggle now taking place around Imphal, Lentaigne, Slim, and Mountbatten decided that the Chindits would be redeployed. Their new task would be to help Stilwell's Chinese-American forces. Lentaigne's plan now envisaged the remaining 4th Brigade, 77th Brigade, 11th Brigade, 14th Brigade, and 3rd West African Brigade attacking Mogaung from the south.

The Chindits were now being drawn more and more into action as conventional troops, the last gasps of 'Operation Thursday' took place. From 6 April 'White City' came under sustained Japanese attack. In fighting on 10–11 April one Japanese battalion alone lost 700 men, and eyewitnesses recalled how the stench of death lay everywhere, with up to 1,000 rapidly putrefying bodies hanging in the wire or rotting in the minefield. The use of flame-throwers to dispose of corpses proved futile, and even pilots evacuating the wounded knew from the smell that they were approaching 'White City'.

On 10 May, 'White City' was finally abandoned and Brigadier John Masters, Lentaigne's successor as commander of 111th Brigade, established a last major stronghold at 'Blackpool' with 2,000 British and Gurkha troops. But by the end of May, things began to go wrong for the garrison at

'Blackpool', which was sited too close to the Japanese garrison at Mogaung. Once 'White City' was evacuated, the Japanese 53rd Infantry Division was able to move safely up the railway corridor unopposed and attack the incomplete 'Blackpool' defences. The creation of 'Blackpool' also ignored vital Chindit principles as defined by Wingate – there was no element of surprise, no floater columns, several of the key leaders were frequently absent from the front line defensive positions, and the concept of avoiding enemy artillery was clearly abandoned as Japanese 105-mm shells and the dreaded 6-in mortars rained incessantly on the Chindit positions. By 25 May the area was evacuated in a virtual mire of mud and rain amidst horrendous scenes, as several critically wounded men had to be dispatched by single shots to avoid imminent capture and possible torture by the Japanese. 'Operation Thursday' was effectively over.

The Aftermath

From 17 May the remaining Chindit Brigades were officially assigned to Stilwell's command, as part of his plan to capture Kamaing, Mogaung, and the Myitkyina airfield. On 26 June a weary 77th Brigade under Calvert, reduced to 150 men after a series of fierce actions and astonishingly without artillery or tank support, finally captured Mogaung. By the end of June it was clear that both the 77th and 111th Brigades were worn out. Many men were ridden with malaria, with the loss of weight averaging three stones per man. Although 14th Brigade remained in action up to 3 August when Myitkyina fell to the Americans, by 27 August the last of the Chindits had been evacuated to India. The total losses of the LRP Chindit Brigades amounted to 3,628 killed, wounded, and missing – roughly one-fifth of the total ultimately deployed. There is no precise figure for Japanese losses incurred specifically at the hands of the Chindits. But the Japanese Fifteenth Army lost 30,502 out of 84,280 men in the Kohima–Imphal battles, and up to 5,000 of these casualties may have been caused by the Chindit operations.

Wingate has been accused of being over-ambitious, unstable, and arrogantly stubborn. His critics have further claimed that his military operations were either ill-planned or ill-conducted and, consequently, tragically wasteful of both men and resources. It is the enemy's view which provides an interesting and possibly more balanced appraisal of the military achievements of 'Operation Thursday'. In the view of many Japanese historians Wingate decisively tipped the scales of the Kohima–Imphal battles by disorganizing their lines of communication, attracting a significant part of their air strength, and, in particular, robbing them of 20 companies of transport which were destroyed on the road to Homalin, the key crossing point of the Chindwin River. Together these actions prevented Mutaguchi's offensive from developing its full momentum, and so by the narrowest of margins it failed. One Japanese officer tellingly recorded in his diary, 'what happened in Burma? We must not forget Major General Wingate. He reduced the Japanese power to wage war on the four Burmese fronts and so fatally affected the balance. In this alone he showed himself a great general'.

EDMUND YORKE

Further Reading

Bidwell, S *The Chindit War* (London, 1979)

Calvert, M *Prisoners of Hope* (London, 1952)

Rooney, D *Wingate and the Chindits* (London, 1994)

Slim, W *Defeat Into Victory* (London, 1956)

THE CITY BATTLES

"What is the position about London? I have a very clear view that we should fight for every inch of it, and that it would devour quite a large invading army." WINSTON CHURCHILL, 2 JULY 1940

THROUGHOUT HISTORY BEFORE the 20th century, military commanders expected to fight battles on land away from towns and cities. The very word 'campaign' derives from the French for 'countryside'. Cities might be fortified, and subject to sieges and even to assaults, but these were regarded as a different aspect of war. It was not until the massive growth of cities in the later 19th century that the prospect emerged of actually having to fight house-to-house through miles of urban stone, brick, and rubble, and this was largely avoided in World War I, at least in the West. The size of 20th-century cities, the manner in which they lent themselves to the defence, the need for heavy firepower from tanks and artillery to blast through, and the way in which they absorbed infantry on all sides, all made the city battles of World War II a distinct and terrible new form of war. Wherever possible, attackers would avoid trying to fight through a city; sometimes there was no choice, or defenders could suck them into such a battle. Once a city battle had started, even getting out of it could prove impossible, while winning was often a case of how far either side was prepared to go.

Stalingrad
The City of the Sword
13 SEPTEMBER 1942 – 2 FEBRUARY 1943

German Sixth Army under General Friedrich Paulus
VERSUS
Soviet 62nd Army under Lieutenant General Vasili Chuikov

CHRONOLOGY

5 April 1942 –	Hitler issues Directive 41
23 August 1942 –	German troops cut the River Volga
12 September 1942 –	Chuikov takes command
14 September 1942 –	The first German attack
27 September 1942 –	The second German attack
14 October 1942 –	The third German attack
19 November 1942 –	Soviet 'Operation Uranus' begins
23 November 1942 –	Sixth Army encircled in Stalingrad
10 January 1943 –	Soviet 'Operation Koltso' begins
31 January 1943 –	Paulus surrenders
2 February 1943 –	End of German resistance in Stalingrad

"The front is a corridor between burnt out rooms; it is the thin ceiling between two floors. Help comes from neighbouring houses by fire escapes and chimneys. There is a ceaseless struggle from noon to night. From story to story, we bombard each other with grenades in the middle of explosions, clouds of dust and smoke, heaps of mortar, floods of blood, fragments of furniture and human beings."
LIEUTENANT WIENER, 24TH PANZER DIVISION

Even among the annals of the city battles of World War II, each of them a hard-fought nightmare of death and destruction, the legendary name of Stalingrad evokes a shudder from all who know of it. The battle of Stalingrad, which lasted from 13 September 1942 until the German surrender on 2 February 1943, represented the spiritual tomb of the German Army. It might have taken three years to confirm, but it was here among the ruins of a shattered, unrecognizable city that the pendulum of victory began to swing towards the Red Army and the outcome of the war on the Eastern Front was decided. General Friedrich Paulus, the commander of the German Sixth Army, had felt confident, when launching the first German assault on Stalingrad, of a rapid and decisive victory. In fact, he had committed his army to a struggle that would last over 100 days and nights, and that would end in its destruction.

The Origins of the Battle

Why, if it was to prove so disastrous, were the Germans fighting for Stalingrad, on the banks of the River Volga, the area generally considered to mark the southern border of Europe and Asia? By 1942 the Third Reich found itself engaged in a war against Britain, with the largest empire in the world, the USA, the greatest economic power in the world, and the Soviet Union, which possessed the largest army in the world. It appeared to be imperative that Germany defeat the Soviet Union in 1942, or deal the Soviets a series of such crushing blows that any continued resistance would represent nothing more than a minor nuisance, enabling Germany to turn west and confront Britain and the USA. The Soviet Union's priority was the rebuilding of its shattered war economy, in order to replenish and retrain the Red Army after the mauling it had suffered in 1941, while protecting the industrial and oil resources of the Stalingrad and Caucasus region. In addition, the Soviet Union would seek to exploit its new links with Britain and the USA while ensuring that Moscow remained secure from German attack.

The German Plan

On 5 April 1942, Hitler issued 'Führer Directive 41' for what came to be code-named *Fall Blau* ('Operation Blue'), deciding that the best way to achieve the emasculation of the Soviet Union would be to destroy its armies in the south and simultaneously starve it of its oil from the Caucasus region by cutting the River Volga, just above Stalingrad. This would render the Red Army immobile, leaving the Soviet Union defenceless and German victory inevitable.

The actual taking of the city of Stalingrad, rather than merely the masking of it, merited no mention in Hitler's directive. This was why General Hans Hube's XIV Panzer Corps arrived on the banks of the Volga on 23 August 1942, cutting the river and with it Soviet oil supplies, thus fulfilling the original mission laid down in Directive 41. Yet, because of the ease with which the Germans had driven the Soviets back to the Volga, Hitler had changed his mind: the city he was to become obsessed with, he now decided, must be taken by Sixth Army.

The Soviet Plan

The speed of the German advance towards Stalingrad in July and August 1942 can be explained by the Soviets' failure to appreciate German intentions. A highly effective German deception plan, 'Operation Kremlin', successfully persuaded Joseph Stalin that the main strategic objective of the German summer offensive was Moscow. As a consequence of this error, the majority of Soviet reserves were pinned down in the Moscow region. Stalin also insisted, against the wishes of senior commanders, on a localized Soviet offensive at Kharkov. This offensive, which lasted from 12 to 17 May, had been anticipated by the Germans, who inflicted a crushing defeat upon the Red Army, which suffered 220,000 casualties in five days.

The absence of these troops, along with the Soviet commitments around Moscow, forced Stalin on 6 July to permit his generals to adopt a strategy of trading space for time. In July and August the Germans took relatively few Soviet prisoners – 54,000, a small number compared to the millions fighting on the Eastern Front. But they drove the dispirited Red Army before them across the River Don and into the city of Stalingrad, where it was envisaged that after a short but futile struggle they would be put to the sword. In their hearts many Soviets agreed with this assessment, including General Alexander Lopatin, the commander of 62nd Army, which was charged with defending the city.

On 12 September, Lopatin was replaced by the man who would become synonymous with the Soviet triumph at Stalingrad: Lieutenant General Vasili Chuikov. He had been the Soviet military attaché to China since the outbreak of war in the east, and had seen no action until June 1942. However, in contrast to the more studious Paulus commanding German Sixth Army, Chuikov was a born fighter – tough, decisive, extraordinarily bloody-minded, and, above all, an optimist. His orders were simple. Given its importance to the Soviet war effort and pivotal position on the Volga lifeline, Stalingrad could not be given up. There was to be no more retreat.

The City of Stalingrad

Stalingrad was no ordinary Soviet city. Originally known as Tsaritsyn (and later renamed Volgograd), it had been the site of a decisive Red Army victory over the Whites in the Russian Civil War of 1918–21. Stalin had been instrumental in this struggle, and later he named the city for himself, a fact that was certainly not lost on Adolf Hitler. Stalingrad had been designated a beacon of revolutionary endeavour and a major industrial centre of the Soviet war effort, with factories and plants, including a large and famous tractor factory that would feature heavily in the battle.

The city was a distinctly odd shape, stretching like a ribbon 15 miles in a north–south direction on the western bank of the Volga, but only 4 miles wide. Chuikov appreciated that the Germans were a formidable enemy, due primarily to their ability to integrate air power, tanks, and infantry in a way that no other army appeared capable of doing. Nevertheless, he also understood that such methods, while devastating in open country, would be difficult to use in the tangled and confined surroundings of a city. The German infantry would have to engage in close-quarter fighting, in circumstances where it would be less than easy to bring armour and air power to bear. Chuikov sought to ensure that Soviet infantry remained as close to their German counterparts as possible, denying the Luftwaffe the opportunity to roam the skies in its usual style and numbers for fear of hitting their own troops. German tanks also found that the claustrophobic city environment prevented them from manoeuvring en masse and blasting holes for the infantry to follow through. Soviet 'tank-killing' squads quickly ensured that German infantry had to fight their own way forward with fixed bayonets, a task with which they were unaccustomed and disliked.

These tactics ensured that the battle, although an awful trial of strength for the Soviet 62nd Army, was fought on terms whereby they stood some chance of success. Soviet troops showed a deadly expertise among the rubble-strewn streets and buildings, especially at night. In contrast Sixth Army, although a powerful opponent, struggled to come to terms with the anarchic nature of street fighting. To soldiers schooled, to an unprecedented degree of excellence, in large-scale manoeuvre, a world of sewers, buildings, grenades, improvised squads, bayonets, shovels, and daggers was one challenge too many.

The First German Assaults

The days when Chuikov could be confident of emerging victorious at Stalingrad were a long way off at the start of the battle. On 14 September, two days after he had taken command, Sixth Army launched a massive assault led by LI Corps which attacked the southern end of the city centre in a two-pronged assault. The German thrust led by 71st Division, 76th Division, and 295th Division tore into the city centre. Simultaneously, 94th Division and 29th Motorized Division supported by 14th Panzer Division and 24th Panzer Division smashed into the southern suburb of Yelshanka. The German objective was the central pier landing stage on the banks of the Volga, which was nearly a mile wide at this point. This would cut the lifeline of the Soviet forces in the city on the western bank from the reserves and supplies on the far side of the Volga. If the Germans could isolate the fighting in the city from the Soviet base on the eastern bank for any prolonged period of time, then the battle would be over before it had really begun.

The northern German thrust headed for the main railway station known as Stalingrad-1. If they took this, they would indeed be able to bring the central landing stage under sustained fire. The Soviet forward defences were overwhelmed, and Chuikov's command post on the high ground known as the Mamayev Kurgan was obliterated, leaving him unable to contact his troops. In the course of 14 September the station changed hands four times but was back under Soviet control before nightfall.

In the southern suburbs the Soviets were being driven back to the river with heavy casualties. It was clear to Chuikov that if his men were to hold on, Major General Alexander Rodimstev's 13th Guards Division had to come across the river into the city, despite the danger of being attacked as they disembarked. During the night, the 13th Guards suffered 1,000 casualties crossing the Volga but were in position to receive the next wave of German attacks at dawn. The fight for the station raged for three more days, and it changed hands 15 times before the Germans finally secured it. The Mamayev Kurgan remained unclaimed, neither side able to muster the strength to evict the other.

By 19 September the fighting died down, but there was no doubt the Germans had won a significant tactical victory. They had reached the river and isolated 62nd Army in the city. The Soviets had barely survived, and it was unlikely they could have defeated another major attack. The 13th Guards Division, 10,000 strong on the morning of 15 September, now mustered barely 2,500 troops. Yet their sacrifice had saved the city. The Germans had suffered grievously for their small triumphs and, faced with shocking casualties and savage resistance, no longer displayed their customary confidence. In the southern outskirts of the city they had come across an enormous grain elevator, which was defended to the last by 50 Soviet soldiers, who managed to drag in three German divisions before being overwhelmed.

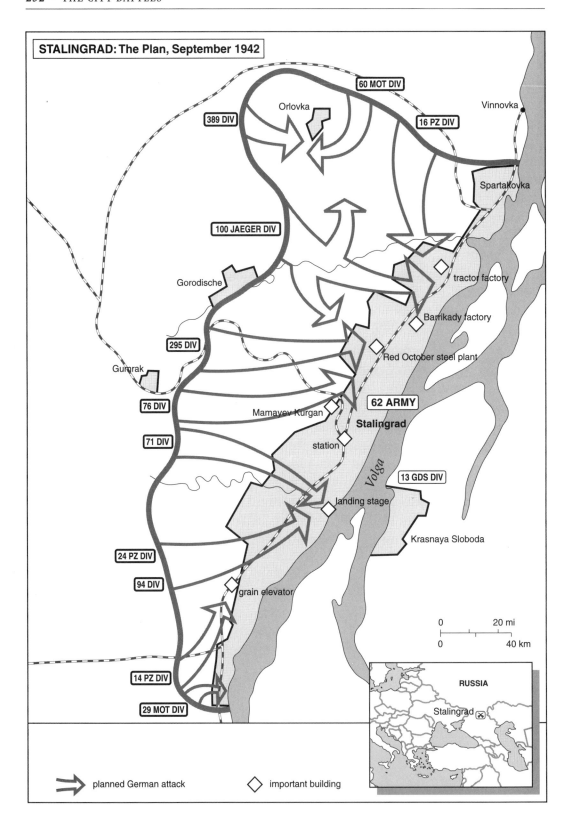

STALINGRAD: The Plan, September 1942

60 MOT DIV

389 DIV

16 PZ DIV

Vinnovka

Orlovka

Spartakovka

100 JAEGER DIV

Gorodische

tractor factory

Barrikady factory

295 DIV

Red October steel plant

Gumrak

76 DIV

62 ARMY

71 DIV

Mamayev Kurgan

Stalingrad

station

Volga

13 GDS DIV

landing stage

Krasnaya Sloboda

24 PZ DIV

94 DIV

grain elevator

0   20 mi

0   40 km

14 PZ DIV

RUSSIA

29 MOT DIV

Stalingrad

⟹ planned German attack   ◇ important building

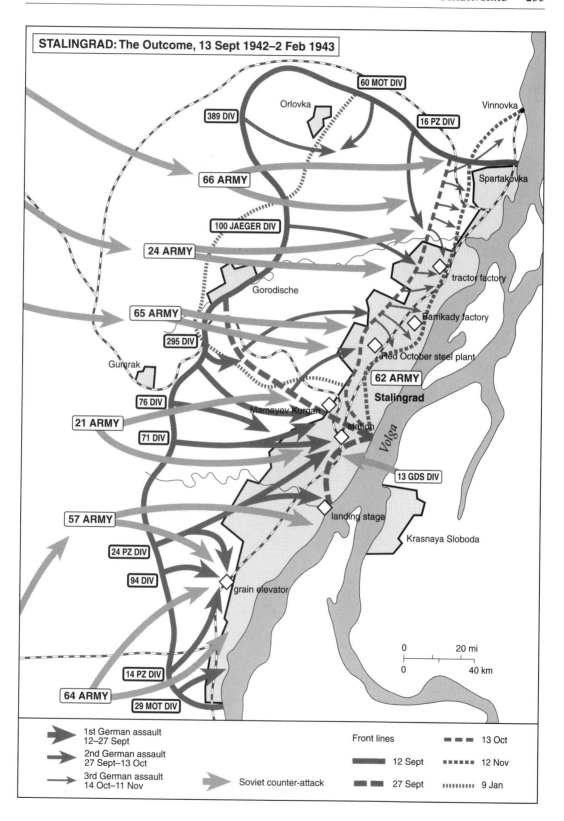

STALINGRAD: The Outcome, 13 Sept 1942–2 Feb 1943

60 MOT DIV

Orlovka

Vinnovka

389 DIV

16 PZ DIV

Spartakovka

66 ARMY

100 JAEGER DIV

24 ARMY

tractor factory

Gorodische

65 ARMY

Barrikady factory

295 DIV

Red October steel plant

Gumrak

62 ARMY

Stalingrad

76 DIV

Mamayev Kurgan

21 ARMY

station

71 DIV

Volga

13 GDS DIV

57 ARMY

landing stage

24 PZ DIV

Krasnaya Sloboda

94 DIV

grain elevator

| 0 | | 20 mi |
| 0 | | 40 km |

14 PZ DIV

64 ARMY

29 MOT DIV

1st German assault
12–27 Sept

Front lines

13 Oct

2nd German assault
27 Sept–13 Oct

12 Sept

12 Nov

3rd German assault
14 Oct–11 Nov

Soviet counter-attack

27 Sept

9 Jan

It quickly became clear to the German soldiers that this was to be a duel to the death such as they had not yet encountered, but to the majority of the 250,000-strong Sixth Army defeat was unthinkable.

The Germans began their second major assault on 27 September, in the north and centre of the city. The Luftwaffe, accepting the risk of hitting German troops, launched an enormous bombardment of the Soviet positions followed by a wave of German attacks. By nightfall the situation of the Soviet forces within the city was perilous. In the north, 24th Panzer Division had driven Soviet 112th Division back over a mile, while Soviet 95th Division had been driven off the Mamayaev Kurgan by German 76th Division. It seemed that Soviet defeat was but a matter of hours away and the normally optimistic Chuikov wrote in his diary 'one more day like this and we will be in the Volga'.

The following day the Luftwaffe, scenting victory, came at dawn with a massive bombardment. By a miracle of endurance the Soviet troops held off the German attacks, and although Chuikov admitted that the situation in the centre was 'poor', he remained optimistic because he felt that the German assaults lacked the cohesion of previous attacks. More by instinct than reason, Chuikov was correct. The Germans had incurred heavy casualties where it hurt most, among their junior officers and section commanders. The Soviets, although driven back in the centre, had once again endured all that Sixth Army could hurl at them. General Paulus implicitly acknowledged this by switching the direction of his attack in the early days of October 1942, to the northern end of the city. Between 30 September and 2 October the Germans overwhelmed the more lightly defended Orlovka salient, reducing the Soviet perimeter at Stalingrad to a critical 12 miles in length along the Volga, its depth varying from a maximum of 3,500 yards to a minimum of 250 yards. The first attack on the tractor factory came on 4 October, but the Germans were stopped dead in their tracks by 37th Guards Division, losing four battalions in two hours. A dismayed Paulus suspended operations as losses on this scale for such paltry return could not be justified. The Germans attacked the tractor factory again on 8 October, but were driven back over 300 yards by 37th Guards Division, an astonishing achievement in a city where progress was quite literally being measured in inches.

The Crisis of the Battle

The Soviets had been doing well in recent encounters, but the illusory nature of this temporary supremacy became clear on 14 October when the Germans launched a huge and frenzied assault on the Soviet lines. Three infantry divisions – 94th Division, 389th Division, and 100th Jaeger Division – with 14th Panzer and 24th Panzer Divisions and five fresh engineer battalions (in total, 90,000 men and 300 tanks with massive air support) plunged into the city towards the 55,000 men of Chuikov's 62nd Army.

This was the day of reckoning for the Red Army, when Soviet plans for a counteroffensive very nearly found a watery grave in the Volga as the defenders reeled back at the hands of German formations keen to avenge their recent reversals. By midnight the Germans had broken through to the Volga in the north and had surrounded the tractor factory. The fighting went on without pause throughout the night, with German and Soviet troops, out of ammunition, pursuing each other around the workshops in murderous hand-to-hand struggles. Paulus threw in an extra division on 15 October, and at the end of the day the fighting was raging almost out of control in the streets, in the sewers, floor by floor, room by room, in the workshops, and in the cellars. On 17 October the Soviets were forced back still further towards the river. The Germans, despite incurring shocking casualties, fought on with grim determination.

By the morning of 23 October the Germans had taken only two-thirds of the tractor factory, and the Barrikady factory which they had also entered on 14 October, and had broken into the city's 'Red October' steel plant. Try as they might in sickening struggles with the remaining Soviet defenders, they could not drive them out of these factories and plants. By the end of October the Germans could no longer sustain the massive effort of the previous two weeks, and fighting would go on in the factories intermittently until February 1943.

By the beginning of November 1942 the Germans held 90% of Stalingrad, and had the remaining sliver of Soviet-held territory under constant fire. Yet, it was not enough. The Soviets were still getting sufficient men and supplies across the river. It was this failure to close off the battle on the western bank from the Soviet resources on the eastern bank that lay at the core of the Sixth Army's failure to win the victory it had been so confident of in September. It appeared that Paulus's forces would be condemned to spend the winter in the shattered, mangled ruins of Stalingrad, a prospect that appealed to no German soldier.

The Soviet Counter-attack

Yet the position of Sixth Army was actually far worse than any of its officers or soldiers realized. On 19 November 1942, General Georgi Zhukov launched 'Operation Uranus', the massive counteroffensive that the Soviet high command had been planning since September, against the long exposed flanks of the Sixth Army, defended principally by the disillusioned allies of Germany, Romanian Third and Fourth Armies.

The trap was sprung from the north, with Soviet troops advancing far to the south and west of the Sixth Army, followed on 20 November by more Soviet troops advancing northwards from the southern side of the city. On 23 November the Soviet pincers met at Kalach, encircling Sixth Army within the ruins of Stalingrad. Sixth Army did not break out in the early weeks of the encirclement because Hitler believed that the Luftwaffe could supply its daily needs. He forbade any breakout attempt, and Paulus was not the kind of man to flout a categorical order from Hitler. By the time that Sixth Army's last hope, an offensive by German troops from the southwest cutting a path through to them, failed in December, Sixth Army no longer possessed the strength to break out on its own. Meanwhile, the life of the men of Chuikov's 62nd Army, although not pleasant, became a great deal more agreeable: supply across the packed ice of the frozen Volga was relatively simple, and fighting became less frequent as the strength of the doomed Sixth Army began to wane.

On 10 January 1943, General Konstantin Rokossovsky began 'Operation Koltso', the final destruction of the surrounded Sixth Army, after the Germans had rejected an offer of honourable surrender two days earlier. In its death throes, Sixth Army fought almost to the bitter end as the remorseless Soviet advance crushed its last hopes. Hitler sang the Sixth Army's praises for its steadfast struggle in the face of overwhelming adversity. On 29 January he raised Paulus to the rank of Field Marshal, ostensibly as a reward for his stoicism in the face of the enemy. In reality, as Hitler knew well, no German Field Marshal had ever allowed himself to be taken prisoner. He was signalling to Paulus that he should kill himself. However, at the last curtain, Paulus surrendered to a Soviet lieutenant on 31 January 1943. It was all over, except for a few remaining German units in the north of the city who capitulated on 2 February. In total, of the 250,000 German troops encircled, 150,000 died in the Stalingrad pocket, while of the 91,000 taken prisoner, only 5,000 ever returned to German soil.

This was not just a defeat, it was a catastrophe. In Germany, three days of national mourning were declared. An unshakeable confidence in the superiority of German arms was replaced by a deep, though rarely acknowledged, sense of foreboding about the prospect of German defeat. Later in 1943, his British allies presented Stalin with a ceremonial trophy, 'The Sword of Stalingrad', to mark this first great victory over Germany. For the Soviet people, Stalingrad represented the moment when they had stopped losing, and the fear of defeat was replaced by a growing confidence that victory, although it would not come easily, would come.

STEPHEN WALSH

Further Reading

Beevor, A *Stalingrad* (London, 1998)

Erickson, J *The Road to Stalingrad* (London, 1975)

Glantz, D M, and House, J *When Titans Clashed* (Kansas, 1995)

Overy, R *Russia's War* (New York, 1997)

The Battle of Manila
MacArthur's Return
3 FEBRUARY – 3 MARCH 1945

United States Sixth and Eighth Armies under General Douglas MacArthur

VERSUS

Japanese Imperial Army and Navy forces under General Tomoyuki Yamashita and Rear Admiral Sanji Iwabuchi

CHRONOLOGY

9 January 1945 –	American forces land on the west coast of Luzon
31 January 1945 –	US 11th Airborne Division lands south of Manila
3 February 1945 –	US forces reach northern Manila
5 February 1945 –	Japanese forces begin setting fire to the city
15 February 1945 –	Rear Admiral Iwabuchi announces a fight to the death
19 February 1945 –	Start of the American assault on the walled city
3 March 1945 –	Last Japanese resistance ends

"We are very glad and grateful for the opportunity of being able to serve our country in this epic battle. Now, with what strength remains, we will daringly engage the enemy. Banzai to the Emperor! We are determined to fight to the last man." SANJI IWABUCHI, 15 FEBRUARY 1945

No ARMY LIKES to attack into a city. In built-up areas commanders find it very difficult to maintain control over their forces, so that overall cohesion breaks down. Moreover, the protection afforded by buildings increases the power of the defender manifold, so that even poorly armed civilians can inflict heavy casualties on well-trained and well-equipped soldiers. For both the Americans and the Japanese, the Battle of Manila was unique. This little-known but murderous battle was the only time in World War II that their armies fought each other in a city. Indeed, it was the largest such battle ever undertaken by either American or Japanese forces. It was also a battle that the American commander did not expect he would have to fight, and a battle that the Japanese commander never intended to fight.

The Strategic Situation

At the start of 1945 the island of Luzon, the main island of the Philippine archipelago, was important for both the Americans and the Japanese. For the Americans it was intended as a staging post for the eventual invasion of the Japanese home islands. Of particular importance was Manila and its harbour, one of the finest in the world, which could accommodate the vast armadas that would be arriving in the western Pacific in the latter part of 1945. Equally important was the desire of the Commander in Chief of the South West Pacific Area, General Douglas MacArthur, to fulfil the promise to return which he had made to the troops he had left behind nearly three years earlier, troops who were now in Japanese prison camps in and around Manila. But of overriding importance was the fact that for much of his life Manila had been MacArthur's home. It had been the place of his happiest memories, the scene of his greatest personal triumphs, and of his most bitter military defeat. MacArthur's desire to retake Manila had little to do with political considerations – it was personal.

The commander of Japanese forces in the Philippines, General Tomoyuki Yamashita, had arrived on Luzon only a few months earlier. A gifted strategist, Yamashita knew the value of Manila to the Americans. He also knew that the only place a sizeable landing could be made on Luzon, apart from heavily defended Manila Bay, was on the shores of Lingayen Gulf on the western side of the island, about 120 miles north of Manila. He therefore anticipated that the Americans would land at Lingayen, and then advance south on Manila as quickly as they could get ashore.

The Japanese Plans

With some 275,000 troops under his command, but with little armour and only 600 aircraft, Yamashita considered his options. Knowing the obliterating weight of American naval firepower, he ruled out opposing the landing on the beaches. His fiercely independent naval and air force commanders agreed, and urged that Yamashita should concentrate on defending Manila, which they argued was the 'centre of gravity' in any campaign on Luzon. Yamashita agreed that the early capture of Manila would almost certainly be the American objective, but he ruled out defending the city of Manila itself, reasoning that what was important was not the city but the harbour, which could be controlled by the 5,200 troops that were dug in on the fortress island of Corregidor, at the entrance to Manila Bay. Indeed, by not defending the city he intended to impose on the Americans the logistic burden of feeding 1 million Filipino civilians. He left a relatively small force of about 20,000 composed largely of naval forces and lines of communication troops in Manila under the command of Rear Admiral Sanji Iwabuchi, tasked with carrying out last-minute demolition before withdrawing in the face of an American advance. Yamashita deployed the bulk of his forces in three groups. Shimbu Group, 80,000-strong, was to dig into the mountains directly east of Manila. The 30,000-strong Kembu Group was deployed about 40 miles north of Manila (80 miles south of Lingayen) to deny MacArthur the vast 200 square mile complex of airstrips and bases known as Clark Field. The bulk of Japanese forces, some 152,000 troops along with virtually all the armour, formed Shobu Group and was under Yamashita's direct command. These he deployed in the rugged northeast of Luzon, from where they could harass any American advance from Lingayen to Manila.

The American Plans

Early on 9 January nearly 1,000 American warships and transports entered Lingayen Gulf, and at 10.00 a.m. the first elements of Lieutenant General Walter Krueger's 200,000-strong Sixth Army began landing. During the next few days, two of Krueger's divisions, advancing to the northeast, ran into Shobu Group, while another division, advancing to the southwest, ran into Kembu Group. This convinced Krueger that any advance directly south to Manila would run the risk of being cut off and encircled. He therefore decided to delay the liberation of the city until he had consolidated his beachhead.

To MacArthur, however, the situation seemed very different. His Chief of Intelligence, Major General Charles Willoughby, was convinced that

Yamashita had only 150,000 men on Luzon, and that consequently Krueger was being overcautious. In addition, Willoughby's men were learning from Japanese radio traffic that troops in Manila were burning code books and other classified documents, which could only mean that they were preparing to evacuate the city. Seventy-two hours after the landing MacArthur urged Krueger to send a flying column to the city. As the days passed, and evidence that the Japanese were pulling out continued to mount, MacArthur lost patience.

Ever since the beginning of the campaign MacArthur had been fanning a simmering rivalry between Krueger and Lieutenant General Robert Eichelberger, the commander of Eighth Army, his other major formation, into raging jealousy. MacArthur now ruthlessly exploited the rivalry by ordering Eichelberger to land Eighth Army's crack 11th Airborne Division under Major General Joseph Swing on the beaches at Nasugbu south of Manila Bay, and advance north on the capital. Having set this in operation, MacArthur then bypassed Krueger and his Corps commanders on 30 January, going directly to Major General Robert S Beightler, commander of 37th Infantry Division, to urge him to advance to the capital. The following day he drove to the headquarters of Major General Vernon D Mudge, commander of the 1st Cavalry Division, and implored him to 'Get to Manila! Go around the Japs, bounce off the Japs, save your men, but get to Manila!' MacArthur had set up an all-out race for the capital.

MacArthur's Fantasy

Swing's division moved rapidly along a two-lane concrete road that ran due north 15 miles from Nasugbu to the 2,000 foot-high Tagaytay Ridge, brushing aside light opposition. On 3 February, Swing aided the advance by parachuting two battalions onto the top of the ridge. From here the paratroopers could look down on Manila, 'shining whitely in the bright Luzon sun' only 30 miles to the north. Two days later the leading elements of 11th Airborne, having been delayed only by mines in the roads and sporadic sniping, reached the perimeter of Nichols Field, an airbase on the southern outskirts of Manila. A delighted Eichelberger wrote to his wife that 11th Airborne 'is right in Manila', the implication being that he had won the race.

Meanwhile 1st Cavalry, having organized itself into three columns, raced south, while 37th Division, most of whose soldiers were marching infantry, struggled to keep pace on the cavalry's right flank. On 3 February the advance guard crossed the line of the city limits, and by evening the easternmost column had reached Malacañan Palace, the 18th-century Spanish mansion which sprawled along the northeastern bank of the Pasig River, which was the seat of government in the Philippines. A few miles to the west, another column reached Santo Tomas University, where more than 5,000 civilians and soldiers were held prisoner. The Japanese guards, completely surprised, barricaded themselves in the administration block, and after hours of tense negotiations were allowed to march under a flag of truce towards the Pasig, beyond which lay central Manila, still under Japanese control. On 4 February the Cavalry liberated more than 1,200 prisoners a few miles further south in Bilibid Prison, and the next morning they were on the northern shore of the Pasig. On 5 February a *Time* magazine correspondent reported that Manila had fallen 'like a ripe plum', while a press release described the raising of the Stars and Stripes in the centre of the city. The following morning MacArthur's headquarters issued a communiqué which confirmed that the liberation of Manila had been completed.

The Japanese Reaction

American intelligence had correctly identified Yamashita's intention to evacuate Manila. But they lacked the sophistication to detect inter-service rivalries, which meant that an Army general's instructions might not necessarily be obeyed by an airforce or a naval officer. The Japanese commander in Manila, Rear Admiral Iwabuchi, treated orders from the Army as suggestions which he might or might not follow, as the mood took him. Like every other Japanese naval officer, Iwabuchi had been stunned by the disastrous defeats that had overwhelmed the Imperial fleet. He was determined both to revenge himself on the Americans and, in so doing, redeem the honour of the navy. Iwabuchi had ordered the burning of the code books because he would soon no longer need them – he intended to die in the city.

Over the preceding weeks Iwabuchi had organized his 20,000 naval personnel and lines of communication troops into a number of provisional battalions. Though poorly trained, they could still give a good account of themselves in fixed positions which they could be expected to defend until dead. The Japanese also had some Filipino allies, the Makapili, a militia formed in October 1944 which had grown to a strength of about 5,000 and which was being used to suppress the increasingly frequent guerrilla activity in the city. Well before the American landing at Lingayen, the Makapili and the Kempati, the Japanese military police, had been at work arresting, interrogating, and eliminating suspects, their net growing ever wider until all non-Asians were at risk. By January, Manila's European population was sheltering in churches, convents, hospitals, and in the 'German Club' – a large building of reinforced concrete which was festooned with Swastika banners.

Iwabuchi's plan of defence was relatively simple. The built-up area of Manila was about 120 square miles, most of it wooden houses with tiled or galvanized iron roofs. Because no part of the city was more than a few feet above sea level, the high water table had made the construction of cellars impossible, so residential accommodation could not be used for defence but could be burnt, which would delay any American advance considerably. The city was divided up by long straight avenues, usually running north–south, which Iwabuchi intended to use as firelanes, delaying any American advance from the east. He proposed to meet any American advance from the north on the southern banks of the Pasig River, thereby abandoning the northern quarter of the city, while in the south he constructed a strong line of fortifications, the Genko Line, along Nichols Field.

Once the Americans had penetrated this outer line, Iwabuchi intended to fall back to the official and business district that formed a semicircle running from the Pasig down to Manila Bay. Because Manila was in a notoriously dangerous earthquake zone the buildings here, such as the Post Office, the Finance Building, and the Manila Hotel, all had deep foundations and were constructed from reinforced concrete supported by steel girders. There were some two dozen of these buildings, each one a potential fortress that could resist attack for several days.

When this line had gone, Iwabuchi intended to make a final stand in Intramuros (literally 'within the walls'), the square mile of the old Spanish stone-built colonial city which was surrounded by wall 20 feet high and 40 feet thick. Salvaging guns from sunken Japanese warships in Manila Bay, Iwabuchi had more artillery than he could properly man and virtually unlimited quantities of ammunition. When the Americans reached the Pasig and Nichols Field he planned to start the systematic demolition of all useful infrastructure and set fire to the outer suburbs, a conflagration which would mark the beginning of the battle. In all this there is no evidence that Iwabuchi considered the fate of Manila's civilian population, 800,000 of them still in the city on 5 February.

The Battle

On 5 February, Americans looking north from Tagaytay and south from the Pasig could see fires breaking out all over Manila. Vast columns of black smoke rose out from the port area, to merge with the white haze rising from the outer suburbs. Pushing north past Nichols Field, the 11th Airborne Division suddenly came under devastating artillery fire from five-inch and six-

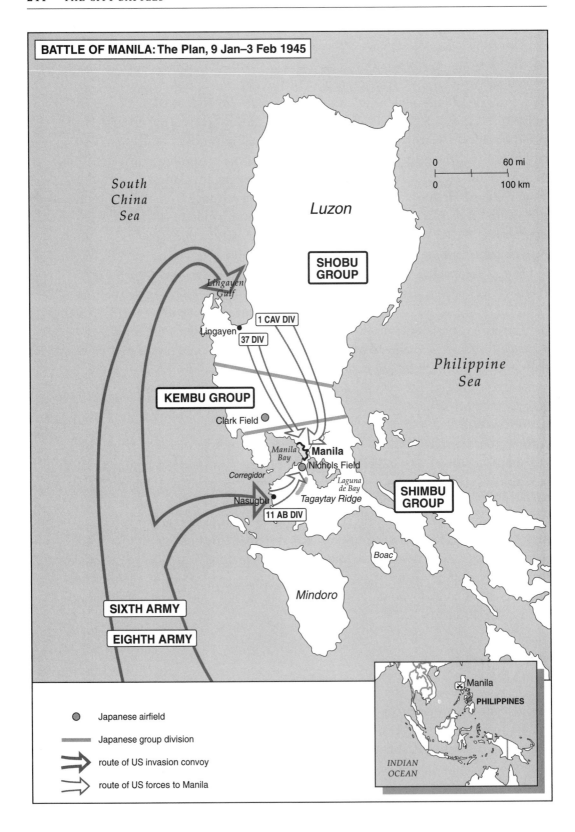

BATTLE OF MANILA: The Plan, 9 Jan–3 Feb 1945

South China Sea

Luzon

SHOBU GROUP

Lingayen Gulf

Lingayen

1 CAV DIV

37 DIV

Philippine Sea

KEMBU GROUP

Clark Field

Manila Bay

Manila

Nichols Field

Corregidor

Laguna de Bay

SHIMBU GROUP

Nasugbu

Tagaytay Ridge

11 AB DIV

Boac

Mindoro

SIXTH ARMY

EIGHTH ARMY

0   60 mi
0   100 km

Manila

PHILIPPINES

INDIAN OCEAN

- ● Japanese airfield
- ▬ Japanese group division
- ➤ route of US invasion convoy
- ➢ route of US forces to Manila

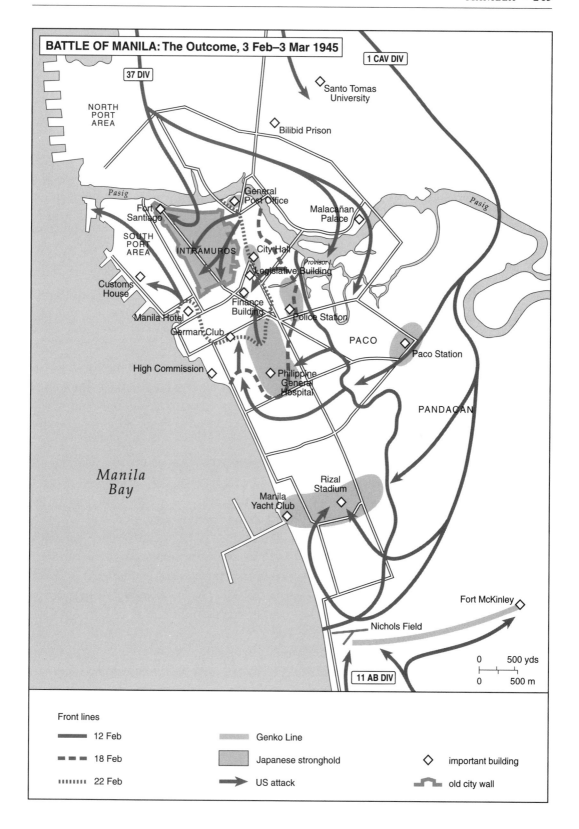

BATTLE OF MANILA: The Outcome, 3 Feb–3 Mar 1945

1 CAV DIV

37 DIV

NORTH
PORT
AREA

Santo Tomas
University

Bilibid Prison

Pasig

Pasig

General
Post Office

Fort
Santiago

Malacañan
Palace

SOUTH
PORT
AREA

INTRAMUROS

City Hall

Provisor

Legislative Building

Customs
House

Finance
Building

Manila Hotel

Police Station

German Club

PACO

High Commission

Paco Station

Philippine
General
Hospital

PANDACAN

Manila
Bay

Rizal
Stadium

Manila
Yacht Club

Fort McKinley

Nichols Field

0   500 yds

0   500 m

11 AB DIV

Front lines

━━━ 12 Feb

▬ ▬ ▬ 18 Feb

▪▪▪▪▪▪▪ 22 Feb

Genko Line

Japanese stronghold

US attack

◇ important building

old city wall

inch naval guns, as well as from smaller calibre weapons. A glider infantry company commander radioed divisional headquarters, 'Tell Admiral Halsey to stop looking for the Jap Fleet. It's dug in here on Nichols Field'. In the fighting to break the Genko Line, 11th Airborne suffered 900 casualties, and was only able to advance slowly behind massed artillery barrages, supplemented by fighter-bombers dropping napalm on suspected Japanese positions.

Meanwhile to the north Beightler had sent his 149th Infantry Regiment across the Pasig on 7 February, to land in the north-central suburbs of Paco and Pandacan. An epic battle developed around Paco railway station, in which 300 Japanese had entrenched themselves. It cost the Americans 335 casualties over two days to break Japanese resistance. Equally vicious was the fighting for the power station a few hundred yards upstream on Proviso Island, which finally fell to 37th Division at a cost of another 285 casualties. As the toll of American dead and wounded mounted, Beightler demanded increased artillery support and air strikes. MacArthur ruled out air power on the grounds that it was too imprecise to use in a built-up area still inhabited by civilians, but grudgingly approved the increased employment of artillery, provided it was used solely for the reduction of enemy strongpoints. In the event, once Sixth Army had been given permission to increase the employment of artillery, it used it with an increasing lack of discrimination until guns were lined up wheel to wheel, literally smashing a swathe of destruction through the city.

While 37th Division had been slogging through north-central Manila, 1st Cavalry Division had advanced in a wide area to the east of the city, and on 10 February they linked up with the right flank of 11th Airborne. Simultaneously another task force had struck directly across the south-central suburbs, and on 12 February reached Manila Bay near the once exclusive Manila Yacht Club. It now moved to eliminate what had become the southern pocket of Japanese resistance, centred on the sporting complex of Rizal Stadium, which was eventually overrun by 1st Cavalry's tanks on 14 February.

On 15 February, Iwabuchi, ensconced in his headquarters in Fort Santiago in the heart of Intramuros, received an order from Yamashita to break out, but rejected it with an emotional broadcast declaring his intention to fight to the death. For the civilian population life in the area remaining under Japanese control steadily degenerated into a vision of hell. Knowing that they were soon to die, Japanese rampaged through the mansions of the Bayside suburbs, raping and murdering women and girls, and butchering all men of European appearance who fell into their hands. A white face was now an automatic death sentence. The worst incident occurred on 15 February when the

Japanese set about the 1,500 refugees in the German Club, killing many hundreds – including some Germans – with bayonets and clubs, or roasting them alive by setting fire to the building.

The Climax

The area now held by the Japanese was only 2,000 yards by 1,500 yards, but included most of the recent buildings in Manila and the walled city of Intramuros, all heavily defended. American techniques of attack varied. Against some objectives squads advanced behind a barrage of high explosives and smoke, breaking into buildings and fighting their way room by room, using bazookas and flame-throwers at close quarters. In others, massed artillery fired at point blank range at the ground floors of buildings, gradually collapsing them floor by floor until all that remained was a pile of rubble. On 21 February the Manila Hotel was destroyed, including the penthouse which had been MacArthur's home. Incredibly, in some cases the Japanese continued to fire from the rubble, and were only silenced when the ruins were sprayed with petrol and set alight.

While the outer perimeter of large buildings was destroyed, American artillery concentrations began to pulverize the walls of Intramuros, and effected the first breach on 19 February. Four days later, advancing behind a colossal bombardment, the 129th Infantry Regiment crossed the Passig and stormed the northern walls of Intramuros, while the 145th Infantry Regiment attacked the southeastern walls. Crouching behind tanks and bulldozers, American infantry destroyed building after building. On 25 February, with American shells smashing against the walls of his headquarters, Iwabuchi and his staff committed ritual suicide. Only the Finance Building, just to the south-east of Intramuros, remained in Japanese hands. The last Japanese stopped firing on 3 March, by which time the building was a heap of rubble.

The Aftermath

On 3 March 1945 American troops could stand on the shore of Manila Bay and look east to open country – not a building of the city remained standing. Over the next few weeks Americans commented on the sickening stench which pervaded Manila, and the swarms of huge black flies that proliferated. The Americans had lost 1,100 dead, and they counted 16,650 Japanese bodies. The Filipino dead were too numerous to count, but the number was certainly not less than 100,000 people. With the single exception of Warsaw, no Allied city had suffered as much in the whole war. To MacArthur, the battle had been an embarrassment; he had declared Manila liberated on 6 February and one month later it was a heap of ruins. He decreed that no mention would be made of the battle in public monuments erected in the Philippines and in the United States to commemorate the campaign. It would be as though the battle had never happened.

DUNCAN ANDERSON

Further Reading

Cannon, H *Triumph in the Philippines* (Washington DC, 1953)

Connaughton, R, Pimlott, J, and Anderson, D *The Battle For Manila* (London, 1995)

Howarth, S *Morning Glory* (London, 1983)

Manchester, W *American Caesar* (Boston, 1978)

The Battle of Berlin
The Final Battle
16 APRIL – 2 MAY 1945

German Army Group 'Weichsel' under Colonel General
Gotthard Heinrici
and part of Army Group 'Mitte' under Colonel General
Ferdinand Schörner

VERSUS

Soviet First Belorussian Front under Marshal Georgi Zhukov,
Second Belorussian Front under
Marshal Konstantin Rokossovsky, and First Ukrainian Front
under Marshal Ivan Koniev

CHRONOLOGY

3 April 1945 –	Stalin approves plans for Berlin operation
16 April 1945 –	The Soviet offensive begins
21 April 1945 –	Soviet troops reach the Berlin suburbs
25 April 1945 –	Soviet forces complete the encirclement of Berlin
29 April 1945 –	Battle for the city centre defence zone begins
30 April 1945 –	Hitler commits suicide, Red Flag raised on the Reichstag
2 May 1945 –	Berlin surrenders

---

*"Tomorrow, on 17 April, the enemy defences on the Seelow Heights
will be breached… I believe that the more troops the enemy throws
against us here, the quicker we will take Berlin, for it is easier to
defeat the enemy on an open field than in a fortified city."*
MARSHAL GEORGI ZHUKOV

CITY FIGHTING IS difficult, time consuming, and destructive. Armies try to avoid it if they possibly can. Generally, it is only when other options are denied that a defender chooses to expose his own urban centres to the damage and civilian suffering that is usually associated with such operations. Similarly, attackers regard being drawn into protracted urban battles as a symptom of failure or weakness, and it requires particular circumstances to persuade them not to select an alternative – for example, encirclement followed by a siege. That such circumstances exist is well illustrated by the battle for Berlin. Here, strenuous efforts were made by the German defenders to avoid a city battle taking place at all. When this policy failed, it was the political and psychological significance of Berlin, together with Hitler's refusal to allow a surrender, that determined that the capital of the Reich should become the scene of a savage and bloody battle. The result was the final collapse of the Nazi state, as well as a human disaster on an appalling scale.

The Strategic Situation

1944 had been a year of tremendous military success for the Allies, but it had not brought them decisive victory in Europe. Backed by the might of Soviet industry and Western lend-lease aid, the Red Army had inflicted a series of crippling defeats on its opponents. Nevertheless, at the end of the year it still stood hundreds of miles from its ultimate objective, the Reich capital of Berlin. Meanwhile, after carving their way through France and Belgium in the second half of 1944, British, Canadian, French, and American units had stalled at the end of their supply lines, only to be subjected to a ferocious German counteroffensive in the Ardennes in December.

Partly in order to relieve pressure on the Western Allies, and partly to further his own ambitions, early in the new year Stalin ordered his forces to resume major operations in central Poland and East Prussia. The effect of these attacks, which began on 12 January 1945, was devastating. Misled by Soviet deception measures, mal-deployed, and with its commanders hamstrung by continual interference from Hitler himself, German Army Group A defending Poland collapsed within days. By the end of the month the Red Army had also advanced to secure bridgeheads over the River Oder, on German soil within 40 miles of Berlin.

These operations were among the most impressive carried out by Soviet forces during World War II. However, despite their success it proved impossible to push the spearheads of Marshal Georgi Zhukov's 1st Belorussian Front (the much smaller Soviet equivalent of an Army Group) the final few dozen miles to the German capital. Melting ice on the Oder hampered reinforcement of the shallow Soviet bridgeheads west of the river, while resistance by bypassed enemy forces in Posen endangered Zhukov's intended main line of supply. Together with threats to his northern flank from German troops in Pomerania, this deterred the Soviet commander from attempting to deliver the *coup de grâce* in February. Instead, as the Germans frantically tried to rebuild their positions, he began preparations for a set-piece offensive that would lead to the fall of Berlin.

The Soviet Plans

As finally agreed in early April, the basic Soviet plan for the capture of Berlin was simple enough. However, before its execution it was necessary to remove the danger on Zhukov's flank and to expand the bridgeheads to the east of Berlin, in order to provide sufficient room for Soviet forces to deploy for their attacks. Doing these things took time, not least because the Germans recognized the value of the Oder bridgeheads and during February tried hard to destroy them with counter-attacks. Nevertheless, by late March Zhukov's forces had succeeded in enlarging their foothold west of the river to a depth of about 6 miles and a breadth of 30 miles. In cooperation with Marshal Konstantin Rokossovsky's 2nd Belorussian Front, they had also cleared the Germans from Pomerania. Meanwhile, south of Zhukov's zone of responsibility, 1st Ukrainian Front under Marshal Ivan Koniev had advanced to the River Neisse, from which it was to launch its own attacks during the battle for Berlin.

At the end of March, having completed their preliminaries, Zhukov and Koniev travelled to Moscow to discuss with Stalin the precise form of the forthcoming operation. Concerned that the Western Allies might still renege on their promise to leave the capture of Berlin to the Soviets, Stalin demanded that the offensive should begin on 16 April. Although this allowed little time for preparations, Zhukov and Koniev had no choice but to agree, and on 3 April they submitted their proposals. As approved, these involved a simultaneous attack by 1st Belorussian Front and 1st Ukrainian Front to break through the German defences west of the Oder–Neisse line and to release powerful mobile forces to encircle Berlin from the north and south. To render German units beyond the immediate battle area incapable of intervening, Soviet armies in Czechoslovakia and Hungary were to carry out fixing attacks. Finally, on 20 April, 2nd Belorussian Front was to launch its own offensive to clear the enemy from northern Germany.

Isolated and almost defenceless, Berlin was expected to fall quickly once encircled, and Stalin tried to ensure this by deliberately encouraging Zhukov and Koniev to race one another to the city. If all went well a junction with the Western Allies would occur on the River Elbe by 1 May. Unless the Nazis made a final stand at their proposed last line of defence, the 'Alpine Redoubt', the largely fictitious creation which was being announced in their propaganda, the war in Europe would be over.

The German Plans

For the Germans, whose actions in the east had unleashed a spirit of terrible Soviet vengeance, the prospect of defeat was an appalling one, and it did much to persuade Hitler and his generals to make a final effort to halt the Soviets outside the gates of Berlin. This was an enormous task, for by April 1945 the German armed forces were utterly exhausted. However, despite severe shortages of manpower, equipment, ammunition, and fuel they still had some defensive capability. Furthermore, the commander of Army Group 'Weichsel', Colonel General Gotthardt Heinrici, was highly experienced in this type of fighting and did his best to help his subordinates make the most of their limited resources. In particular, by exploiting terrain features and constructing successive defensive belts within which Soviet momentum would be absorbed, he hoped at worst to delay the enemy breakthrough long enough to evacuate German troops and civilians towards the west. Here, by falling into British or American hands, they would at least avoid the nightmare of Soviet captivity.

Heinrici had no intention of waging a street-by-street battle for Berlin. He knew that doing so would mean catastrophe for the population and that although the city was nominally designated as a 'fortified place', in reality its three million inhabitants remained virtually undefended. Admittedly, on paper they were protected by a series of obstacle zones and defence positions both in and outside Berlin. However, few of these actually existed in their intended form, and even fewer were likely to pose problems for a determined attacker. Command authority within the city's defence sectors was confused, signals communications grossly inadequate, and the quality of the garrison pitiful. Indeed, other than a few thousand SS personnel protecting government buildings in the city centre, most of Berlin's 70,000 defenders were old men and boys thrown together in *Volkssturm* ('home guard') and Hitler Youth units, whose fanaticism was in some cases intense, but whose fighting power was generally negligible.

Given the indefensibility of Berlin itself, Heinrici's plan stressed the need to stop the Soviets as close as possible to the River Oder. Efforts were therefore made to prepare deep defensive positions containing minefields, anti-tank obstacles, strongpoints, and mobile reserves, whose role it was to destroy enemy penetrations. Particular attention was paid to building up General Theodor Busse's Ninth Army, which had the task of preventing a breakthrough along the anticipated main axis of attack, the Küstrin–Seelow–Berlin highway. Third and Fourth Panzer Armies, the latter deployed along the River Neisse opposite Koniev's forces as part of Army Group 'Mitte', also attempted to improve their defences.

Even so, despite combing rear services and using airforce, naval, and *Volkssturm* personnel to reinforce their units, by mid-April the Germans could muster on the Oder–Neisse line barely 700,000 men, supported by fewer than 9,000 artillery pieces, 1,500 tanks and self-propelled guns, and a few hundred aircraft. Against them the three Soviet fronts involved in the Berlin operation could deploy 2,500,000 soldiers, over 41,000 guns and mortars, 6,250 tanks and self-propelled guns, and 7,500 aircraft. For all Heinrici's efforts, only a miracle could save Nazi Germany once the Soviet offensive began.

The Opening Moves

At 3.00 a.m. (local time – Soviet time was two hours ahead) on 16 April the battle for Berlin commenced. Packed almost wheel to wheel inside the bridgehead around Küstrin, thousands of Russian guns unleashed a devastating bombardment against the forward German positions west of the Oder. However, they struck mostly at thin air. Heinrici knew that the offensive was coming, and on the night of 15 April had ordered his forces to withdraw towards their second defence line on the escarpment that marked the western limit of the Oder valley. As a result, when 1st Belorussian Front's infantry attacked at 3.30 a.m. their energies were largely wasted. Their confusion only increased when searchlights set up on Zhukov's orders to provide artificial illumination blinded them instead. Within a few hours, as they came under heavy artillery fire in the maze of canals and flooded ditches that criss-crossed the area, their attacks began to falter.

With casualties mounting rapidly, Zhukov decided in the afternoon to seize the initiative by releasing his armoured reserves – the formidable 1st Guards Tank Army and 2nd Guards Tank Army – earlier than he had originally planned. The only effects, however, were to cause further chaos and to present the Germans with even more targets. By the evening, responding to a furious telephone call from Stalin, Zhukov was reduced to arguing that the stronger the enemy's resistance near the Oder, the easier it would be to capture Berlin itself. In a sense this was true, but it was also making a virtue out of necessity.

Despite the gloomy situation facing 1st Belorussian Front, not everything

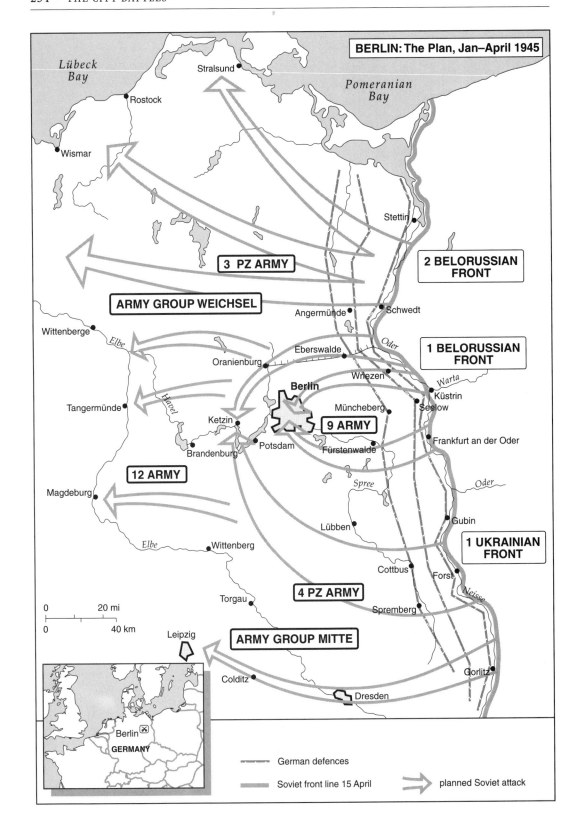

BERLIN: The Plan, Jan–April 1945

Lübeck Bay

Pomeranian Bay

Stralsund

Rostock

Wismar

3 PZ ARMY

2 BELORUSSIAN FRONT

ARMY GROUP WEICHSEL

Stettin

Angermünde • Schwedt

Oder

1 BELORUSSIAN FRONT

Wittenberge

Elbe

Eberswalde

Oranienburg

Wriezen

Warta

Berlin

Küstrin

Tangermünde

Havel

Ketzin

Müncheberg

Seelow

9 ARMY

Brandenburg

Potsdam

Fürstenwalde

Frankfurt an der Oder

12 ARMY

Magdeburg

Spree

Oder

Lübben

Gubin

Elbe

Wittenberg

1 UKRAINIAN FRONT

Cottbus

Forst

4 PZ ARMY

Torgau

Spremberg

Neisse

ARMY GROUP MITTE

Leipzig

Görlitz

Colditz

Dresden

0   20 mi
0   40 km

Berlin
GERMANY

- - - German defences

Soviet front line 15 April

planned Soviet attack

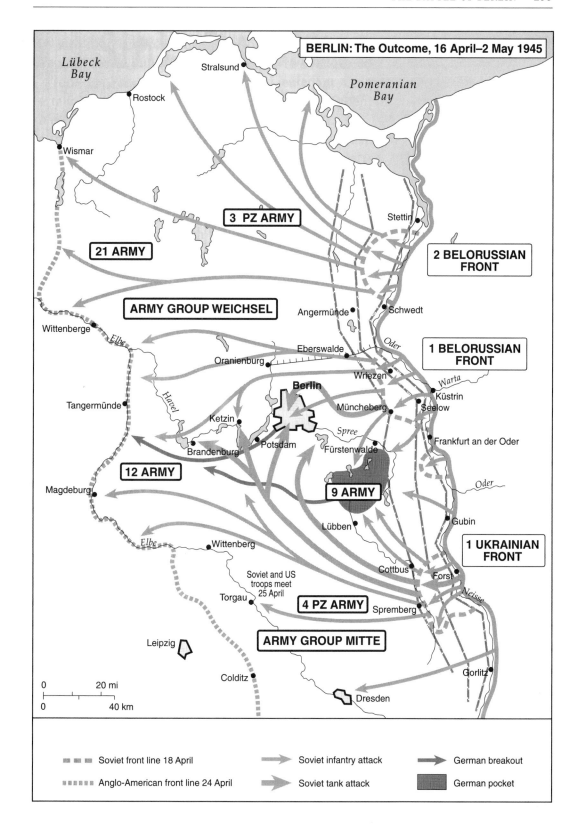

BERLIN: The Outcome, 16 April–2 May 1945

Lübeck Bay

Pomeranian Bay

Stralsund

Rostock

Wismar

3 PZ ARMY

Stettin

21 ARMY

2 BELORUSSIAN FRONT

ARMY GROUP WEICHSEL

Angermünde ● Schwedt

Wittenberge ● Elbe

Eberswalde

Oranienburg

Wriezen

Oder

Warta

Küstrin

1 BELORUSSIAN FRONT

Berlin

Tangermünde ●

Ketzin

Müncheberg

Seelow

Havel

Brandenburg

Potsdam

Spree

Fürstenwalde

Frankfurt an der Oder

12 ARMY

Magdeburg ●

9 ARMY

Oder

Lübben

Gubin

Wittenberg

1 UKRAINIAN FRONT

Elbe

Soviet and US troops meet 25 April

Cottbus

Forst

Torgau

Neisse

4 PZ ARMY

Spremberg

ARMY GROUP MITTE

Leipzig

Colditz

Gorlitz

Dresden

| 0 | 20 mi |
| 0 | 40 km |

Soviet front line 18 April
Anglo-American front line 24 April
Soviet infantry attack
Soviet tank attack
German breakout
German pocket

that happened on 16 April was disastrous for the Soviets. To the south, Koniev's forces achieved much greater success in their attacks across the River Neisse, where Fourth Panzer Army had to commit a large proportion of its mobile reserves to prevent a breakthrough. Furthermore, even in Zhukov's zone there were reasons for optimism. East of Wriezen, Soviet troops advanced six miles into the enemy's defences, while in the central sector, sheer weight of numbers helped General Vasili Chuikov's 8th Guards Army push forward to the base of the Seelow escarpment. Several German front line divisions were shattered, Ninth Army used up large amounts of ammunition, and Busse lost some precious armoured assets in unsuccessful counter-attacks. Although they were fighting hard, the Germans were bleeding to death. And the simple fact was that unlike their opponents, Heinrici's forces could not afford their losses.

The Climax of the Battle

That the balance was swinging in the Soviets' favour became clear on the second and third days of the offensive. Throwing every available unit into battle, the Germans even sent suicide aircraft to crash onto the Oder bridges in the hope of cutting the Red Army's supply lines. Virtually all of Ninth Army's armoured formations were soon engaged in heavy fighting on the Seelow Heights, requiring Busse to request reinforcements from Third Panzer Army, which had so far not been attacked.

In the face of such massive numerical superiority, gaps rapidly began to appear in the German defences, and into these poured Zhukov's tanks. Helped by improving weather, which allowed more effective air support than at the start of the offensive, 1st Belorussian Front broke through the German CI Corps' lines at Wriezen on 18 April. On the same day General Helmuth Weidling's LVI Panzer Corps was pushed back along the Seelow–Berlin highway to Müncheberg. Only in the areas held by XI SS Panzer Corps and V SS Mountain Corps did Ninth Army's front remain reasonably firm. But this was largely immaterial, for in the adjacent sector of Fourth Panzer Army Koniev's breakthrough was almost complete. Keen to exploit his success, on the evening of 17 April Stalin had already given permission for 1st Ukrainian Front's tank armies to be directed towards the southern outskirts of Berlin. Bypassing pockets of enemy resistance in order to maintain momentum, 24 hours later they were well on their way.

By 20 April it was clear that Heinrici's plan to stop the Red Army on the Oder–Neisse line had failed. Although for the first few days the limited size of their bridgeheads had forced the Soviets to carry out unsophisticated and costly frontal assaults, once the enemy's defences were broken it was easy for their armoured formations to thrust deep into the German rear. In a desperate attempt to halt the flood a few battalions from the Berlin garrison were sent east, but these were either crushed immediately or swept back towards the city. Third Panzer Army might have counter-attacked the right flank of Zhukov's forces as they moved north of Berlin, but on 20 April it was struck a blow by 2nd Belorussian Front that left it fighting for its own life. Meanwhile, southeast of the city the remains of Ninth Army, together with fragments of Fourth Panzer Army and thousands of civilians, were driven into a huge encirclement by their much superior enemy. On the morning of 21 April, the centre of Berlin itself came under long-range artillery bombardment for the first time.

The imminent arrival of the Red Army in Berlin's suburbs, and the threat of encirclement by Soviet forces advancing towards the River Havel, threw many in the Reich capital into a state of panic. Refugees from the east were already pouring into the city, while others – among them, numerous high-ranking Nazis – streamed out towards the west. In Hitler's bunker under the Chancellery an air of unreality dominated proceedings, as rumours flew and the Führer ordered relief attempts and redeployments by formations that were at best shattered remnants of their former selves. Southwest of Berlin, Lieutenant General Walter Wenck's Twelfth Army was, in fact, in a position to come to the defenders' aid. However – like Busse and Heinrici – Wenck's priority by this point lay in saving his own men together with as many civilians as possible from capture by the Soviets. The defenders of Berlin were now, to all intents and purposes, alone.

The Capture of Berlin

On 25 April elements of 4th Guards Tank Army from 1st Ukrainian Front and 47th Army from 1st Belorussian Front met at Ketzin, completing the encirclement of Berlin. By then, clashes were already occurring within the main urban area. In view of the balance of forces there was no doubting the outcome. However, given Hitler's refusal to allow a surrender, it was clear that the Red Army would have to fight its way to the Reichstag, the building that still represented symbolically the seat of German government.

Furthermore, several factors meant that the battle would not be utterly one-sided. Firstly, many German troops, especially survivors of LVI Panzer Corps, had retreated into Berlin before the encirclement was complete. On 23 April Hitler ordered their commander, General Weidling, to take over the city's defences, and his 15,000 men and 60 tanks significantly increased the fighting power of Berlin's garrison. Secondly, Soviet infantry losses in the breakthrough battles had been very high. In city fighting such troops were at a premium, not least to protect Soviet armour, which was otherwise easy prey for any German armed with a *Panzerfaust* (anti-tank grenade launcher). This lack of infantry slowed down what might otherwise have been a more rapid Soviet penetration. The city and suburbs were also already heavily damaged by several years of Allied bombing, and under intense artillery bombardment roads soon became choked with further debris, making movement extremely difficult. Finally, the effects of propaganda, Nazi ideology, terror of the Red Army, or fear of the roving SS court-martials that executed deserters out of hand, all meant that many Germans were indeed willing to fight to the bitter end.

The final week of the battle for Berlin was characterized by a methodical Soviet tightening of the noose, rather than by a sudden dash for the Reichstag. Koniev's forces had arrived at the city before Zhukov's. However, by the time they were ready for the urban battle, forces from 1st Belorussian Front had bypassed them, and the fighting within Berlin was therefore conducted mainly by Zhukov's troops. Using heavy firepower to blast their way forward, or infiltrating through underground railway tunnels and areas where German defences were weak, they gradually pushed towards the city centre. Occasionally they encountered significant obstacles, most notably several massive concrete Flak towers mounting powerful anti-aircraft guns, which became the last bastions of German defence. However, the fields of fire from these positions were limited, and the Soviets were usually able to find a way round them. By 27 April they were closing on Berlin's innermost defence zone (designated as the '*Zitadelle*'), bounded to the north by the River Spree and to the south by the Landwehr Canal. This was where most of the government buildings were located. It was also the site of Hitler's headquarters bunker.

The End of the Battle

In the early morning of 29 April the battle for Berlin's centre reached a crescendo. Amid a maelstrom of smoke, flame, and noise, forces from 3rd Shock Army poured south across the Moltke bridge over the Spree. They met savage resistance. Nevertheless, in hand-to-hand fighting they fought their way into the diplomatic quarter and the buildings of the Ministry of the Interior, cleared both, and pushed on to the open ground in front of the Reichstag.

Desperate to fulfil Stalin's demand that the Red Flag be raised on the building by 1 May ('May Day' being celebrated as a revolutionary holiday in the Soviet Union), and almost irrespective of losses, the Soviet commanders drove their men forward. Smashing through the Reichstag's bricked-up entrance, and hacking their way from room to room, on the evening of 30 April soldiers from LXXIX Rifle Corps headed for their final objective. An hour and ten minutes before midnight, with fighting raging in the building beneath them, they planted the Red Flag on the roof of the Reichstag.

The end had come. Told that the battle would finish within 24 hours, Adolf Hitler and his new wife Eva Braun committed suicide on the afternoon of 30 April. This did not end the fighting immediately, as the subsequent surrender negotiations dragged on for another day. Because many of Berlin's defenders were determined to avoid Soviet captivity, breakout attempts continued for some time. Most of these failed, adding thousands to an already enormous casualty list. Some of the garrison, however, did escape, largely because General Wenck was determined to salvage something from the wreckage and several days before had pushed his Twelfth Army to the southwestern corner of the city, rescuing many soldiers and civilians. After an equally desperate fight to escape, elements of Busse's Ninth Army also managed to reach Wenck's positions, and together with some 300,000 civilians they crossed into American captivity. But by then Berlin lay in silent ruins. And so too did the Nazis' dreams of their 'Thousand Year Reich'.

SIMON TREW

Further Reading

Glantz, D M, and House, J *When Titans Clashed* (Kansas, 1995)

Le Tissier, T *The Battle of Berlin 1945* (London, 1988)

Le Tissier, T *Zhukov at the Oder* (London, 1996)

Victor Madeja, W *The Russo-German War* (Allentown, 1987)

Index